Cougar Pr

The Walls Talk

Cougar Pr

The Walls Talk

Historic House Museums of Colorado

Patricia Werner

Filter Press, LLC
Palmer Lake, Colorado

Dedication

For my good fairy, Maxine,
who makes everything possible

ISBN: 978-0-86541-095-4
Library of Congress Control Number: 2010920626
Copyright © 2010 James Werner

P.O. Box 95 • Palmer Lake, CO 80133
888-570-2663
FilterPressBooks.com

Printed in the United States of America

Contents

Preface

The house museums included in this book tell the stories of the families who lived in these dwellings. It was these stories that I wanted to bring to life.

I had hoped to represent all the cultures that left behind dwellings that are now house museums and whose organizations wished them included. Sadly, no Native American dwellings of known families have survived in Colorado, so the rich culture of that thread is missing here.

Many worthy living history museums were not included in this volume, as they were not family specific. Likewise, ruins, though some have been preserved at great expense, were not included. Historical museums housed in historic houses were not included unless the majority of their exhibits depicted the lives of those who dwelled within.

Above all, I strived for complete accuracy, relying on primary sources as much as possible as well as personal conversations with directors and curators. The truth of these stories was fascinating enough. There was no need to embellish with the folklore that many of these places inherited from the 1960s and 1970s, when articles and oral histories paid little mind to accurate details.

I wrote this book so that I could know the people who lived in these dwellings. I hope you enjoy knowing them, too.

Acknowledgments

Many people deserve thanks for patiently assisting me in gathering the data for this book. Among them are:

The staff at the Western History and Genealogy Department, Denver Public Library

Rebecca Laurie, Public Relations; Rebecca Lintz, Director; and all the staff, Stephen H. Hart Library, Colorado Historical Society

Ann Rutledge, Archivist, Summit Historical Society

Doris Baker, Editor and Publisher, Filter Press

Sarah Ewalt and Ann McCampbell, Illustrators

Tina Nowlin, Researcher and adventurer

Edna Pelzmann, Manager of Visitor Services, Colorado State Capital

Nancy Donahoo, Curator; Kathi Hill, former curator, A.J. Eaton House Museum

Beth Higgins, Public Relations and Development Coordinator, Auntie Stone Cabin, Fort Collins Museum

Jane Hail, Docent; Joann M. Thomas, President, Poudre Landmarks Foundation, Avery House

Paula Manini, Director; Janet Miller and Priscilla Opper, Interpreters; Mary Ellen Hadad, Trinidad Historical Society, Trinidad History Museum, Colorado Historical Society, Baca and Bloom Houses

Karen Musolf, Ph.D., Docent; Laurie Best, Breckenridge Town Planner, Barney Ford House Museum

Karen Musolf, Briggle House

Kevin Graymer, Director, Byers-Evans House

John Lake, Docent; Meg Anderson, Docent; Terry Williams, Executive Director; Donna Wilson, CEO, Cherokee Ranch and Castle

Grand County Historical Association; Elizabeth Cook, Regis University; Sally White, Museums Coordinator for the Town of Morrison, Cozens Ranch Museum

Barbara Gibson, Executive Director; Don Schuderer, Docent, Four Mile Historic Park

Dana K. Abrahamson, Executive Director, Historic Georgetown, Inc., Hamill House

Maureen Scanlon, Director; Ellen Boettcher, Docent, Healy House

Terry Blevins, Hugo Preservation Advisory Board Secretary; Karen Hedlund Scott, Fran Hedlund Mitterer, and Thomas Hedlund, descendants, Hedlund House Museum

John Steinle, Administrator, Hiwan Historical Museum

Peggy Shaw, Director; Lois Lange, Historian and President, Humphrey Memorial Park and Museum

Evelyn Tibbits, Town Clerk, Jack Dempsey Cabin

Michelle Bahe, Curator of Collections, Aurora History Museum; Michael Thompson, Museum Education, John Gully Homestead

Wallace Yvonne Tollette, Executive Director, Justina Ford House

Lee Harrison, Lula Myers Ranch House

Eric D. Adams, Executive Director; Gladys Thomson, Historian, MacGregor Ranch

Carol Davis, Curator/Director, South Park City Historical Foundation; Linda Bjorklund, Park County Archives, Mayer House

Barbara Gately, Curator, McAllister House

Peggy A. Ford, Research and Education Coordinator; Sue LaBrette, staff, Meeker Home Museum

Robin Johnston, Public Relations, Miramont Castle Museum

Kerri Atter, former Director and Curator; Annie Robb, Director, Molly Brown House

Betty Aragon-Mitotes, Chair and founding member; Juliet Romero Chavez, descendant; Janet Devlin, Treasurer, Poudre Landmark Foundation; Katherine Woods, Assistant Project Manager, Museo de las Tres Colonias

Charlotte Bumgarner, Manager, The Old Homestead House Museum

Connie Jo Fox, Researcher, Orum House

Cheryl Catalano, Chief Interpreter, Rock Ledge Ranch Historic Site

Deb Darrow, Executive Director; Susan Kittinger, Collections Manager, Rosemount Museum

Win Ferrill, Lead Curator; Mary Hatlestad, Docent, Streer-Peterson House

Linda Hollenback, Director of Administrative Services, Tabor Home; Sandra Smith, former Docent; Kayla Koucherik, Supervisor, Matchless Mine

James J. Prochaska, Executive Director; Robbie Martin, Docent, Thomas House

Bridget Bacon, Museum Coordinator, Tomeo House

Shirley Esher, Executive Director, The Historical Society of Idaho Springs; Marjorie Bell, Museum Curator; Don Allan, photographer, Underhill Museum

Claudia Worth and Charlotte Wetsel, Wheat Ridge Historical Society

A special thanks to Karen Musolf, Ph.D., who traipsed around Breckenridge, Leadville, and Dillon digging into archives, asking questions, and acquiring photos for me. Without her help, Summit County would have proved less rich indeed. And special thanks to my husband, James, who enthusiastically trekked to most of the houses, took pictures, and turned our trips into mini-vacations—and who read every single chapter aloud so that I could hear what I needed to change.

In Memoriam
Pat Werner
November 11, 1947 – November 22, 2007

*P*at wrote *The Walls Talk* to invite readers into the lives of the pioneer families who settled Colorado and built their homes, rude or grand, that eventually became the Historic House Museums of Colorado. If you share a curiosity about the challenges and uncertainties of frontier life, about enduring hunger and cold and Indian attacks to amass a fortune in silver and gold or to raise a family in rough times when barter, not cash, was king, you will enjoy Pat's creation. Each family left a visible contribution to the history of Colorado with their homes. This book invites you to share some moments of their lives.

There is an inside story to the writing of this book and the final months of Pat's life that highlights the qualities I so admired in her—her persistence, intention and passion for writing that overcame incredible obstacles.

In May 2007, Pat checked into the hospital with shortness of breath. It had been two years since her ovarian cancer returned to settle in the lungs, and we had been through several rounds of chemo therapy already. We didn't know if relief was available for her breathing difficulties.

After several days in the hospital, her doctor told us it was just a matter of weeks. Pat's immediate reaction was, "I'm a Scientologist and not afraid of dying, but it is damned inconvenient. I've been writing a book for six years and need till the end of summer to finish it and find a publisher!" The doctor said he thought he could help.

We spent a glorious summer together visiting and revisiting historic house museums across Colorado, verifying facts, taking more photos, interviewing descendants. It was Pat's vision that *The Walls Talk* should tell the settlers' stories and that the house museums should be a frame for their lives and add accent to the daily details of their living.

All summer long she read family letters and diaries and interviewed family descendants. It was original research which she loved doing, and she made many friends in the process.

Summer passed, and in the fall Pat finished the book with time for the families and museums to approve their copy. We were still without a publisher. Pat was very particular about who that should be. She wanted someone local so she could easily collaborate. Someone with a feel for her project who could give it the attention it deserved. Someone with a passion for regional history. She found a kindred spirit in Doris Baker and Filter Press and a deal was shortly struck.

There's much more to writing a book than doing the research and putting the words on paper. Many details remained to be organized after the manuscript was complete: Original and digital photos organized, permissions obtained, fees negotiated, credits cross-checked; a database of all the retail outlets and bookstores and museums who might carry her book; instructions to send an author's copy to the families and museums who had contributed so much; a powerpoint presentation created for book signings. The list was long.

When all the interviews and research was done, all the words written and proofread, all the materials, photos, and permissions organized for her publisher, she put the manuscript in a box and gave me written directions to deliver the manuscript to Filter Press in December.

Her work was done, and two weeks later Pat passed at home in bed sleeping peacefully with her two cats curled by her feet.

There are many stories to Pat's life, but I wanted readers to know about her enduring passion for writing and history and what she overcame to complete *The Walls Talk*.

Jim Werner

House Locator

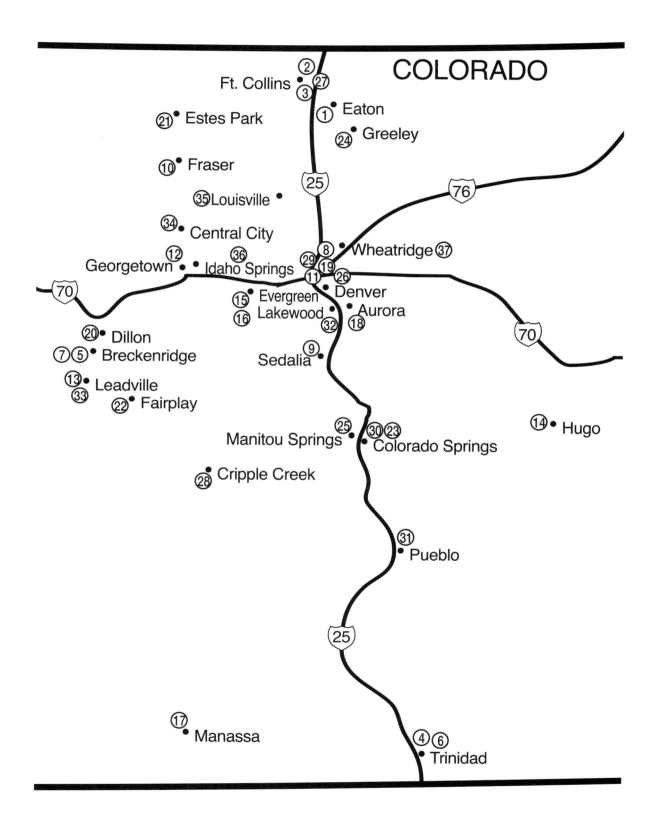

COLORADO

1 A. J. Eaton House Museum

A wedding gift of muslin was meant for aprons, curtains, and shirts. Rebecca Eaton used it to cover the sod ceiling to protect her room from falling debris.

Courtesy of James Werner

Aaron James (A. J.) Eaton was born in 1857 in West Bedford, Ohio. His parents were Benjamin and Delilah Eaton. Delilah died a month after A. J.'s birth.

Benjamin was a teacher, and in 1858 he moved to Iowa. His baby son, A. J., stayed in Ohio with his mother and sisters. Becoming dissatisfied in Iowa and intrigued by the call of the goldfields in Kansas Territory, Benjamin moved farther west. He first engaged in mining and agriculture in southern Colorado. But he didn't like the wearisome farming processes used there, so he moved to Denver, a hotbed of mining activity. There he met Jim Hill, and the two men panned for gold at Clear Creek.

A. J. Eaton House Museum. Denver Square two-story brick built in 1888. Symmetrical front, dormer window in attic. Full-width front porch, a two-story bay window on the south, and a rear porch. Neoclassical Italianate plaster sculptures on the walls and ceilings.

However, Benjamin was not born to be a miner, and he set his heart on prairie land to the north. In 1863, he and Jim claimed a homestead on the Cache la Poudre River, two miles south of the present town of Windsor. There they built a rude cabin on their claim. Benjamin had worked on the Erie Canal and understood irrigation. So he brought water to his claim and made the prairie bloom.

In 1863, Benjamin and Jim returned to visit their families in Ohio and Iowa. The following year, Benjamin married Jim's sister, Rebecca Hill. Their wedding trip was the trip west by covered wagon. Friends sent them off with parched corn, dried apples and peaches, and goose down for pillows and feather beds. One group of women gave them a bolt of unbleached muslin sheeting. It was meant for aprons, curtains, and shirts.

Rebecca's father gave them an iron cook stove of the latest fashion. It was embellished with bright nickel plate and was regulated with numerous dampers and levers. Rebecca also packed her big trunk of clothing and her hope chest of linens. An enclosed box in the front of the wagon held supplies needed for meal preparations and served as a seat for the driver. Rebecca even took plantings of the lavender wisteria that climbed beneath her bedroom window, trumpet vine from the dooryard, and yellow roses that grew against the fence. She took seedlings of oak and maple as well as roots of asparagus and rhubarb.

Ben and Jim also outfitted larger wagons that held tools and farm implements and were pulled by oxen. Little A. J., now 6, remained with Ben's family in Ohio.

When Rebecca picked up the reins to gently slap her span of mules into action, little did she know what lay ahead. They took the ferry crossing at the Missouri, and in Omaha, they were told that they would have to wait for a caravan to be formed, which would provide sufficient protection from any hostile Indian raids.

When the required number of men had been assembled to take the wagon train through, they got started. The pace was slow enough to accommodate the plodding oxen and their heavy loads. Rebecca learned the routine of trail life: circling to make camp at night, building a fire with buffalo chips, and preparing meals.

At Fort Kearney, they learned that a party of Cheyenne had recently attacked a wagon train. A military escort was provided for a short way. Stage stations and ranches along the way also provided a fragile thread of civilization. Westward from Fort Kearney, the plains grew more empty and barren. But when they reached Julesburg, Colorado, they again enjoyed a larger settlement. They paused at the Robert Boyd farm for their last evening of camp. The Boyds had

spent four years building a riverside farm, and Rebecca admired the graciousness and friendliness of the place.

When Rebecca finally arrived at Ben's claim, she asked where the home was that had been built for her. Much like Augusta Tabor's reaction when she first set eyes on Horace's rude cabin on his claim in Kansas Territory, Rebecca wept at the sight of the cabin before her. And like Augusta, she soon made the best of the situation.

Once on the claim, Ben and Rebecca built a log cabin that could be expanded as their needs grew. But the threat of attacks by Indians drove them to a fort the neighbors had constructed. One sod room sheltered Rebecca, and she used her wedding gift of muslin to partition her kitchen from her living space and to cover the sod ceiling to protect her room from debris falling from the roof. Meanwhile, Ben freighted hay and later mining machinery into the mountains to the mining camps. He didn't tell her about the dangers and discomforts of freighting in the winter.

Minnie and A. J. Eaton's
wedding photograph

Springtime saw them back in their cabin, where Rebecca put in a garden and Ben labored in the field. They called their place the Eaton Hay Ranch. The couple had three children: Abraham Lincoln, Bruce, and Jennie. Abraham died of diphtheria at age fourteen.

In the years they lived in their homestead, many changes took place in the surrounding area. Cattle were driven up from Texas on the famous cattle trails—trails once used by Indians because of the availability of grass and water along the way. Settlers organized local governments, and Ben was appointed justice of the peace. In 1866, the settlers near Ben and Rebecca built a school.

In 1870, when A. J. was 12, his aunt, Miss Emily Eaton, brought him out to Colorado to join his father and stepmother. Also that year, the Union

Around the World itinerary for
the A. J. Eaton family

Colony settled the town that would become Greeley.

Ben was elected to the territorial legislature, which convened in January 1872. With A. J. of high school age, Ben moved his family to Greeley in 1873 to be near a school. Living there would also give his family greater security.

From the time A. J. arrived, he involved himself in activities that had to do with his father's business. When he was a senior in high school, his father needed him to work on irrigation ditch projects. He left school to help his father and never returned to formal schooling.

Irrigation Ditches

Benjamin Eaton was the driving force behind the Eaton Canal. He worked on a number of canals, including Denver's Highline Canal. He also constructed the Eaton Mill for farmers to dispose of their grain, and he contributed to the development of the Eaton sugar beet factories.

Ben purchased more land and had it surveyed. Then in 1882, he founded the town Eatonton on that land. A. J. and Jim Hill opened the first general store there, in a 16-by-24-foot structure that was the third building on the town site. In September, the post office was located in their store. A. J. was now 23. The town name was later shortened to Eaton.

Because A. J. had opened the first "little" store in town, he became known as Eaton's Father of Commerce. Ben financed the construction of a two-story brick building in 1883, and A. J. and Jim moved their stock into the "big" store. A. J. bought out Jim's interest in 1884 and served as the town's second postmaster for eight years.

A. J. married Minnie Goodman in 1885. Their wedding present from Ben was

the property where the house museum now stands. A. J. and Minnie lived in the big store until the house was completed in 1888. The new house loomed over the tiny fruit and shade trees surrounding it.

The couple had seven children, but three died in infancy. Minnie was an organizer of the Eaton Woman's Club and was active in the Congregationalist Church.

In 1897, A. J. became director of the Larimer and Weld irrigation ditch. When Ben became active in politics and eventually became Colorado's fourth governor, the responsibilities of the farms fell to A. J. He was also active in banking.

In 1904, A. J.'s family moved to Los Angeles because of illness in the family. They spent winters in California and summers in Colorado. In 1911–1912, the Eaton family traveled around the world on a Grand Tour. The master bedroom in the present house museum shows the preparations: a trunk being packed, clothing ready to be ironed, and so forth.

In 1918, at age sixty-one, A. J. had a stroke and from that time forward remained an invalid. Minnie turned the Eaton house into a boardinghouse to gain additional income. Their son Ralph, his wife, Beulah, four children, and two servants lived in the house, They paid thirty dollars a month in rent. Other boarders lived in the house in the 1930s and 1940s. A. J. remained in California, never to return to Colorado, but Minnie returned from time to time, to run the house. A. J. died in 1944 in Los Angeles.

Becoming a House Museum

Minnie also died in 1944 at age seventy-seven. The family sold the house after her death. A subsequent owner, F. Pat Maylott, transformed the interior in the French traditions of Louis XIV, Regency, Louis XV, and Louis XVI.

In 2003, the town of Eaton purchased the house from then owner Patricia Simonds. The house is operated by the Eaton Area Historical Society.

About the A. J. Eaton House Museum

Address: 207 Elm Avenue, Eaton, Colorado 80615

Phone: (970) 454-3660

Hours: Tuesday, Thursday, and Saturday, 2:00–4:00 p.m.

Admission: Free

Driving directions: I-25 to Exit 262, Windsor. Turn east onto County Road 392. Drive 6.1 miles. Drive through the town of Windsor. At the intersection with County Road 19, turn left (north). Go 2.8 miles to the intersection with County Road 74. Turn right (east). Drive 9.5 miles. Once in town, County Road 74 becomes Collins Street. Go to Elm Street. A statue of Benjamin Eaton is on the northwest corner. Turn left (north) and go 0.2 mile.

Parking: Free on street

Memberships: Membership in the Eaton Historical Society is available at varying levels of support. Call (970) 454-3660.

Web site: http://www.eatonco.org/eaton-house-museum.htm

2 Auntie Stone Cabin

In her sixties, Elizabeth Stone saw opportunities for the development of industries in the frontier settlement of Camp Collins.

Photographer, Pat Werner; Courtesy James Werner

The Auntie Stone Cabin. Two-story log cabin.

Elizabeth "Auntie" Stone was born in 1801 in Hartford, Connecticut. In 1824, at the age of twenty-two, she married physician Ezekiel Robbins in Watertown, New York. Four years later, the Robbins family moved to St. Louis, Missouri, to establish a store in that French frontier trading post during the fur trade era. They stayed in St. Louis for ten years. The family grew to include eight children.

In 1838, they moved to Illinois and settled on a farm. Ezekiel became a representative in the Illinois General Assembly and, in 1847, a member of the Illinois Constitutional Convention.

He died in 1852, leaving Elizabeth a small fortune and responsibility for several children in their teens and twenties. With a large family to support, she returned to New York State. She stayed in New York for a year before deciding

to try her luck on the Minnesota prairie. In St. Paul, she met Lewis Stone, and in 1857, at the age of fifty-five, she married him. The couple headed west.

They arrived in Denver, the "Queen City of the Plains", in 1862. They purchased twelve lots at the site of Union Station, built a house, and rented the house for a restaurant. One of Lewis's sons took care of the restaurant property while the Stones homesteaded along the St. Vrain River. Dr. T. M. Smith, acting surgeon at Camp Collins, urged the Stones to move there, thinking they might be interested in boarding army officers.

The Stones moved to Camp Collins in 1864. The camp consisted of some tents and a few log houses. Soldiers were stationed there to protect the white settlers from Indian raids. Elizabeth was the first white woman to settle in Camp Collins and the only woman for nearly a year.

The Stones built a structure to be used as an officers' mess. The two-story log structure was completed in October 1864. The logs were cut from trees in nearby hills, hewed by hand, and hauled by ox team to Camp Collins. The living room and dining room were downstairs. Steep stairs led to sleeping rooms overhead. The second bedroom was occupied by Elizabeth's niece, Elizabeth Keays, who used her room as the first school. The interior of the cabin was lined with canvas, which came from worn-out shelter tents. Soldiers cut lumber for a lean-to at the rear. Auntie Stone's cabin served as the mess house for the Camp Collins officers.

In January 1866, Elizabeth became a widow for the second time when Lewis died. At the age of 64, she became known as Auntie Stone. She saw the need for new industries and applied herself to several businesses. In 1868, she and H. C. Peterson built a flour mill. Then in 1870, she and Peterson built a brick kiln. From this kiln came the bricks for the first brick houses in Fort Collins. She expanded the mess house into a hotel.

In 1873, the Agricultural Hotel was erected. Auntie Stone's cabin was moved to the rear of the new hotel and used as a kitchen and laundry. In 1877, Englishman David Harris, purchased the hotel, changed its name to Commercial Hotel, and later moved the hotel. Auntie Stone's cabin was left standing alone.

An advocate of women's suffrage, Auntie lived to cast her first vote in the Fort Collins municipal elections of 1894. She died in 1895 at the age of 94.

Becoming a House Museum

The cabin was improved, decorated, and used as a residence by Mr. and Mrs. James F. Vandewark until 1907. In 1908, the logs were covered with siding and painted white. The building was used as a paint shop until 1909.

In 1908, the Association of Pioneer Women of the Cache la Poudre Valley

discussed the question of buying and preserving the cabin because of its historical interest. By 1913, the society had finished paying for the structure. A porch was added, and the interior was plastered. It served as a meeting place for the Larimer County Pioneer Association and as a small museum.

In 1959, the porch was removed, the logs bared, and the cabin moved to its present location. It now has a permanent home in the Heritage Courtyard at the Fort Collins Museum and Discovery Science Center.

About the Auntie Stone Cabin

Address: 200 Mathews Street, Library Park, Fort Collins, Colorado 80524

Phone: (970) 221-6738

Hours: Tuesday–Saturday 10:00 a.m.–5:00 p.m., Sunday Noon–5:00 p.m. Closed Mondays and holidays

Admission: Adults (13-59) $4.00, Seniors (60+) $3.00, Child 3–12 $3.00, Members and Children under 2 free

Driving directions: I-25 to Exit 269B onto Mulberry Street. Turn west toward Fort Collins. Drive 3.4 miles. Turn slight right on Riverside Avenue. Drive 0.4 mile. Turn slight left on East Oak Street. (The sign is hard to see.) Drive 0.2 mile. Turn left onto Mathews Street. The museum is within 0.1 mile.

Or from Highway 287 or College Avenue, turn east on Olive Street. Turn left on Mathews Street (the second stop sign). The museum is on the right in Library Park. The Auntie Stone Cabin is to the right after entering the Heritage Courtyard on the museum grounds.

Parking: On-street parking surrounds Library Park; a downtown parking garage is two blocks away on Mountain Avenue.

Membership: Membership in the Fort Collins Museum and Discovery Science Center at various levels of support is available. Call (970) 221-6738.

Web site: www.fcmdsc.org/museum/courtyard.html

3 Avery House

Franklin Avery laid out the streets in Fort Collins wide enough so that a freight wagon pulled by horses could turn around in the street without having to back up.

Photographer, Pat Werner; Courtesy James Werner

Fort Collins military fort was originally established to guard the travelers and settlers along the Colorado branch of the Overland Stage Line. It served as a military post between 1862 and 1866. A disastrous flood took the old military camp near the Laporte stagecoach stop in June 1864, and a new permanent post was established five miles downstream on the Poudre River. But less than three years later, the area was declared safe from Indian raids, and the fort was abandoned. Settlers took over the abandoned army buildings as fast as they were vacated.

Avery House.
Center-gable Gothic Revival design. Two-color sandstone house with steep gabled roof, flared eaves, and corner turret west side. Mansard roof on northeast corner (built when porch was enclosed). Sandstone from local quarries.

Franklin Avery

Franklin Capen Avery was born in 1849 in the Finger Lakes area of New York. He entered Cazenovia Seminary in 1868 where he studied surveying. December 13, 1869, he wrote to Nathan Meeker, agricultural editor of Horace Greeley's *New York Tribune*, who was advertising for individuals of temperance to start a new town in Colorado. Avery assured Meeker that, "I never had any desire to drink nor use tobacco."

Avery joined Meeker's Union Colony and came to Greeley with the group in 1870. He lived and worked in Greeley for two years, helping to survey and plat the new town and helping to lay out the new ditches. In the fall of 1871, he embarked in the cattle business near Laporte in Larimer County.

Other agricultural communities were springing up, among them the abandoned army post of Fort Collins, upriver from Greeley. Avery went to Fort Collins in the fall of 1872, at age 23, to survey and plat the new community. He gave the east-west streets names of trees, with the idea that trees matching the names would be planted along those streets. The north-south streets were named for pioneers of the town. The exceptionally broad streets he provided remain today. Some say that he made them wide enough so that a freight wagon pulled by horses could turn around in the street without having to back up.

He was elected county surveyor in 1872 and re-elected in 1874. He acquired town property as well as farmland in Larimer and Weld counties.

In 1876, Avery returned to New York to marry Sara Edson. Back in Fort Collins, they first lived in a small white house on Mountain and Meldrum. Railroad connections between Cheyenne and Denver had been completed in 1870, and the town was growing.

Avery owned the entire block where the house museum now sits, and the first structure on the property was a barn, built in 1878. The next year, he built the gable front and wing section of the house that make up the left side of the present façade. The girls' bedroom upstairs has a secret hiding place under the eaves behind a bookshelf.

In November 1880, Avery founded the Larimer County Bank. Two years later, the name was changed to the First National Bank. He served as president from 1881 to 1910.

Sara's sisters followed her out west and found husbands in the little town. Their parents eventually joined them in Fort Collins. However, Mrs. Edson used to sit in the Averys' backyard and watch the trains arrive at the depot, wishing she could take one back east. Two of Avery's brothers followed him to Fort Collins, and his sister moved with her family to Greeley.

The Averys continued to add to the house. Franklin selected Harlan Thomas, an acclaimed Denver architect who had lived in Fort Collins, to design an addition. In 1881, a kitchen wing was added followed by the right wing two years later. The addition of the right wing of the house created a center-gabled whole. Because the Fort Collins Water Works was completed in 1883, plumbing was probably added to the house soon after. The electric light plant was completed in 1887, and electricity was added to the house by 1890.

Growing Family

Franklin and Sara had five children, but only three survived: Edgar, Ethel, and Louise. The family had a pony and two cows. Chubby, the pony, pulled the cart that Sara used visit her friends. Edgar also used the cart and a small wagon to drive about the countryside. Chubby and two cows used the Avery property up to Laporte Avenue on the north side as a pasture.

Sara Avery

In addition to his interests in banking and other businesses, Franklin and his brother William had a cousin bring them a hundred head of Merino sheep from Vermont in 1884.

An ice cream social, complete with Chinese lanterns, was held in July 1888 on the lawn to raise money for the Methodist minister's salary. Guests were entertained by vocal and instrumental music. Sixty dollars was raised.

Franklin built the Avery block downtown in 1897, containing ten stores and a large number of offices. The Avery block was also home to the First National Bank for many years. Avery erected a number of other buildings and had an interest in the building of the Opera House block.

He was also one of the organizers and promoters of the Larimer County Ditch Company, which became the Water Supply and Storage Company. He was president of that company for several years. It was his idea to use a trans-mountain diversion ditch to bring water from the Laramie River across the divide to the Cache la Poudre watershed. The project brought water to thousands of acres of unproductive land.

Avery served as alderman on the Fort Collins City Council three times and had much to do with shaping municipal affairs. He was also treasurer and first baseman of the Standard Baseball Club of Fort Collins.

At the turn of the century, part of the Avery block was sold to the Catholic Church. In 1901, Franklin and Sara built a house to the east of their own as a wedding gift for Edgar Avery and his bride, Mabel Gordon.

Growing House

Meanwhile, Franklin's house continued to grow. The gazebo and front fountain are shown in pictures by 1890. In 1893, they added the back parlor, a Queen Anne tower on the right side, and a wraparound porch. About 1905, they built the carriage house to replace the original barn. The carriage house had a loft for hay storage and ground-level stalls for horses and cows, a tack room, and a grain room. Large double doors in the central area of the structure opened on the Meldrum Street side.

Courtesy Fort Collins Public Library

Franklin Avery

Also in 1905, the left-rear bedroom was enlarged by squaring off the corner and adding a turret. The original dormer window was moved to the carriage house loft. The upstairs porch off the Queen Anne tower was enclosed, and the stairway landing and entrance were remodeled to look as they do now. In 1906, the Averys added the back porch and upstairs sleeping porch. In later years, Edgar's youngest son, William H., slept on the porch year-round.

Sandstone from local quarries was used for all of the work, and the exterior details were carefully matched, so that the house presents a unified design. Franklin's last big public event was a gala reception when the First National Bank moved to a new location on the southeast corner of Mountain and College. The event was hosted in part by Sara, daughter Ethel, and nieces Pauline and Beth. A hidden orchestra provided music.

In 1910, Franklin retired from the bank. He and Sara took a steamship to China and Japan that year.

In 1916, Franklin and Sara moved to California. Franklin hoped the lower altitude would improve his health. Edgar and his family moved into the main house when Franklin and Sara left. Franklin died in 1923 at age 74, and Sara returned to live in Fort Collins where she died two years later.

Edgar became the cashier of the First National Bank, the city treasurer, and worked in the real estate and loan businesses.

Becoming a House Museum

The house remained in the Avery family until 1964. It was sold and used as a rental property for ten years. When the owners wanted to sell the property, many possibilities were suggested. But the Fort Collins Historic Landmarks Commission and other civic interests requested that the city purchase the house as part of a capital improvements project called Designing Tomorrow Today.

The voters passed a one-cent sales tax for the projects, which included the Lincoln Center, the Library, and the Avery House. The City Council purchased the house in 1974. June Bennett, an interior designer and wife of the mayor, was instrumental in getting the tax passed as well as obtaining grants for the many repairs.

The city pays utilities and maintains the exterior of the house. The Poudre Landmarks Foundation and the Avery House Historic District Guild are responsible for the restoration and operation.

About the Avery House Museum

Address: 328 West Mountain Avenue, Fort Collins, Colorado 80521

Phone: (970) 221-0533

Hours: Wednesdays and Sundays, 1:00–3:00 p.m. Closed holidays

Admission: Free; donations appreciated

Driving directions: I-25 to Exit 269B, Mulberry Street. Turn west toward Fort Collins. Go 4.5 miles. Turn right on Meldrum Street. Go 0.4 mile.

Parking: Free on street

Membership: Membership in Poudre Landmarks Foundation is available at varying levels of support. Call (970) 221-0533.

Web site: www.poudrelandmarks.com/plf_avery_house.shtml

4 Baca House

Felipe and Delores Baca paid for their house with 22,000 pounds of wool.

In 1860, Felipe Baca was on his way to Denver from the Mora Valley in New Mexico territory. He and a friend were hauling four wagonloads of flour to sell to prospectors in the gold camps along Cherry Creek. They stopped by the Purgatoire River to camp. Baca was impressed with the lush vegetation. When they stopped again on their way home, Baca made up his mind to locate here. The rich bottomlands would make excellent farming and grazing.

In the fall of 1861, Baca left his wife and family at home in Mora and returned to the Purgatoire with workers and enough provisions to plant a tract of land a mile long, east of today's Commercial Street. According to one source, he built a *jacal* (a hut with walls built of thin vertical

Baca House.
Side view with gardens in back. Greek Revival with columned porch. Territorial style two-story adobe with tin hip roof. New England embellishment: widow's walk.

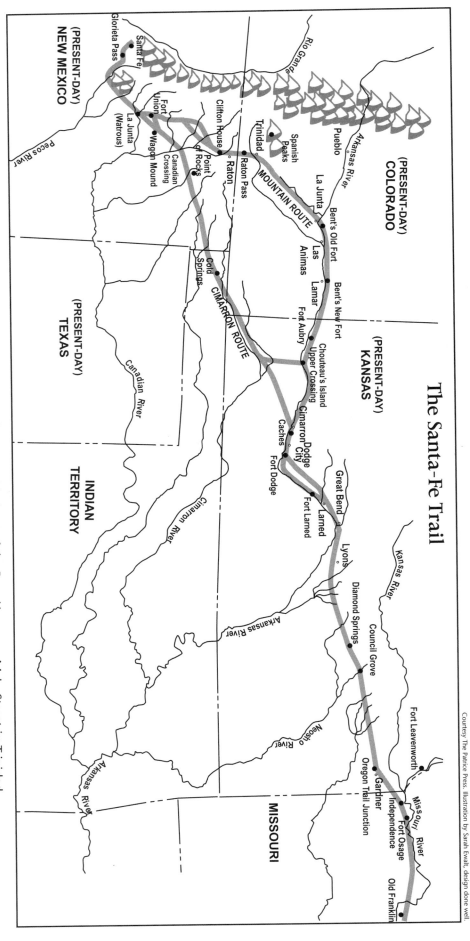

The Santa-Fe Trail

(PRESENT-DAY) COLORADO

(PRESENT-DAY) NEW MEXICO

(PRESENT-DAY) TEXAS

(PRESENT-DAY) KANSAS

INDIAN TERRITORY

MISSOURI

Rio Grande
Arkansas River
Pecos River
Canadian River
Cimarron River
Arkansas River
Neosho River
Kansas River
Missouri River
Arkansas River

Glorieta Pass
Santa Fe
Fort Union
La Junta (Watrous)
Wagon Mound
Canadian Crossing
Clifton House
Point of Rocks
Raton
Raton Pass
Trinidad
Spanish Peaks
Pueblo
La Junta
Bent's Old Fort
Las Animas
Lamar
Bent's New Fort
Fort Aubry
Chouteau's Island
Upper Crossing
Cold Springs
Dodge City
Cimarron
Caches
Fort Dodge
Larned
Fort Larned
Great Bend
Lyons
Diamond Springs
Council Grove
Gardner
Oregon Trail Junction
Fort Leavenworth
Fort Osage
Independence
Old Franklin

MOUNTAIN ROUTE
CIMARRON ROUTE

The Santa Fe Trail, showing the Mountain Route that passed in front of the Baca House on Main Street in Trinidad. Some modern locations are shown for the reader's orientation.

Courtesy The Patrice Press. Illustration by Sarah Ewalt, design done well.

poles filled in and plastered over with mud) at the western boundary of his farm. Baca always made it a point to be on good terms with the Indians, and he advised his companions to do the same.

This proved to be a smart idea. According to the story his wife, Dolores, later told their son Facundo, on one occasion before Baca's family moved from Mora County, he was called back to New Mexico because Dolores was ill. Baca started from Trinidad on horseback. Fifty miles into the trip, his horse took sick. The nearest person was twenty miles away. Sighting a campfire about five miles away, he decided to head in that direction, hoping to find hunters. Instead, he found a band of Indians. Holding up a flag of truce, he prayed for the best. The chief of the Indians recognized him, for Baca had once treated the chief royally. The chief declared that he would do likewise. Baca was saved.

Thereafter, quite a number of Indian chiefs visited Baca, who always furnished them with flour and cornmeal. He asked in return that their people not molest his herds or herders. In this way, he was able to increase his sheep herd with little trouble from the natives.

In 1860, adobe houses and log structures started to appear along the Santa Fe Trail. The clump of buildings would become the town of Trinidad. The first survey of the town

The Santa Fe Trail was established in 1821 when William Becknell, an American trader, made the first recorded trading expedition from Missouri to Santa Fe. Prior to Mexico's independence, Spain had jealously protected the borders of its colony, but now with Mexican independence, trade boomed along the trail.

What became known as the Mountain Route of the Santa Fe Trail followed the Arkansas and Purgatoire Rivers, which provided water to the traders. Before travelers heading south undertook the grueling climb up the pass, many camped on the banks of the Purgatoire to prepare. One traveler commented, "The trail was a faint wheel mark winding in and out over fallen trees and huge boulders."[1]

Those traveling north also rested along the banks of the Purgatoire after the difficult trek over the pass. It was a natural spot for a trading town to grow up.

After Mexico's freedom from Spain in 1821, land grants were made in what is now southern Colorado by the governor of New Mexico. Trouble developed between the United States and Mexico as a result of Anglo settlers moving west. In 1846, war broke out, and U.S. forces took control of New Mexico province. The Treaty of Guadalupe Hidalgo ended the war in 1848. The United States took possession of what is now California, Nevada, Utah, most of Arizona and New Mexico, and parts of Colorado and Wyoming.

New Mexico province was now U.S. territory. And still the wagons rolled. Some preferred the Cimarron Route of the Santa Fe Trail, which avoided the mountain pass but left travelers without plentiful water and vulnerable to Indian attacks.

site was done in 1861 on land furn-ished by Baca. That portion of the trail along which businesses had already sprung up became Main Street. When Commercial Street was laid out due north from Main Street, it failed to coincide with the old wagon road where settlers had already built corrals. The settlers didn't like this new straight street cutting through their property. Taking a rope, they marked off their claims, which followed the crooked wagon way. Commercial Street remained from then until now a crooked road.

Racial Tensions

A majority of the early Trinidad residents were Spanish Americans. Relations between the Spanish and the English Americans and other pioneers from the East were mostly harmonious, although a conflict in 1862 was dubbed—some say erroneously—the "Trinidad Race War." Common challenges of settling the land and dealing with the Native Americans encouraged cooperation. And because there were almost no English American or European women in the early years, many pioneer men married Spanish American women, uniting their families in kinship.

Occasional clashes occurred when scoundrels from "the states" stirred up trouble. (See Chapter 6, Bloom Mansion for one such riot.)

Felipe Baca was against statehood, and he participated in the anti-statehood convention in Pueblo in 1869. He felt that with statehood, the large Hispanic community in southern Colorado would be forgotten. They would be dominated by the Anglo and European politicians in Denver. Baca also served in the Territorial Legislature from 1870 to 1872, campaigning against statehood.

Leading the Rest

Baca dug the first irrigation ditch in the area and eventually cultivated 400 acres. In the fall of 1862, he returned home to Mora County, taking a load of grains, melons, and other produce. His friends back home were impressed.

Twelve other families loaded 20 wagons and gathered livestock to migrate north with him. Back on the Purgatoire River, Baca built an adobe plaza (a large home surrounding an open courtyard), which Dolores managed. Between 1850 and 1870, she gave birth to ten children— Maria Dionisia, Juan Pedro, Maria Catarina, Maria Apolonia, Maria de la Luz, Maria Rosa, Luis, Gregorita, Felix, and Facundo. One died in infancy.

Two-story Adobe

By the time merchant John Hough got to Trinidad in 1869, the town had a telegraph line, a post office, sawmill, and four general stores. (One of the general stores was run by Frank Bloom.) Five stagecoaches a week stopped here. In 1870, Hough built a two-story Greek Revival–style house out of adobe.

Heavy, durable adobe bricks are made from a thick mixture of mud and straw poured into rectangular molds and left in the sun to harden. When the bricks are laid, mud mortar glues them together. Adobe stucco spread over the walls seals them against the elements.

Adobe was common for building, but unusual for a two-story structure. The house perched right above Main Street, which had been laid out on the Santa Fe Trail as it curved along the Purgatoire River. An unusual feature of the house was the widow's walk atop the roof.

In 1873, when Hough wanted to move his family to West Las Animas, he wasn't sure he would be able to sell such an expensive house. But successful businessman Felipe Baca and his wife were interested. They gave Hough $7,000 worth of wool (22,000 pounds) for the property. For an additional $1,500 worth of wool, the Bacas bargained for furniture from the Houghs. The two wives bargained in different languages. Mrs. Hough spoke only English, and Mrs. Baca spoke Spanish.

Once settled in the grand two-story adobe, the Bacas added a kitchen garden behind the house. They also built an adobe structure at the back of the courtyard to serve as a barn and to house their domestic help in two side wings.

Felipe Baca died at age 46, only a year after moving into the house. At the time of his death, he was respected as a founder of the town and was thought to be the wealthiest man in Las Animas County.

Felipe Baca

Dolores Baca

"Whereas, the great Supreme Architect has seen fit to remove from our midst, our fellow member, FELIPE BACA; thereof be it

Resolved, That in the decease of our late associate, we have lost an earnest and energetic co-worker, a genial companion, a faithful friend and an upright citizen.

Resolved, That to the family of our departed brother, we tender our warmest sympathy and condolence in this loss, of a faithful husband and an indulgent father."

Trinidad Enterprise, Trinidad, Las Animas County, April 16, 1874.[2]

He left each of his three youngest male children 245 ewes, which the executor was instructed to sell. The proceeds were to pay for the boys' educations. One became an engineer, one a doctor, and one a lawyer. Baca also left ewes to three of his daughters, with no stipulation regarding their sale or the girls' educations. One daughter became a nun. Dolores lived in the house for 41 more years with her younger children. She died at home in 1915 at age 83.

About the Baca House and Trinidad History Museum

The Trinidad History Museum consists of the Baca House, Bloom Mansion, Santa Fe Trail Museum, and Historic Gardens. The museum complex also has a bookstore and is home to the Trinidad and Santa Fe Trail Information Center.

Address: 312 East Main Street, Trinidad, Colorado 81082

Phone: (719) 846-7217

Hours: May 1–September 30, 9 a.m.–4 p.m. Monday–Saturday
October 1–April 30, Santa Fe Trail Museum is open 9 a.m.–1 p.m. Monday–Friday. Historic homes are open by appointment.

Admission: Adults $8.00, Seniors (65+) $6.00, Children (6-16) $3.00. Colorado Historical Society members, Trinidad Historical Society members, Friends of Historical Trinidad, and children age five and under are admitted free.

Driving directions: I-25 to Exit 13B, Main Street. Go straight 0.5 mile. The museum complex is on your right, at 312 East Main, across from the post office.

Parking: Free on the street

Memberships: Membership in the Colorado Historical Society is available at varying levels of support. Visit www.coloradohistory.org/join_us/membership_benfts.htm.

Web site: http://www.coloradohistory.org/hist_sites/trinidad/bacahouse.htm

5 Barney Ford House Museum

Barney Ford, a runaway slave, came west to find gold but ended up building luxury hotels.

Courtesy of James Werner

Barney Ford House.
1882 Victorian home of Barney Ford in Breckenridge, Colorado. One-story frame house with bay windows. An attic spans part of the house.

Barney Ford was born in 1822 in a slave cabin near Stafford Courthouse, Virginia, the progeny of a white plantation owner and a slave house servant. He had no surname. At this time in the antebellum South, teaching slaves the rudiments of reading, writing, and arithmetic was forbidden. Even so, Barney's mother encouraged her son to learn to read and write.

Eventually, his owner sold him to a Georgia slaveholder, who put him to work driving hogs and mules, handling cotton on barges, and working in goldfields at Auraria, Georgia. There Barney acquired the gold fever that would eventually carry him west.

He was hired out as a cook and steward on Mississippi River steamboats. At age twenty-six, while his boat was tied up at Quincy, Illinois, he jumped ship

Barney L. Ford

Colorado Historical Society # 10031421

for freedom. He made his way to Chicago via the Underground Railroad.

He fell in love with and married Julia A. Lyoni, the sister-in-law of freed man Henry O. Wagoner, who operated a livery stable that served as a station in the Underground Railroad. At Julia's suggestion, Barney took the name Barney L. Ford, after a steam engine named Lancelot Ford. He bought barber clippers and learned the barber's trade because a black man could earn good money in tips from white customers.

The 1849 news of gold discovered in California fanned his gold fever. Barney and Julia booked steerage passage for California, stopping off in Nicaragua. However, Barney came down with a fever, and the couple stayed in Greytown until his health improved. They abandoned their California plans, bought a building, and opened a small hotel to serve passengers traveling to and from the coasts. The hotel offered home-cooked American meals.

The business thrived. Unfortunately, during a conflict between United States and British interests, the hotel was destroyed in a naval bombardment. Barney went to work as a steward on a riverboat for a year, but then opened another hotel on Lake Nicaragua. Further political unrest in the area and a new president who was a proponent of slavery prompted the Fords to sell the hotel and return to Chicago.[1]

Barney and Julia joined Henry Wagoner in operating the livery stable. Barney made a modest income, but lost money on an ill-advised lightning-rod business. In 1859, just when the Pikes Peak gold fever was taking hold, the Fords went broke.

Barney went west without Julia and staked two claims in the Gregory Diggings near present-day Central City. The claims were jumped by armed white

men. Barney had no recourse. Colorado territorial law barred blacks from filing a mining claim or homestead.

He headed for Breckenridge with two other black prospectors and panned for gold in French Gulch. Again, they were driven away, this time by the sheriff, who said Barney had filed a false claim. Nearly broke again, he headed back to Denver, where he established a barbershop in a fifteen-foot shack. Presently, Wagoner brought Julia from Chicago.

In 1863, fire destroyed most of Denver's business district, including Barney's shop. The next day, he sought out banker Luther Kountze. He asked if a black man with a total of less than fifty dollars could qualify for a loan of a thousand dollars to rebuild his business. "No," replied Kountze. "I won't lend you a thousand, because you can't possibly earn a living with such a small amount. Go out and find what it'll cost to build you a two-story building and I'll see that you get the money. You're a good business man, Barney; you pay your bills and you have a reputation for integrity."[2]

Barney's new establishment opened in August 1863. It had a restaurant, bar, barbershop, and hairdressing salon. He paid off his loan in ninety days. He also began to acquire a considerable amount of unimproved real estate.

FORD'S PEOPLE'S RESTAURANT,

Blake Street, Denver.

B. L. Ford would respectfully invite his old patrons and the public generally to call and see him at his new and commodious

Saloon, Restaurant and Barber Shop,

on the site of his old stand. Gentlemen will find at ALL HOURS his tables supplied with the

MOST CHOICE AND DELICATE LUXURIES OF COLORADO AND THE EAST.

Private parties of Ladies and Gents can be accommodated with special meals, and Oyster Suppers to order, in his upstairs saloon.

HIS BAR IS STOCKED WITH

The Very Finest Liquors and Cigars

that gold or greenbacks can control of first hands in the eastern markets. Denver and Mountain Lager received daily.

Game of all kinds, Trout, &c., constantly on hand for regular and transient customers, and served up in a style second to no other restaurant in the west.

A Shaving and Hairdressing Saloon

is connected with the establishment, in the basement, wherein competent artists are ever pleased to wait on customers in first class style.

☞ Our motto is to please and satisfy.   aug26dtf

Denver Public Library, Western History Collection, Z-8869

Newspaper advertisement announcing Barney Ford's new establishment.

Political Leader

In 1859, Barney began to follow political movements promoting a new territory called Jefferson, a precursor of the Colorado Territory. He was lukewarm about the proposal because, although the bill introduced in Congress provided that slavery would have no legal status, it didn't prohibit slavery. Barney also disapproved of the 1861 bill creating the Territory of Colorado, which sidestepped the issue of slavery.

In July 1862, Congress passed an act prohibiting slavery in the territories. Barney was delighted. But in 1864, during the administration of Governor John Evans, the territorial legislature amended election laws by inserting a sentence extending the vote to "every male person of the age of 21 years or upward," with the qualifying words, "not being a Negro or mulatto."[3]

Barney was dismayed that Evans, a Lincoln supporter and advocate of emancipation had approved the amendment. Now the statehood movement was taking hold in Colorado, and Barney plunged into the fray to prevent the disenfranchisement of blacks. The constitutional convention of 1865 sidestepped black suffrage. It went on record against slavery but barred blacks from voting, 32 to 9.

Barney decided to leave Colorado. He sold his restaurant to John J. Riethmann and leased out the building. After signing the care of the rest of his property to a lawyer, the Fords moved to Chicago.

With the Civil War ended, the Thirteenth Amendment barred slavery. Wagoner wrote to Barney telling him that Colorado blacks were leaderless. John Evans and Jerome R. Chaffee were designated as provisional U.S. senators. If statehood were granted, the antislavery amendment to the territorial constitution, as it stood without Negro suffrage, would be incorporated into the state constitution.

Barney took the next train to Washington to lobby against the statehood bill. Evans flatly denied that as governor he had helped disenfranchise the black man and insisted that the question of black suffrage had not been raised during his administration. Barney was shocked; the record showed differently.

Eventually, a bill was called up prohibiting any territory from denying the vote to any adult male because of race or color. It passed both houses of Congress and became law. Now blacks could vote in Colorado and in any territory.

The suffrage issue was eventually settled in March 1870 with ratification of the Fifteenth Amendment to the Constitution, stating that the right to vote could not be denied on account of race or color.

Barney continued to support the fight for Colorado statehood, which was finally achieved on August 1, 1876.

Boom and Bust

Back in Chicago, Barney learned that the lawyer he had left in charge of his Denver affairs had left with another man's wife and a great deal of his clients' cash, including Barney's. Barney took the next train for Denver. After selling his Chicago home and fifteen parcels of Denver real estate, he was once again in

stable financial condition.

The Union Pacific was building westward up the Platte River valley from Omaha, Nebraska. It was to meet the Central Pacific Railroad of California, which was building eastward from Sacramento, California. When the railroad bypassed Denver to go through Cheyenne, it appeared that Cheyenne would become the metropolis of the Rockies. So Barney built a restaurant in Cheyenne. It was destroyed by fire in 1870, leaving him $30,000 poorer.

However, he contributed to the fund to build a spur line from Cheyenne to Denver and bought a new restaurant at 42 Blake Street, opposite Denver's new railroad station. When the train pulled into the station on June 15, 1870, Denver entered a new era.

Barney also helped organize a new bank, along with former Governor Evans, with whom he had evidently reconciled. Other founding members were Jerome R. Chaffee, William N. Byers of the *Rocky Mountain News*, Edward M. McCook, who was appointed governor in 1869, and Daniel Witter. The Dime Savings Bank was capitalized at $100,000.

Construction of railroads brought many black laborers to Denver. Now that they could vote, they became important to political leaders. Barney was named a member of the Republican County Central Committee, and when the Republican Club was organized, he was elected its vice president.

He sold his Blake Street restaurant in 1872 to operate a combination hotel and restaurant called Ford's Hotel and Ford's People's Restaurant. This business did so well that Barney was able to construct an even bigger hotel two years later. In 1874, he built the four-story Inter-Ocean Hotel at a cost of $53,000. It became one of Denver's foremost luxury hotels. This building still stands at Sixteenth and Blake Streets. Barney later sold the building for $75,000.

Barney's Inter-Ocean Hotel had proven to be such a civic asset that the city of Cheyenne offered to donate a site if he would build a similar a hotel there. He mortgaged his Denver property to raise the needed funds, and the new Inter-Ocean was opened in Cheyenne in 1875. But business there declined due to a series of droughts and grasshopper plagues. His fortune of a quarter of a million dollars melted away to almost nothing.

He moved to San Francisco and tried to run a restaurant, but it also failed. Then he ran a lunch counter in Bodie, California, a mining community on the California-Nevada border and earned enough to return to Denver in 1878.

In 1880, he became the first black businessman in Breckenridge when he opened a small restaurant called Ford's Restaurant and Chop Stand. The Fords lived in the back of the restaurant and hired the town's best builder, Elias Nashold, to construct their home, which is the present house museum, on the

Inter-Ocean Hotel at Sixteenth and Blake Streets, Denver. This building still stands.

adjoining lot. It was completed in 1882. With its numerous rooms and luxurious furnishings, the house contrasted sharply with the rude dwellings of most other Breckenridge residents. The Fords lived there with their three children.

Ford's Restaurant and Chop Stand was considered the best place to get a good meal. Menu items included fresh mountain trout, oysters, chicken, hot corn cakes, frog legs, pigs' feet, and tripe. Fire destroyed the Chop Stand, but Barney soon opened another Breckenridge restaurant called The Saddle Rock. In addition, in 1883, he bought another eatery in Denver, Ford's Oyster Ocean and Chophouse, and began to divide his time between Denver and Breckenridge.

Four years later, Barney made a mining investment in Breckenridge that paid off. At age sixty-eight, he sold his Breckenridge restaurant, retired to Denver, and bought a home at 1569 High Street in the heart of Denver's then fashionable Capitol Hill district.

Three years later, in 1893, silver prices dropped, and panic ensued in Colorado, bringing an abrupt end to prosperity. Barney opened a barbershop to pay taxes on several parcels of his real estate.

Tribute

The Colorado Association of Pioneers was originally limited to white males who had become residents prior to December 31, 1860. Wolfe Londoner, a leading merchant and later mayor, had the constitution of the association amended so that Barney could be admitted.

In 1898, Mrs. B. L. Ford appeared in the Social Register Yearbook. She died the following year at age seventy-one. Barney, then eighty-one, went to live with a niece. He died in 1902 and was buried beside his wife in Riverside Pioneer Cemetery.

Barney Ford had gained and lost several fortunes. He fought for the civil rights of his people. Today, he is gratefully remembered with a stained glass window portrait directly behind the speaker's desk in the state capitol's House of Representative.

Becoming a House Museum

After the Fords left the house, it was occupied by several owners and renters until the Theobolds bought it about 1946. That family made additions and enhancements to the house and occupied it until about 1970. Then it was abandoned. In 2002, Patty and Robin Theobold established the Saddle Rock Society and donated the house to the group.

The Barney Ford house was restored in 2004 by the Saddle Rock Society with assistance from the town of Breckenridge. Owned by by the Saddle Rock Society, the house is operated by the Breckenridge Heritage Alliance.

About the Barney Ford House Museum

Address: 111 East Washington Street, Breckenridge, Colorado 80424

Phone: (970) 453-5761

Hours: 11 a.m.–3 p.m. Tuesday–Sunday.

Admission: Free; $5 donation suggested.

Driving directions: I-70 to Exit 203, Colorado 9 to Frisco/Breckenridge. Take Colorado 9 south to Breckenridge. Go 9.1 miles. At traffic circle, take first exit onto N. Main Street. Go 0.7 miles. Turn left onto Washington Street. Barney Ford House is on the right.

Parking: Free parking lot on east side of the museum

Membership: Membership is available in the Saddle Rock Society. Call (970) 453-5761.

Web site: http://www.breckheritage.com/barney-ford

6 Bloom Mansion

When Frank Bloom was thrown by a bull, he hung onto the bull by the ring in its nose to keep it from charging again.

Denver Public Library, Western History Collection, X-1923

On April 27, 1880, a bull threw Frank Bloom over its head, tearing open a gash of seven to eight inches in his leg. When the bull came after him again, Frank caught three fingers in the ring of the animal's nose, held him, and called for help.

Jack Littleton heard the call, came running, put a rope through the bull's nose, and tied him to a post. The doctor tended the leg twice a day for ninety days. He had to make a five-inch cut under the knee and a three-inch cut in his calf to keep infection out of the foot. The bull was sold for $150 two weeks after the accident, and Frank did not get back in the saddle for nearly seven months.[1]

Bloom Mansion.
Second Empire Victorian: a French design popular after the Civil War. Central tower, wide veranda, prominent cornerstones, ornate woodwork, iron trim, mansard roof. Built of bricks manufactured in Trinidad.

How It All Started

Frank Bloom was the eldest of five sons growing up in Pennsylvania. He was close friends with John and Mahlon Thatcher and worked for their father in the Thatcher General Store. Frank was also courting the boys' sister, Sarah.

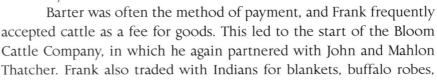

When the Thatcher brothers left Pennsylvania for the West, Frank joined them in March 1866. His adventures coming west are recounted in chapter 31 (Rosemount Museum). In October 1866, the Thatchers sent him to Four Mile Creek, four miles below Canon City, to open a store. The store thrived, but after John Thatcher visited Trinidad, he decided Trinidad would be a better place for a store. So Frank moved the store's inventory to Trinidad in the fall of 1867.

When he stepped off the stagecoach in Trinidad, after a sixteen-hour ride from Pueblo, he saw a town of 150 with fewer than twenty adobe buildings. The first Thatcher Brothers & Company store (Frank said that "and Company" referred to him) had a leaky dirt roof. Eventually, he moved the store to Main and Commercial, where he stayed for five years.

Barter was often the method of payment, and Frank frequently accepted cattle as a fee for goods. This led to the start of the Bloom Cattle Company, in which he again partnered with John and Mahlon Thatcher. Frank also traded with Indians for blankets, buffalo robes, and the like.

Colorado Historical Society # 10026061

Frank Bloom

On one occasion, some Indians came to the store to trade. One of them admired a large coffeepot. Frank saw the Indian put his blanket over the pot and feared he would try to take the coffeepot without any exchange. But Frank didn't want to risk trouble. A big tomcat happened to be sleeping on the counter, tail hanging down behind. Frank walked away from the man, and as he passed the cat, he pinched its tail. The animal leapt onto the Indian's shoulder, claws extended. The man jumped, and the coffeepot clattered to the floor. Mustering as much dignity as he could, the man quietly withdrew. Frank was certain that the man thought the cat knew his intentions.

On a Sunday ride in the foothills, Frank noticed dark streaks showing on embankments. This observation led Frank to open one of the first coal mines in the area.

Married at Last

Sarah Thatcher had been patiently waiting to marry until Frank was well

enough established to convince her father that he could support a wife. They married July 22, 1869, after a five-year, long-distance engagement. They traveled from Pennsylvania by railroad as far as the terminus at Sheridan, Kansas. Because of Indian attacks, the train ran only during the day. From Sheridan, they took the stagecoach, stopping at Bent's Fort for a rest on the way.

They visited with the Thatchers in Pueblo for three days, then took the coach on to Trinidad. While awaiting their household goods, they stayed at the Colorado Hotel, where "chickens roosted on the mantelpiece of the hotel and she [Sarah] had to pass through the bar to get to their room."[2] There were only ten English or European pioneer families in Trinidad at the time.

When they moved into their house at Main and Maple streets, each week Sarah received visits from Native Americans who came to the back door seeking fresh bread, potatoes, or meat.

In the early 1880s, Frank traded seven steers for a saddle mule named Topsy. He trained Topsy and rode her for eight years, thinking that she was the best mule he had ever encountered. Later, he sold her to John Thatcher's brother Judge Henry Thatcher.

Frank and Sarah had four children. Only one, Alberta, lived to adulthood.

The Mansion

In August 1882, the Bloom family moved into their new brick Second Empire Victorian, three-story house on the corner of Main and Walnut streets in Trinidad. The house was located on the same block as the home of Felipe and Delores Baca and their large family (*see* Chapter 4, Baca House). It

> **Herefords.**
> Messrs. D. B. Berry, of Pueblo county, and Frank Bloom, of Las Animas county, received a few days since a number of fine Hereford bulls, which they purchased of Messrs. Wm. Powell and Constable, Hereford breeders, at Beecher, Illinois. The Hereford stock is far superior to the short horns for beef purposes, and we are pleased to find that our leading cattle growers are discovering this fact. With good Hereford bulls in a few years the long-legged Texas characteristics would altogether disappear from our herds and the improved animals would bring a far greater profit to the breeder.

Colorado Weekly Chieftan, Pueblo, Colorado, March 20, 1879, Colorado's Historic Newspaper Collection.

Race Riot

Trinidad experienced racial tensions in 1867–1868, when a party of English American and European pioneers rescued one of their own being held in jail on suspicion of murder. The rescue party took refuge in the Colorado Hotel and a house opposite it.

The Hispanic sheriff raised a posse of almost entirely Spanish Americans to retake the prisoner. A riot ensued, with casualties on both sides. Ironically, the Anglo pioneer leaders of the affray escaped from the hotel and deserted their comrades.

The two groups began negotiation, and in the end, the European pioneers surrendered. The arrival of U.S. troops under the command of Brevet Brigadier General Penrose of Fort Lyon also helped restore order.

was daughter Alberta's seventh birthday, and because of the move, she had no birthday cake. But the house had a tower that she liked to go up to. She got to watch the animals being unloaded when the circus came to town.

Alberta Bloom, June 16, 1893

When she grew up, Alberta was supposed to attend Smith College in Massachusetts. But the Silver Panic of 1893 changed things (*see* sidebar in Chapter 12, Hamill House). Instead, she attended the University of Denver (DU), where she met her future husband, William W. Iliff, son of John Wesley Iliff, who was known as the "Cattle King." After Alberta and William became engaged, Sarah decided that Alberta didn't know enough about housekeeping. So she was taken out of school to learn how to run a household. She returned to DU and graduatee in 1897.

Alberta Bloom Iliff's daughter, also named Alberta, remembers visiting her grandparents at their house. Like her mother, she would go up to the tower and watch everything going on in town. She loved to sit in the tower and read.

Household Tasks

In the Victorian West, specific days of the week were designated for various household tasks. Sarah Bloom and her Thatcher sisters-in-law most likely followed a schedule something like this.[3]

Monday Laundry. Sort, wash delicates and whites, ginghams, calicos, and woolens last. Clean detachable lace collars and cuffs by hand. Use spot-treating fluids for taffeta, velvet, and so on. Monday evening, sprinkle and roll clothes to be ironed. Serve cold meals from Sunday dinner leftovers. *Tuesday* Iron using various-shaped irons heated on the stove. Beware of maids who daydream and scorch the pillowcases. *Wednesday* Baking and marketing. Most women ran an account at the shops, which their husbands settled monthly. *Thursday* Gardening, arranging flowers. *Friday* Heavy cleaning. Take rugs outdoors to beat clean. *Saturday* Polish the silver, furniture, and brass. *Sunday* Rest.

Alberta Bloom Iliff inherited the house after her father died in 1930. She held onto it for about ten years and then had to let it go for back taxes. It was operated as a rooming house after that.

When the Bloom house was dedicated as a property of the Colorado Historical Society in 1961, Alberta Bloom Iliff, then in her eighties, attended. She was presented with a cake, which was a replica of the house, to make up for the one she had missed out on when she turned seven.

Were the Bacas and Blooms Friends?

Alberta Iliff Shattuck recalls that her grandparents, the Blooms, had many friends in the Methodist church. The Bacas were active in the Catholic church. The church groups were somewhat separate from each other. And the families had different cultural backgrounds: the Bacas were Hispanic, the Blooms were Anglo. Baca raised sheep, Bloom cattle. But both men were involved in building the town and must have known each other in business.

So did the women borrow cups of sugar from each other because they lived next door? According to Paula Manini, Director of the Trinidad History Museum, we don't know. We can only surmise that they were cordial neighbors. There is no evidence to the contrary.

About the Bloom Mansion

The Trinidad History Museum consists of the Baca House, Bloom Mansion, Santa Fe Trail Museum, and Historic Gardens. The museum complex also has a bookstore and is home to the Trinidad and Santa Fe Trail Information Center.

Address: 312 East Main Street, Trinidad, Colorado 81082

Phone: (719) 846-7217

Hours: May 1–September 30, 10 a.m.–4 p.m. Monday–Saturday. October 1–April 30, Santa Fe Trail Museum is open 10 a.m.–1 p.m. Monday–Friday. Historic homes are open by appointment.

Admission: Adults: $8.00, Seniors (65+): $6.00, Children (6 – 16): $3.00. Colorado Historical Society members, Trinidad Historical Society members, Friends of Historical Trinidad, and children age five and under are admitted free.

Driving directions: I-25 to Exit 13B, Main Street. Go straight 0.5 mile.

Parking: Free on the street

Memberships: Membership in the Colorado Historical Society is available at varying levels of support. Visit www.coloradohistory.org/join_us/ membership_benfts.htm.

Web site: http://www.coloradohistory.org/hist_sites/trinidad/bloommansion.htm

7 Briggle House

Mr. and Mrs. Briggle often carried off the honors in six-handed euchre and whist at the many parties held in their home.

With thanks to Karen Musolf for collaboration on this chapter.

Courtesy of Maureen Nicholls, Breckenridge, Colorado

William Briggle was born in Ohio in 1861. He came to Breckenridge from Canton, Ohio, to work as the cashier at his brother-in-law's bank, the Engle Brothers Exchange Bank. Kathleen (Katie) Trotter was born and raised in Hamilton, Ontario, Canada. When William married Kathleen in 1896, the couple bought a circa-1896 one-room log cabin and immediately enlarged it by six rooms downstairs and three rooms upstairs. They then clapboarded the entire structure.

He soon became involved in politics, serving as mayor in 1903 and 1904. When the railroads threatened to cut off service, Briggle was active with the Chamber of Commerce to keep the trains coming.

The Briggle House in 1898. One and one-half stories local vernacular style with high gable roof. The Romanesque Revival exterior signifies wealth and prominence. Dark-green trim represents dollar bills. Silver, incorporated into the primer, lies underneath white clapboard. Large windows in dining room and front parlor resemble bank windows. Clapboard sheathing.

He was a director of the Metal Mining Association, thus aiding the town's most important industry.

He was also involved in the local chapter of the Knights of Pythias, the Kiowa tribe, and the Breckenridge Fire Department as a member of the Blue River Hose Company.

Entertaining

Katie, an accomplished musician, played five instruments and taught piano lessons. She owned an upright piano and often played all five of her instruments in a single concert. Her love of music is reflected in the front parlor, which was well-positioned for the many concerts held there.

A piano, accordion, and mandolin occupy one corner of the room, while a cabinet with sheet music occupies another.

Inside are extravagances that further differentiated the Briggles from most townspeople. At a time when closets were taxed as rooms, the couple had a dressing room that contained three closets. Visitors nowadays can see what Katie's neighbors envied most: her cold pantry, which is really two rooms. The inner room has a gravity-pull sink and well-stocked shelves of kitchenware; the outer room served as a refrigerator. She liked to bake, and she contributed several recipes to a 1908 high-altitude cookbook—pumpkin pie, cherry cake, orange marmalade, and chili sauce.

Kathleen Trotter Briggle

The Briggles entertained frequently, holding luncheons, dinners, fund-raisers, and receptions. Games were played at many of these, and the Briggles often took the prizes in six-handed euchre and whist.

Off the bedroom is a dressing room. On one wall, a door leads to a cut-in, would-be cedar closet. Katie couldn't obtain real cedar, so she had the closet wall covered with cedar-like wallpaper.

The Briggles had no children, but they did own a dog. William died in 1924. At the time of his death, he was a county commissioner.

Becoming a House Museum

In 1982, the Victor A. Kormeier Jr. family of Houston, Texas, gave the Summit Historical Society $80,000 so the organization could purchase the Victorian home. Two years later, the family gave another $10,000 gift to continue the restoration project.

About Briggle House

The Briggle House is owned by Summit Historical Society and operated by the Breckenridge Heritage Alliance.

Address: 104 North Harris Street, Breckenridge, Colorado 80424

Phone: Summit Historical Society: (970) 453-9022. Breckenridge Heritage Alliance: (800) 980-1859.

Hours: The house is available for viewing. Call (800) 980-1859 for information.

Admission: Free, $5 suggested donation.

Driving directions: I-70 to Exit 203, Colorado 9 to Frisco/Breckenridge. Take Colorado 9 south to Breckenridge. Go 9.1 miles. At traffic circle, take first exit onto N. Main Street. At the stoplight at Main and Lincoln, turn left (east) and proceed three blocks to Harris. The Briggle House is located in Milne Park, which is on the northeast corner of the intersection of Harris and Lincoln. Briggle House is the largest house in the park and is adjacent to the Milne House.

Parking: Free on street or in the parking lot of nearby Colorado Mountain College

Web sites: http://www.breckheritage.com/william-h-briggle

8 Byers-Evans House Museum

William Byers established the first newspaper in Denver. Elizabeth Byers named it the Rocky Mountain News.

Denver Public Library, Western History Collection, X-26104

Byers-Evans House.

Dark red Italianate architecture

In 1864, William Byers was with the first party to attempt an ascent of Long's Peak. After camping overnight near tree line, the party undertook the summit the next day. They never made it. Byers wrote, "We had been almost all around the Peak; so far that we could see all sides of it. We are quite sure that no living creature, unless it had wings to fly, was ever upon its summit, and we believe we run no risk in predicting that no man ever will be, though it is barely possible that the ascent can be made."[1]

William was born in Madison County, Ohio, in 1831. His father was a farmer, and because William was needed for chores, he went to school only three months a year for eight years. Later, after the family moved to Iowa, he attended a village academy where he took a course in surveying. He was employed as a surveyor in western Iowa. At age nineteen, he went to California with a surveying party.

In the fall of 1852, he followed the gold rush to Oregon. When he arrived, he had twenty-five cents and a ragged suit of clothes. He chopped railroad timbers and sawed logs until he got a government surveying job. After a year in Oregon, he took a ship for New York by way of Central America.

When the Kansas and Nebraska Act of 1854 opened those two territories for settlement, Byers went to west to the settlement that would become Omaha, Nebraska. Though still wilderness, that location at the confluence of the Missouri and Platte rivers became the gateway to the west. He became the county surveyor and directed the first surveying and platting of a large part of Omaha. He was appointed the first Deputy United States Surveyor for Nebraska. He also invested in real estate.

William N. Byers, early years

He returned to Iowa in the fall of 1854 and courted and married Elizabeth Sumner. She was the granddaughter of Governor Lucas, an early governor of Ohio, who was also the last territorial governor and the first state governor of Iowa. When the couple returned to Omaha, William entered politics. When the city government of Omaha was established, he was elected an alderman. In 1854–1855, he was a member of the first Territorial Legislative Assembly of Nebraska.

Denver and Auraria

William Green Russell had gained mining experience in the goldfields of Georgia, where he grew up working family mining claims with his father. Gold had been found on Cherokee land in that region in 1828.

William was related by marriage to the Cherokee Indians and was chosen to lead an expedition of his wife's people to the California goldfields in 1848. His brothers Levi and Oliver accompanied him. Along the way, he noticed promising outcroppings along the front range of the Rocky Mountains, but that year, it was "California or Bust," so they didn't stop.

William prospered in the Sierra Nevada and returned home to Georgia with enough money to buy a plantation. Levi went to medical

school, and Oliver mined in the Georgia hills. In the evenings, the Russell brothers remembered the Rockies. They decided to organize a party to prospect for gold in Pikes Peak country.

In February 1858, the three brothers and six companions set out from Georgia for the West. They rendezvoused with Cherokee friends from Indian Territory (in present-day Oklahoma) on the Arkansas River, and as they continued west, other fortune seekers joined them. By May 23, they reached the site where Cherry Creek flows into the Platte River. They found nothing for twenty days, and some of the men in the party returned home. But the Russell brothers and ten other men remained.

In early July, they found gold at the mouth of Dry Creek, where it emptied into the Platte. Present-day Dartmouth Avenue in Englewood now crosses the Platte where the Russells found their gold. They only panned a few hundred dollars of gold dust, but from this discovery, the Pikes Peak gold rush began. The Russell group spread out, looking for more gold.

A second group of men arrived from Kansas Territory. This group was led by John Easter, a butcher from Lawrence in Kansas Territory. He had heard an Indian guide's story about finding gold when he bent over a stream to drink. As the Lawrence party moved west, they, too, were joined by others. They came by way of the Santa Fe Trail and then moved up the Arkansas Valley. They prospected at the foot of Pikes Peak but found no gold. Hearing the news that the Russells had found gold at Cherry Creek, they hurried north.

News had spread from mountain traders who had met the Russells at Dry Creek that there was gold to be found in the Pikes Peak region. When the Russell group returned to their camp, they found the group from Lawrence. Within a few weeks, gold seekers from the East began to arrive.

The Lawrence party first staked out a town north of Dry Creek. But this venture died when the promoters decided a better location was on the east side of Cherry Creek. There they staked out a town they called St. Charles. They left one man to defend their new metropolis while the rest of the Lawrence group headed back to Kansas to gain a charter for their new town from the territorial legislature. Theirs was a business venture, requiring settlers to buy shares in their organization.

More people gathered at Cherry Creek. In October 1858, the settlers held a public meeting and formed a new town on the west side of Cherry Creek. They called the new organization Auraria Town

Company, named after a gold region in Georgia where the Russells had come from. Each of the company's organizers was entitled to receive a town lot measuring 66 feet by 132 feet, on the condition that the owner immediately build a house "at least sixteen feet square and comfortable to live in."[2] As a result, a collection of austere log cabins and rude frame dwellings were built.

William and Levi Russell returned to Georgia to visit family, buy supplies, and recruit men to return to Auraria in spring. Oliver stayed to winter in the Auraria cabin.

In mid-November, General William Larimer led yet another group of men from Kansas Territory. These men carried with them commissions as officers of Arapahoe County signed by the governor of Kansas Territory. At the time, Arapahoe County included in its boundaries all of Kansas Territory west of the 103rd meridian. (The 103rd meridian is the line of longitude that passes through Las Animas, Colorado. A line drawn north from the westernmost border of Oklahoma approximates the 103rd meridian.)

The Larimer group decided to acquire the St. Charles site thinking it had been abandoned. The one man left to defend St. Charles later claimed that the Larimer group served him whiskey and jumped the claim. Larimer and his men gained control. They renamed the town Denver City, after the governor of Kansas Territory, General James W. Denver. They platted the streets to parallel the river and the creek.

In December 1858, Larimer waded across the South Platte and staked out the town of Highland. He also mapped out another addition on the hill east of Denver City. He even staked out the Mount Prospect Cemetery at the site of the present-day Denver Botanic Gardens and Cheesman Park.

Cherry Creek separated the two rival towns, Auraria and Denver City. During the fall and winter of 1858–1859, the men built cabins and waited for spring.

Denver gained supremacy with the arrival of the first stagecoach in the spring of 1859. When the Russells returned from Georgia in May, they found that Auraria was losing population and business to Denver City. Hotels, saloons, and other businesses sprang up around the stage depot built on a site Larimer had donated. In early 1860, the two towns were consolidated and took the name of Denver. The Auraria neighborhood was known as West Denver.

Going West

William Byers felt the call of gold from the diggings at Cherry Creek. And the most popular route to the new diggings began in Omaha.

Byers decided to become the first full-time public relations man for the Pikes Peak region. In 1859, he set out from Omaha intending to publish the first newspaper in the goldfields. A wagon brought the press. But because he had no idea where he might set up shop, a name for the paper eluded him. Elizabeth had suggested it be known as the *Rocky Mountain News*. He set up office in a building on piles in the middle of Cherry Creek. The first issue was peeled from the press on April 23, 1859. Elizabeth arrived later that spring with their children, Mollie and Frank.

The Byers' first home was a rude shack common to all newcomers. When Elizabeth saw it, she wept. But they soon settled in a house behind the newspaper in Auraria. The Byers moved often, and later they homesteaded on a piece of land three miles from Denver. In October 1860, fire destroyed the house and furnishings. Elizabeth and the two older children escaped, and the baby was snatched out of his burning crib. The infant died four months later of natural causes. They built a new home at East Colfax and Sherman streets.

The *Rocky Mountain News* built its first building on stilts over the bed of Cherry Creek near Market Street in 1859.

From the beginning, Elizabeth was interested in the community. In the raw boomtown, many people roamed the streets homeless, hungry, and sick.

Governor John and Margaret Evans had come to Denver in May 1862. They became good friends with the Byers. Elizabeth and Margaret enlisted the help of some of the few other women there to form the Ladies Union Aid Society, to provide relief to the poor.

Denver Public Library, Western History Collection, Z-2318

Mrs. William N. Byers

At Gunpoint

Byers published tirades again the lawless element taking over the settlement on Cherry Creek. He demanded that they be run out of town. Many of these desperadoes hung out in the Criterion Saloon on Larimer Street. One morning, the gang was particularly incensed over the editorials and stormed the *News* office.

One young pressman raced to the attic for his gun. When the intruders made clear that they intended to take Byers at gunpoint, the pressman threatened to shoot. Byers admonished his protector not to shoot and quietly accompanied his captors back to the Criterion. The kingpin of the gang, Charles Harrison, arrived and took charge. After dismissing the others, he escorted Byers into the back room. No one knows what they said, but Byers was released out the alley door and advised not to linger.

When darkness descended, the outlaws dashed past the *News* on horseback, firing twice into the office. Two *News* employees returned fire. Those in the gang who were not shot were rounded up and the leaders were escorted out of town. They were advised that the hanging tree awaited any who returned.

Harrison also left Denver but claimed thereafter the courageous newspaper editor a friend. Byers' opinion of Harrison was never recorded. Harrison sent him a gold ring as a gift, which Byers kept but never wore.

The incident led to the formation of a Vigilance Committee that brought miscreants to trial before a people's court. Byers was a charter member.

Free Press

Byers occasionally published the names of delinquent newspaper subscribers. This brought a challenge to a duel from a ferryman on the South Platte River. In an editorial, Byers answered that the ferryman was wasting his time. "You may murder us," he said, "but never on the so-called field of honor

under the dignified name of a duel. While we do live and conduct a public press, it shall be free and unfettered, fearless to rebuke the wrong and uphold the right."[3]

The Byers lived in a small ranch house on the east bank of the South Platte River. On May 19, 1864, Cherry Creek suddenly flooded. The water rose so quickly that there was no time to escape. Elizabeth, William, and the children climbed onto the roof and frantically cried out for help. Troops from Camp Weld near Denver rescued them, taking them by raft them to dry ground.[4] For ten days, the Byers stayed at the home of the Evans.

The flood of 1864 wiped out the newspaper plant, and the press was buried under the river. Byers borrowed money and started over again. Also in 1864, President Lincoln appointed Byers postmaster of Denver, a position he held until 1867, when he resigned.

Life on the frontier was hard for Elizabeth. Years later, she said, "It was the constant anxiety of not knowing what would happen next, rather than any terrible things that actually did happen that made life on the frontier so hard."[5]

Moving On

Byers sold the *Rocky Mountain News* in 1879. He served a second term as postmaster of Denver from 1879 to 1883. In 1883, the Byers moved into the house on Bannock Street, which is the present house museum.

While he lived in the Bannock Street house, he devoted countless hours to the work of the Denver Tramway Company and to the progress of the Denver, Texas and Fort Worth Railroad, which was completed in 1888. Gatherings in the home led to plans for many organizations that thrive today. The State Historical and Natural History Society, and the Denver Chamber of Commerce were among the groups that held meetings there.

Elizabeth was always involved in many civic improvements. In her twilight years, she said, "I always considered I raised Denver. Yes, indeed, we pioneer women raised her from a lusty, noisy infant to the sedate, beautiful City she is today."

William Byers also helped establish the first telegraph line in the state. He left the newspaper in the hands of his staff and worked on the telegraph for several months. He walked the entire distance from Denver to Santa Fe, finding the best route and pacing off positions for every telegraph pole on the line.[6]

In 1889, six years after the home's completion, the Byers sold the house to William G. Evans, the eldest son of their good friend, Governor John Evans. The Evans family stayed in the house for ninety-two years.

The Flood of 1864

The early settlers of Denver and Auraria, which was across Cherry Creek, considered the creek to be a dry stream. Many buildings were put up on piles in the very bed of the creek itself. The bridges were low wooden structures, also raised on piles a little above the sand. Indians and mountainmen had warned the settlers that the creek sometimes flooded. But the settlers thought the stories were folklore and scare tactics.

A few days prior to the great flood of 1864, an abnormal amount of rain fell along the Continental Divide, where the headwaters of Cherry Creek and Plum Creek are. William Byers' diary tells us that it also rained in Denver.

About midnight, Thursday, May 19, when most citizens were in bed, a great roar was heard like the approach of a tremendous locomotive. Those awake attempted to wake their neighbors, and the alarm spread. The torrent swept up trees and houses, rolling with maddening momentum toward the Larimer Street Bridge.

The low bridge served as an obstruction to the wave, causing the water to rebound and strike adjoining buildings. It upheaved the bridge, the Methodist Church, and other structures. Onward it went, carrying broken buildings, bedsteads, baggage, and logs. Those who could got out of its way on higher ground but had no time to take anything with them.

The *Rocky Mountain News* had been publishing for five years and one month in a building on stilts built over the sands of the creek. It sank down into the waters, press and all. Five men had been asleep in the building. Upon awakening and realizing their peril, they jumped out a side window down into eddying water. They made it to shore in time to see their building, stock, and material torn up and scattered.

The water raced toward the Blake Street and Ferry Street bridges, which both fell. For four or five hours, floodwaters spread over Denver, Auraria, and the Platte bottomlands east and west of town. Houses were flooded three to six feet deep with water. Many stranded families had to be rescued. The flood took the city safe, probate records, and court records, which were never found.

After the flood, Auraria, came to be called West Denver. It suffered the most because it was on lower ground. Many people moved to Denver City, on the higher ground. Thereafter, Denver City acquired more prominence and importance, ending the old rivalry with Auraria.

Evans Family

William G. Evans was born in 1855 to John and Margaret Evans. William, his wife, Cornelia, and their two young children, John and Josephine, settled into the house in 1889. Margaret was born in the home that December, and their fourth child, Katherine, was born there five years later.

Bannock Street was now tree-lined, and mothers cautioned children to be wary of runaway horses and carelessly driven carriages. In the summers, a sprinkler wagon passed up and down the street to settle the dust. Flagstone walks lined the street. It wasn't paved until 1892, when asphalt paving was first used in Denver.

Colorado Historical Society # 10028128

William Gray Evans

William Evans served as secretary of the Denver Tramway Company and was a director on a number of boards in both the banking and railroad industries. Again meetings were held in the home, where ideas and planning took place for various organizations. He was also influential in politics. In 1894, he had a proposal adopted by the City Council that provided for the establishment of a comprehensive park system in Denver. The proposal met with a storm of protest from the press and public. The financial panic of 1893, occasioned by the repeal of the Sherman Silver Purchase Act, had left a number of businessmen impoverished (*see* sidebar in Chapter 12, Hamill House).

Years later the proposal for a park system, much as it had originally been presented, was put into effect by Mayor Robert W. Speer.

When Governor Evans died in 1897, William invited his mother, Margaret, and his sister Anne, who had never married, to come and live in the house. A two-story addition was built onto the house that created a separate apartment for the two women. This addition can be seen as part of the current house museum.

The title to the house was put in Cornelia Gray Evans's name after 1897. Cornelia's widowed father, Captain William P. Gray, also moved into the home. Cornelia's father and William's mother, Margaret Gray Evans, were brother and sister.

William and Cornelia's son, John, graduated from Massachusetts Institute of Technology in electrical engineering. He married Gladys Cheesman and moved to his own home. Margaret went to Paris to further her musical training.

Josephine pursued her artistic talents in Paris and at the Art Institute of Chicago. Katherine attended Miss Reed's school.

Anne Evans

Anne Evans was the daughter of John and Margaret Evans, and was sixteen years younger than her brother William. She had been born in London in 1871. Her adulthood was filled with active participation in Denver's cultural life. She was a founder of the Denver Artists' Club, which grew into the Denver Art Museum. Her expertise was Southwestern art, and in1936 she opened a gallery in the art museum. Her collection was instrumental in gaining national recognition of the art of Native Americans.

In the Depression years, she also contributed her time and money to Central City's determination to build an opera house and became chair of the Central City Opera House Committee. It was her idea to raise funds by having chairs in the opera house carved with prominent names in Colorado history. Progeny of these families donated one hundred dollars for each chair inscribed with the name of a forebear. The opening of the opera house was a great success.

She advised the Denver Public Library in selecting books from 1914 to 1941. Both the University of Denver and Colorado College conferred honorary degrees on her.

In the winter, she worked on her philanthropic projects. But in the summer, she retreated to her home at the Evans' ranch at the base of Mount Evans, which had been named for her father.

Becoming a House Museum

Anne died at the Bannock Street house in 1941, at age sixty-nine. Josephine Evans died in the house in 1969 at age eighty-two. Katherine Evans died in Denver in 1977, at eighty-three. William's son, John, died in 1978. His heirs along with Margaret Evans Davis's heirs decided to give the house to the Colorado Historical Society, reserving for Margaret a lifetime interest. Margaret died in 1981, at age ninety-two, the first of the Evans to be born at the house and the last of the family to live there.

About the Byers-Evans House Museum

Address: 1310 Bannock Street, Denver, Colorado 80204

Phone: (303) 620-4933

Hours: Open daily, except Sundays, 10:30 a.m.–2:30 p.m.

Admission: Adults $3.00, Seniors (65+) $2.50, Children (6–16) $1.50, Children (under 6) free, Colorado Historical Society members free

Driving directions: I-25 to Exit 207A, Lincoln/Broadway. Go north on Lincoln Street. Continue on Lincoln Street 1.7 miles. Turn left on Speer Boulevard. Go 0.3 mile. Turn right on Bannock Street. Go 0.5 mile

Parking: Hourly parking is available in lots throughout the area. The most convenient parking is at the Civic Center Cultural Complex Garage at Broadway and 12th Avenue, directly across the street from the Denver Art Museum and the Denver Public Library. The Byers-Evans House Museum is diagonal to the parking garage. Metered parking is also available throughout the area.

Membership: Membership in the Colorado Historical Society is available at varying levels of support. Visit www.coloradohistory.org/join_us/membership_benfts.htm.

Web site: www.coloradohistory.org/histsites/ByersEvans/byersevans.htm

9 Cherokee Ranch and Castle

Tweet Kimball once had her Italian butler put on his jeans and made him the cattle foreman for the day.

Denver Public Library, Western History Collection, X-13537.

rederick Gerald Flower renounced his English citizenship in Chicago in 1892 and applied for American citizenship. On August 6, 1894, he filed for a homestead.

He began construction of his stone house on the homestead and moved in with his wife, Amy, and his sister, Beatrice, on January 15, 1895. On his homestead claim form, filled out in 1900 to patent his land, Flower wrote that he had plowed twelve acres and strung barbed wire to contain his livestock. Local lore says that the twelve acres were used to raise potatoes.

The Flower family sited their home on a ridge at the edge of a high plateau, with stunning views of the

Cherokee Ranch and Castle. Castle with three-story tower and design elements of 15th-century English and Scottish castles. Castle and guesthouse contain twenty-four rooms, eight baths, and eight fireplaces. Great hall with timber-vaulted ceiling and two-and-a-half-story ridgepole. Built of native rhyolite stone quarried on the property. Artifacts from the circa 1300 A.D. period have been found on the land, and mountain man trails from the 1840s cross the area.

Front Range. The long trail to the house begins at the old territorial road, now named Daniels Park Road. U.S. Geological Survey maps from the period indicate that on this rough terrain, there were very few inhabitants nearby. In his homestead claim form, Flower listed a stone house, a well, a cow shed, three stables, a chicken house, tool house, buggy shed, and a water closet. The Flower house was finely crafted with walls of sixteen-inch-thick rhyolite. The stone is exposed on both the inside and outside faces of two main rooms and a hall. The house is visible at the top of the hill to the left as guests approach the castle driving up Deer Trail Road.

Frederick Flower prospered and added land to his holdings. At the time of the sale of his ranch to Charles Johnson in 1924, the property was approximately 2,380 acres.

The Johnson Period

When Charles Alfred Johnson, a wealthy Denver real estate tycoon, bought the Flower property, he thought he just wanted a hunting lodge. But as he and his wife began to make plans, one thing led to another, and they began to envision a castle.

Johnson hired the Denver architectural firm of Holt and Holt to construct a year-round residence with the architectural details of English and Scottish castles and country homes. The design was to be original and not a copy of any existing European castle. The site for the mansion was about 6,500 feet above sea level at the extreme northwestern edge of a mesa capped with conglomerate rock. It was just west of the Flower home. The towering location afforded a breathtaking view of the Front Range from Pikes Peak to Long's Peak as well as the grasslands in the valley below. There elk bugled in the fall, and a bear was once seen bathing in the pond in summer. The castle took two and a half years to build.

During the Johnson era, a graceful horse barn and two well houses were built. The barn, designed by Burnham Hoyt, is a wood frame construction, two stories high, with a gambrel roof. A porch was also added to the Flower house, with rustic supports fabled to be the branches of an apple tree. The two well houses are octagonal, with beautiful, still-functional pumps.

The Johnsons owned the property for thirty years. They called the mansion "Charlford," after Charles and Alice's son, Charles Jr., and her son Gifford from a previous marriage. But when Alice died, her husband began to spend time in California. Her two sons used the house until 1954, when they sold it.

Tweet Kimball

Mildred Montague Genevieve Kimball was born into a prominent Tennessee family at Fort Oglethorpe, Georgia. Her father, Richard Huntington Kimball, sent illustrated letters from his military post to his wife before Mildred was born. The illustrations depicted a little character named Tweet. When their daughter was born in Chattanooga, Tennessee, she inherited the nickname.

Tweet Kimball and her prize-winning cattle

Tweet's great-grandfather had purchased a million acres of land in Texas during the Civil War. But because no one knew how the war would turn out, he had two surveyors, one from the North and one from the South, write titles to the land so he would not be in danger of losing it either way. The Kimball family continued to accumulate wealth from eleven different businesses over the generations.

Tweet was raised in Chattanooga and attended the Shipley School of Pennsylvania. She studied at Bryn Mawr College in 1932 and majored in art history and architecture.

In 1938, Tweet became engaged to her first husband, Merritt Ruddock. In 1948, he was named sixth secretary of the American Embassy in London, and they spent four years living in a house near Ascot. There Tweet collected art. With her training in Southern hospitality, she learned to entertain diplomatic style.

The couple adopted two children, Kirk and Richard. After Merritt resigned from the diplomatic corps, the couple moved to California, but they divorced in 1956.

Merritt didn't want Tweet to return to Tennessee where she would talk about him to all her cousins, so he offered to help her buy property west of the Mississippi. She took him up on his offer and looked for a place near her friend Freddie Lincoln of Evergreen, Colorado.

When Tweet set eyes on Charlford, she decided this was the place for her. She bought the property and five additional ranches around 1954 and renamed it "Cherokee Ranch," after the Indian tribe that had lived on the land where she grew up in Tennessee. She also purchased additional property, bringing the ranch to 7,000 acres.

Tweet Kimball was an avid equestrian and served on the board of the National Western Stock Show. She rode both English and Western and hosted an annual ride for the Arapahoe Hunt Club on Cherokee Ranch.

Santa Gertrudis Cattle

The Santa Gertrudis cattle breed is a mix of three-eighths Guzerat Brahman and five-eighths beef and milking Shorthorn. The breed was established between 1908 and 1920 by the King Ranch in Texas. In 1940, it was the first new breed of beef cattle to be recognized in the United States. The Santa Gertrudis name comes from the Spanish land grant given to the King family.

Tweet had seen Santa Gertrudis cattle in 1938 and never forgot them. Once settled at Cherokee Ranch, she imported twenty-nine cows and two bulls. While the breed is known to survive dry and hot conditions, they had never been raised in a cold climate. When they arrived, her ranch foreman refused to unload them, saying it was a death sentence. Tweet fired him on the spot and came up to the castle to tell her Italian butler to put on his jeans. Together, they unloaded the cattle and began a fifty-year legacy.

Santa Gertrudis cattle flourished at the ranch, and Tweet was the first woman in the world to breed this type of cattle. She also founded the Rocky Mountain Santa Gertrudis Breeders Association. The cattle provided more meat per pound than Herefords. They are gentle and intelligent. Tweet's ton-sized bulls could be led around easily on halters.

Tweet said, "They are gentle, and we keep them that way. If we catch any employee abusing them, he is fired that day."[1]

Many awards and ribbons on display in the Ranch Room of Cherokee Castle were won at several state fairs and the National Western Stock Show. Cattle from Cherokee Ranch have been sold all over the world, including in Taiwan, Australia, South America, South Africa, and Canada.

Tweet was frequently found in the pens, working the cattle. She named each of her bulls and cows powerful names, such as Cherokee Commander,

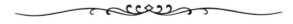

Cherokee Minotaur, and Cherokee Governor. Minotaur, along with Little Governor and Tallahassee (a cow) are buried near a large boulder with a bronze plaque along the driveway. These animals were important to the development of the present herd.

There is an interesting story about the storm of 1965 that Tweet told to writer Lee Pitts and published in *Livestock Magazine* in September 1981. In 1965, a deadly storm struck Douglas County, leaving four bridges destroyed, with debris and dead animals piled up in large numbers. Tweet recalls, "That storm took 12 feet of top soil from the fields. The Santa Gertrudis cattle during the storm were in single sire herds along the creek. Due to the commanding leadership of the Santa Gertrudis bulls who shepherded their cows and calves to high ground, not one animal was lost when an adjoining ranch lost 40 cows and all their calves. The Santa Gertrudis have shown an extraordinary ability to accept new climate and rugged terrain."[2]

From forty to seventy head of Santa Gertrudis cattle are now raised on Cherokee Ranch each year.

Becoming a House Museum

During the time Tweet Kimball resided at Cherokee Ranch, the original Flower home was used as employee housing. Wooden additions were made to the house over the years to accommodate families of the ranch workers.

Tweet lived in the castle from 1954 to 1999. Along with European artwork, antique furniture, maps and other documents, silver, and china, she collected hats. She also spent fourteen years on the board of the Denver Art Museum as accessions chair.

In 1996, Tweet sold a conservation easement of 3,140 acres to Douglas County, reserving five building envelopes, including the Flower home. Of Tweet's original 8,000 acres, her children received some land. In 1996, she established the Cherokee Ranch and Castle Foundation. The preserved land lies next to already-preserved county open space and Pike National Forest, creating a long wildlife corridor. The castle and ranch land will be preserved in perpetuity as open space for wildlife. It is not for use by people. Tweet did not want people interfering with the wildlife.

About Cherokee Ranch and Castle

Address: 6113 North Daniels Park Road, Sedalia, Colorado 80135-8716

Phone: (303) 688-5555

Hours: Guided tours are available to adults and children ages 12 and older. Tours are conducted on the following days: Wednesdays at 9:30 a.m. Thursdays at 9:30 a.m. Saturdays at 9:30 a.m. Call for reservations.

Admission: Adults $15

Driving directions: I-25 to exit 188 (Castle Pines Parkway). Turn right and go 2.7 miles until Castle Pines Parkway ends. Turn left on Daniels Park Road and go 1.6 miles. Entrance is on the right. Inside the gate, turn right. Go 2 miles up the driveway.

Or take Colorado 85 to Daniels Park Road, which is 2.6 miles south of Sedalia. Turn north and go 1.3 miles. Entrance is on the left. Go 2 miles up the driveway.

Parking: Parking lot is at the site. For handicap parking, proceed to the front of the castle and park in the auto court.

Web site: www.cherokeeranch.org

10 Cozens Ranch and Stage Stop Museum

Mary Cozens's employer wanted her to work as a prostitute. His wife objected, and there were many quarrels.

Courtesy of Archives and Special Collections of Regis University

William Zane Cozens was born in Canada in 1830. He grew up in New York, and at age eighteen began supporting himself as a carpenter. Like so many others, he came to Colorado in 1859 during the gold rush.

Mary York was born in England in 1830, where her father was a royal gardener at Windsor Castle. In 1842, when Mary was twelve, the family immigrated to Canada. Mary's father died en route, and her mother died three months later.

Mary found work as a servant in New York and Baltimore, and when her last employers, the McGees of Baltimore, decided to move to California, they asked Mary to go along. Mary agreed to go, for she hoped to become more than a servant in the new territory. However, Mr. McGee wanted to turn her into a prostitute. His wife objected, and there were many quarrels.

Cozens Ranch House in Fraser, Grand County, Colorado. Seven-bedroom frame construction. White clapboard, green roof and trim. Said to be the oldest building in Grand County. Sign on the house says Fraser Post Office.

When they reached the Platte River, Mary left the McGees. A man dipping water from the river, John H. Gregory of Georgia, listened to Mary's story. He was with a party of prospectors on their way to what became Central City. He offered his protection, and Mary accompanied the group, cooking and washing for the men.

At the mining camp, Mary set up a boardinghouse. There the petite, five-foot-tall Mary met the six-foot-two William Cozens. They married in 1860 and lived in a two-story house on Eureka Street, up the hill from the present opera house. When Jesse L. Pritchard was elected sheriff of Gilpin County, he named Cozens his deputy. A few months later, Pritchard left to join the Second Colorado Volunteers, so Cozens took over as sheriff.

Mary and William had seven children, three of whom, Sarah, Mary Elizabeth, and Billy, survived to adulthood.

Fraser Valley

The Cozens had vacationed in the valley below the junction of the Vasquez and Fraser rivers, and William paid squatter's rights for a claim on the left bank of the Fraser River in Grand County. In 1875, he moved his family there, where they spent the first winter in a cabin. Travelers began to stop there to enjoy Mary's hearty meals of trout and game, and to graze their teams.

In 1874, William began building the white clapboard house that is the present house museum. It was finished in 1876. The ranch house served as a stage stop on the route between Georgetown and Hot Sulphur Springs. Travelers facing the daunting Berthoud Pass could be assured of warm hospitality. Overnight guests were housed in six small, windowless rooms upstairs. Eastern sportsmen also came to hunt, fish, and stay on the ranch. William was served as postmaster for twenty-eight years.

In the 1885 Colorado census, Cozens listed his ranch as follows: 320 improved acres with 70 acres in mown hay; land and buildings worth $6,000; $800 in livestock, including three horses; and $300 in farming equipment. Hired hands worked sixteen weeks and received $200 in wages, including Mary and the girls who cooked. The farm grossed $816 for the year.[1]

Eventually, a grocery store, machine shop, and small cabins sprang up on the property. When son Billy was elected justice of the peace at age twenty-one, the Cozens' store became a courthouse.

The Jesuits

Around the turn of the century, a group of Jesuits traveled annually from Denver to the mountains for vacation, study, and prayer. During one return trip,

they broke a wagon wheel near the Cozens ranch. The group asked the family's permission to camp in tents on the property. The Cozens and the Jesuits became good friends, and William extended an invitation to them to visit the following summer.

William offered the leader of the group, Father Bertram, eighty acres of land so they could build permanent structures for the annual retreats. The Jesuits bought the land for $1,200. Father Bertram then deeded the property to Sacred Heart College (now Regis University). They called their property Maryvale.

William died in 1904, and Mary survived him by five years. None of their three children married. The Jesuits remained close to the Cozens children and spent every summer at Maryvale. They even constructed facilities to house and entertain guests. The priests also became involved in community activities and held Mass in a chapel on the property.

Denver Public Library, Western History Collection, Z-4868

Sheriff William Cozens appears with unidentified men in this studio portrait. Sheriff Cozens is seated in the center with a full beard.

After Sarah died in 1923, Mary Elizabeth and Billy deeded the remaining 732 acres of property to the Jesuits. The deed agreement specified care for Billy and Mary Elizabeth until death. Billy survived his sister, and he spent his final years with the Jesuits in Denver. He spent summers at the ranch for as long as his health permitted. Father Verdict of the Jesuits held many conversations with Billy up until his death in 1938. He recorded what he learned from Billy in a lengthy manuscript, which he finished in 1955. Unfortunately, that manuscript has been lost.

The Jesuits continued to use Maryvale as a vacation retreat for Jesuits from all around the country. The ranch house was used as a chapel for twenty-five years, until the 1980s, when it was used for storage after the Jesuits began to develop the property for commercial, residential, and recreational use.

About the Cozens Ranch Museum

Address: Located on the east side of U.S. Highway 40 between Winter Park and Fraser

Phone: (970) 725-3939

Hours: Summers: Tuesday–Saturday, 10 a.m.–5 p.m. Winter: Closed.

Admission: Adults $4, Seniors (62 and older) $3, Students $2, Children under 6 free. Members of Grand County Historical Association free.

Driving directions: I-70 to Exit 232 (U.S. 40) toward Empire/Grandby. Continue on U.S. 40 for 28.8 mi. through Winter Park. Cozens' Ranch is on the east side of the street before you get to Fraser.

Parking: Free parking lot.

Memberships: Membership in the Grand County Historical Association is available at varying levels of support. Call (970) 725-3939.

Web site: www.grandcountymuseum.com/CozensRanch.htm

11 Four Mile House

When Millie Booth couldn't put out a roof fire with water, she called for an axe, chopped away the burning roof boards, and sent them flying over the yard.

Mile houses were named for the number of miles they were located from a certain destination. They served as rest stops for horses and riders alike. Four Mile House lies four miles from where a number of trails converged near Denver in the late 1800s. It sat on Cherry Creek where the Cherokee Trail and the Smoky Hill Trail merged. It is the oldest standing structure in the Denver metro area still in its original location.

Stagecoach travel was a grueling and tiring way to travel. Four Mile House was a good place to stop, refresh, and prepare to make a grand entrance into Denver with a fresh team of horses (*see* Appendix A, The Smoky Hill Trail).

Four Mile House, located inside Four Mile Historic Park. Originally a two-story log structure covered with clapboard siding. In 1883, a brick addition added twice the square footage including parlor, study, bedroom, basement dining room, and kitchen. Brick and frame home with chimneys, arched windows, and a covered porch with spindle work and steps.

The Brantner Brothers

Samuel and Jonas Brantner built the hewn log structure in 1859 as a home for Samuel and his wife, Elizabeth. Stone for the foundation was quarried from a bluff to the north. The cabin measured twenty-two-by-thirty feet. That year, Samuel and Elizabeth's daughter, Izamba Anna, was born in the new home.

There is no evidence that the Brantners operated their home as a wayside inn. However, a rancher's home along a trail traditionally offered hospitality to travelers.

The Brantners planned to enter the livestock business and had brought fifty head of cattle with them. However, business was disappointing. In the late summer of 1860, they moved north of Denver and settled there.

Mary Cawker

Mary Cawker and her husband had managed taverns in Chicago and Milwaukee. When he died in 1850, she came west from Wisconsin and started a boardinghouse in Central City with a friend. That didn't work out, so in 1860, at the age of forty-eight and with a teenage son and daughter, she bought Four Mile House from the Brantners. Very few women pioneered here in the raw, wild West, and for a widow to take over the place was most unusual. Mary ran it as an inn, with a tavern downstairs for men only.

Widow Mary Cawker

Mary allowed women to use her living quarters to freshen up, mend torn clothes, rest on a daybed, or use the community toothbrush to brush their teeth. Beyond the sitting room was Mary's six-by-twelve-foot bedroom, which she shared with her children. Upstairs was an unpartitioned bedroom where guests may have stayed.

She started catering to the teamsters and migrants who come across the Smoky Hill Trail. Four Mile House gained a reputation as a warm, friendly stage stop before the final run into Denver. A barn and corral housed teams of horses, so a fresh team could be used to dash into Denver.

Dances were held on Saturday nights at the house. At eleven o'clock, Mary chased everybody out so that the travelers who paid her could sleep.

After the Cherry Creek flood of 1864, Mary sold the place to Levi and Millie Booth, who had stopped to camp by the creek for a short time. (*see* sidebar on

the flood in Chapter 8, Byers-Evans House). After leaving Four Mile House, Mary's managerial abilities served her well in several businesses. She ran a boardinghouse in Denver for variety theater performers and others. She also platted the Jersey subdivision in Denver. Later, she made her home in Southern California, where she lived into her nineties.

Millie and Levi Booth

Levi Booth was a lawyer. He went to Leadville to look for silver but didn't do very well. After he bought Four Mile House in 1864, he ran the place as a trading post, where furs, soap, food, firewater, and other merchandise were bought, sold, or traded. He also had a very successful farming operation.

One traveler wrote, "The ride down Cherry Creek, through sand and dust, on the banks of the muddy stream, was the most tiresome part of the overland journey. Mile after mile went slowly by, and still there was no sign of cultivation. At last, four miles from the town, we reached a neat little tavern, beside which grew some cotton-woods. Here there were two or three ranches in the process of establishment. The water from the wells was very sweet and cold."[1]

When the Booths bought the house, their son Gillett was eight years old, and Lillie Belle was less than a year old. Daughter Grace was born in the house in 1868.

Grace Booth Working later recalled an incident when the house was set afire:

> Mother and the hired girl were busy doing the family washing...A boiler of white clothes had been placed on the stove over a brisk fire. When Mother went to stir the clothes she found charred black pieces in the boiling pan. Looking overhead, she saw the roof was on fire....
>
> The hired girl cried and wrung her hands in panic, but Mother flew into action. She dashed water on her skirts, seized two buckets of water, climbed up the outside corner of the kitchen on the ends of the logs, and poured the water where it would

Levi Booth

Millie Booth

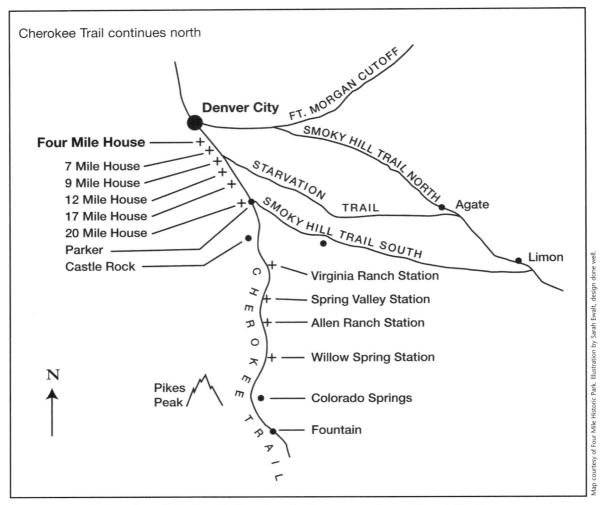

Cherokee Trail continues north

Denver City

FT. MORGAN CUTOFF

SMOKY HILL TRAIL NORTH

Four Mile House — +

7 Mile House — +

9 Mile House — +

12 Mile House — +

17 Mile House — +

20 Mile House —

Parker —

Castle Rock —

STARVATION TRAIL

SMOKY HILL TRAIL SOUTH

Agate

Limon

CHEROKEE TRAIL

+ — Virginia Ranch Station

+ — Spring Valley Station

+ — Allen Ranch Station

+ — Willow Spring Station

Pikes Peak

● — Colorado Springs

● — Fountain

N

Map courtesy of Four Mile Historic Park. Illustration by Sarah Ewalt, design done well.

The Smoky Hill Trail and Cherokee Trail converged near Four Mile House.

do the most good.... Mother saw they could not put it out in this manner. So she called for them to hand up an axe. She then chopped away the burning roof boards, sending them flying over the yard.... Late that afternoon when the men, riding back over the prairie, came in sight of the house, Father exclaimed, 'What's the matter with the kitchen roof?'[2]

After the railroad came in 1870 and the stagecoach declined, the Booths partitioned the second-floor room into three bedrooms. The divisions can still be seen in the ceiling and the floor, though the restoration put the

unpartitioned room back to its original shape. Levi built a schoolhouse on the property in about 1871. It stood southeast of the residence near the apple orchard.

By 1881, the Booths built a new house. Levi may have placed siding over the original log structure at this time. In 1883, he added the larger, brick wing. The new wing added twice the square footage and had a parlor, study, bedroom, basement dining room, and kitchen. The family did most of their living in the basement, where the kitchen and dining rooms were situated. It was cool in summer and warm in winter.

Levi was also justice of the peace. Millie made and sold butter, stamping it with her own seal of a rose. She also sold honey from her beehives. In addition to taking care of her family, the laundry, and the cooking, she also ran two cottage industries. She was very active in the association of honey producers.

Grace Working recalls that, "We went up to the mountains to get those Blue Spruce trees there in the yard. I was nine, and the trip took three days."[3] Some of those same trees stand in the grove on the south side of the house.

Becoming a House Museum

In 1945, the Four Mile House and a small amount of surrounding acreage were purchased by the Glen A. Boulton family from Texas. They worked the land and then leased it to others to work over the years. Boulton built a greenhouse and grew flowers, strawberries, asparagus, barley, and young evergreen trees. He also raised sheep and rented horses. He used the old log section of the house for storage.

In 1977, Four Mile House Historic Park, Inc., a nonprofit corporation, was established for perpetual and continuing development of the house as a history museum and the land as a public historic park.

About Four Mile Historic Park

Address: Four Mile Historic Park, 715 South Forest Street, Denver, Colorado 80246

Phone: (720) 865-0800

Hours: April 1–September 30: Wednesday–Friday noon–4:00 p.m., Saturday and Sunday 10:00 a.m.–4:00 p.m. October 1–March 31: Wednesday–Sunday noon–4:00 p.m.

Admission: Museum tours: Adults $3.50, Seniors (65+) and children 6–15 $2.00, Children under 6 free

Driving directions: I-25 to Exit #204. Turn right on South Colorado Boulevard. Go 1.5 miles. Turn right on East Bayaud Avenue. Go less than 0.1 mile. Turn right on Leetsdale Drive. Go 0.9 mile. Turn right on South Forest Street. Go 0.3 mile. Turn right on Exposition Avenue. Go 0.2 mile.

Parking: Free in parking lot

Memberships: Membership in Four Mile Historic Park is available at varying levels of support. Call (720) 865-0803.

Web site: www.fourmilepark.org

12 Hamill House Museum

William Hamill's imposing office was meant to impress and make visitors feel they were stepping into a bank.

Courtesy of James Werner

William A. Hamill was born in Liverpool, England, in 1836. When he came to the United States as a young man, he took a job in the office of a shipbuilder in Philadelphia. He met and married Priscilla McKee in 1859, who was from a wealthy Quaker family. With the outbreak of the Civil War, Hamill served briefly as a commissioned officer with the 156th Voluntary Infantry. In 1863, he was discharged.

The original two-story frame house that would eventually be known as the Hamill House was begun in 1867 by J. W. Watson. Watson was a miner and lumberman who came to Georgetown when he laid claim to a mine there. He was married to Hamill's sister, Nancy Ann. In July 1865, William arrived in Georgetown and took employment at his brother-in-law's tobacco store. Priscilla joined him in 1867.

Hamill House showing the greenhouse on west side. A corner of the spacious six-seat privy is at far left.
Early Gothic revival style. Pointed gabled roof and center front arched window. Steep, gabled, shingled roof with gabled dormers and brick chimneys.

Courtesy of James Werner

Visitors to Hamill's office were greeted at this imposing counter.

After some hard luck, Watson left Georgetown for Salt Lake in 1871. He took a mortgage on the house to pay for his journey to Salt Lake. Under the terms, the loan plus interest was to be paid within six months or the house would be sold at public auction. At the time Watson left, William and his wife were living in a small log cabin on the property. Because Nancy Ann was left alone in the house without any supplies or fuel, William deemed it his duty to move into the house to take care of his sister's needs. He moved in April 15, 1871, and was severely criticized for it.

Watson defaulted on the loan, and the house was sold at auction to James Clark for $3,882.50 in August 1872. William purchased the trust deed on the house from him for $4,308.84 in January 1874. The house was a two-story frame building at this time. From 1874 to 1882, William made additions to the house and property, making it a showplace in Georgetown.

He prospected in the area but had more luck managing some of the wealthiest mines around Georgetown. It was through his interest in the Terrible Mine that he became associated with Jerome B. Chaffee, the leader of the

Republican Party in Colorado.

In 1877, William became manager of the Consolidated Colorado United Mining Company, serving as a member of the company's board of trustees. He also managed several other mining companies that had been backed by English investors. The Colorado United Mining Company con-structed mills necessary for the reduction of the ore as it was taken from the mines. This was easier than shipping the ore to a reduction plant. As manager of the mines, Hamill gained a reputation for having an unparalleled know-ledge of mining operations.

Hamill's mine holdings led to involvement in numerous litiga-tions, and although he had no legal training, he tried all his own legal cases during this period. He acquired an enviable reputation in the field of law.

His position as a leader in the mining industry, led to an involvement in politics. He served numerous times as a delegate to the state conventions from Clear Creek County. In 1876, he was elected to the state senate. After Jerome B. Chaffee resigned in 1876 as chairman of the Republican State Committee due to ill health, Hamill was elected to serve as chairman in 1878.

In 1879, he resigned from this position. When a U.S. Senate seat came open for appointment, he was considered for the post. Personal grudges stemming from mining litigation were blamed for his failure to be appointed.

The Sherman Silver Purchase Act

By 1890, U.S. farmers were straining under growing debt and sharply falling prices. Farmers asked the government to put more money into circulation, either paper money or silver coins. They felt that this would increase farm prices and make it easier for farmers to pay their debts. Western mining companies were eager to expand the market for their silver, and they also exerted pressure on Congress.

With the Sherman Silver Purchase Act, the U. S. Treasury purchased 4.5 million ounces (or 281,250 pounds) of silver each month at market rates—almost the total monthly output from the mines in the country. The Act increased the amount of silver that could be coined. The Treasury issued notes redeemable in either gold or silver. However, the increased supply of silver drove down the price.

As the price of silver declined, holders of the government notes redeemed them for gold rather than silver. Because of this, the fear of a drain on the Treasury's gold reserves helped cause a financial panic in 1893.

The Act failed to expand the money supply as had been hoped. Because gold reserves dwindled to a dangerous point, President Cleveland called a special session of Congress in 1893 and secured a repeal of the Act. Overnight, Colorado fortunes based on silver mining were lost and hard times ensued.

Also that year Hamill began construction on the office building at the rear of his property where he could manage his wide range of business interests. In 1881, he began construction of a glass solarium that served as a greenhouse on the west side of the house. He added bay windows to the north and south sides, constructed a fountain in the yard, and planted ornamental trees.

Before he completed the upper floors of the office building, the silver crash of 1893 came to Georgetown and impacted his wealth. He couldn't afford to complete the suspended staircase in his office building.

Community Contributions

Hamill laid the first stone sidewalk in Georgetown. In 1880, when the fire department needed a new fire bell for the city, he paid for the casting and transportation of the bell from the East. The bell was inscribed with his name and placed in the tower of the Alpine Hose House. It rang every day at noon to signal the time.

In 1881, Hamill began construction of a two-story brick block for the business district. Known as the Hamill Block, it contained the First National Bank of Georgetown and Strousse's Clothing Store. A portion of the buildings still stands today.

In addition to mining, Hamill purchased the Junction Ranch in Middle Park in 1883. There he raised cattle. His oldest son, W. A. Hamill Jr., managed the ranch. William also helped organize the Georgetown and Middle Park Company to construct a wagon road between the two areas in 1881. He also owned a farm near Denver, from which fresh vegetables were brought up to Georgetown for household use in the summer.

Becoming a House Museum

William and Priscilla Hamill had five children: William Jr., Henry, Hannah Elizabeth, James, and Thomas. The family fortunes were greatly affected by the silver crash of 1893, and Hamill moved to Denver shortly thereafter. His wife remained in Georgetown with most of the family. William died in 1904, and Priscilla died in 1910. The last of the Hamills left Georgetown in 1915. The house was acquired by Historic Georgetown, Inc., in 1971.

Hamill descendants visit Hamill House from time to time. The best known is actor Mark Hamill, star of the *Star Wars* movies.

About the Hamill House Museum

Address: 305 Argentine Street, Georgetown, Colorado 80444

Phone: (303) 569-2840

Hours: Summer hours: 10:00 a.m.–4:00 p.m. daily. September through December: 10:00 a.m.–4:00 p.m. Saturday and Sunday

Admission: Adults $4, Seniors (over 65) $3, Students $3, Children under 8 free

Driving directions: I-70 to Exit 228. Turn toward Georgetown. Go 0.2 mile. Turn left on 15th Street. Go 0.1 mile. Turn right on Argentine Street. Argentine Street becomes Brownell Street. Go 0.6 mile. Turn left on 6th Street and then right onto Argentine Street. Hamill House is on the right.

Parking: Free on street

Memberships in Historic Georgetown: Memberships in Historic Georgetown, Inc., are available at varying levels of support. Call (303) 569-2840.

Web site: http://www.historicgeorgetown.org/houses/hamill.htm

13 Healy House Museum

Nellie Healy could not marry and keep her job as a teacher. It was assumed that her time could not be divided between family and her job.

Courtesy of James Werner

Healy House.
A three-story wood frame building built in 1878. Greek Revival clapboard siding. Window shutters, pediment-shaped window heads on the windows, hipped roof with flat top, and two chimneys. The porch has decorative balusters, straight posts and moldings, and a bay window on the south side.

August R. Meyer was born in St. Louis, Missouri, in 1851. At age fourteen, he was sent to Switzerland, where he studied chemistry and geology in the Cantonal College of Zurich. He completed his education in mining and metallurgy at the University of Berlin. He returned to St. Louis in 1873 and the following year, came to Colorado to accept the position of territorial assayer in the district of Fairplay.

He went to California Gulch, near present-day Leadville, in August 1876 to examine and report on the first carbonate discoveries for eastern investors. Seeing the potential of carbonate in the area, he bought the first carbonate ore in September, and hauled the ore by oxen to the railroad at Colorado Springs.

He built the August R. Meyer Ore Milling & Sampling Company, to ship ore, coke, and bullion. Meyer built roads at his company's expense to connect the mining areas. He organized regular freighting to supply the camp. When local teamsters refused to ship freight at reasonable rates, Meyer brought in large

shipping outfits from outside the area. To help develop the camp, he charged merchants a lower rate for shipping over his roads. He also helped the miners by paying large prices for small and odd lots of ore.

Meyer's company also handled the banking of the camp at California Gulch. For these efforts, he became known as "the father of the carbonate camp."

In 1878, together with Alvinus B. Wood and George L. Henderson, he laid out the town of Leadville and procured a post office.

That same year, Meyer built the house that is the present-day house museum. It was built for his bride, Emma J. Hixon atop Harrison Avenue Hill. Emma had come to Leadville early in the year and worked for the Tabors in their store and post office. The two were married in the Tabor home. Some of the items on display in the present house museum are originally from the Tabor House.

Meyer's two-story house was one of the first substantial residences built in Leadville. The Meyers lived in the house for three years.

Carbonate Camp

When gold was discovered in California Gulch, its name was changed to Oro City, *oro* meaning gold in Spanish. By midsummer of 1860, 5,000 fortune seekers had poured in. Augusta Tabor was the first woman to live in Oro City. She and her husband, Horace, set up a small general store to meet the needs of miners. In less than five years, the placer claims were stripped of their gold. By the mid-1860s, Oro City claimed fewer than 500 residents.

The few miners left cursed the gritty black sand that clogged their sluices. Then sometime between 1873 and 1876, William H. Stevens and Alvinus B. Wood had the black sand assayed. The sand was lead carbonate—ore brimming with silver. They kept their secret for over a year, buying up gold claims along the seven-mile-long California Gulch. Word of the silver strike got out. By early 1877, the rush was on. Leadville was named after the lead carbonate that bore its silver.

In 1881, Meyer left Colorado to return to live in Missouri. He sold the home to the Methodist Episcopal Church of Leadville. From 1881 until 1886, the house served as the parsonage and social hall.

The Kelly and Healy Connection

In 1886, Patrick A. and Ellen Healy Kelly bought the house and rented out rooms to boarders. It became known as the "Kelly House on the Hill." Patrick had the barn moved and attached to the original small kitchen to provide a larger kitchen and servants' quarters above. The larger kitchen made it easier to cook for so many people. Baths were provided in a galvanized tub in the

Daniel Healy

Nellie Healy

kitchen behind a privacy screen. Napkins were washed weekly, so everyone had his or her own napkin ring and saved their napkins.

Ellen's brother Daniel Healy was born in Ireland in 1858. He came to America with his parents when he was four. Following graduation from the Northern Indiana Normal School at Valparaiso, Inidana in 1884, Daniel joined the Kellys in Leadville.

In 1887, he served as a post office carrier. Two years later, he was assistant postmaster. By 1894, he was involved in real estate. He bought the house from the Kellys. The Kellys' names do not appear in city directories after 1895. It is presumed that they left the area.

Daniel had an insurance business as well as real estate. He also bought some mining claims. He served as senator from the 6th senatorial district in the 14th General Assembly of Colorado.

He continued to live in the house and in 1897 hired Mr. and Mrs. Harper to manage it as a boardinghouse primarily to schoolteachers. In 1898, a third story was added to accommodate more boarders.

Daniel's cousin Nellie A. Healy came from Michigan to Leadville to teach. Nellie had been raised in the East and educated at a convent in Canada. She lived in the house from 1892 to 1928 and continued to use the house in summers until 1937.

Following Daniel's death in 1912, Nellie and other relatives inherited the house, and Nellie took over the insurance agency. She did not renew her teaching certificate after 1912.

During World War I, Nellie hosted USO dances in the dining room. Visitors today can still see the raised floor that accommodated the dancing.

Nellie continued to run the boardinghouse, though in the 1920s there were only a few boarders. During the 1930s, she was the only resident and only in the summertime. She spent the rest of her time in Utah, and the house fell into disrepair.

Becoming a House Museum

In 1936, Nellie donated the house to the Leadville Historical Association. She died in 1946. After World War II, the association didn't have enough money to run the house successfully as a museum. It was deeded to the Colorado Historical Society in 1947.

Unmarried teachers

In the Victorian West, teachers were expected to be the perfect model of decorum for their students. Teachers were not permitted to marry without giving up their jobs. They could not divide their attention between a family and their jobs. Their spare time was often spent attending school functions and preparing lessons for the next school day.

About the Healy House Museum

Address: 912 Harrison Avenue, Leadville, Colorado 80461

Phone: (719) 486-0487

Hours: Mid-May through September: 10 a.m.–4:30 p.m. daily

Admission: Adults $6.00, Seniors (65+) $5.50, Children (6–6) $4.50, Children (under 6) free. Colorado Historical Society members free.

Driving directions: I-70 to Exit 195. Take Colorado 91 south toward Leadville. Go 22.6 miles. Colorado 91 ends at the edge of Leadville and becomes U.S. 24. From there, go 1.1 mile. Turn right on Harrison Avenue. Go 1 block and turn right onto 10th Street.

Parking: Free on 10th Street

Memberships: Membership in the Colorado Historical Society is available at varying levels of support. Visit www.coloradohistory.org/join_us/membership_benfts.htm.

Web sites: www.coloradohistory.org/hist_sites/healyhouse/H_general.htm

14 Hedlund House Museum

Two kitchens were used to prepare meals. Food was cooked in Ellen's kitchen and served in Mertle's.

Courtesy of Karen Hedlund Scott

Hedlund House Museum. Single detached frame structure. One-and-one-half story main gable is oriented east to west, with a north-to-south one-story gabled wing to the south of the higher portion. The exterior is covered in wood clapboard.

William Augustus Hill was born in 1837 at Derry, New Hampshire. At the commencement of the Civil War, he enlisted in a New Hampshire regiment of volunteers, serving as first lieutenant. He was wounded in battle and kept the offending musket ball as a souvenir.

Hill arrived at a spot between the Willow Springs and the Lake stage stations on the Smoky Hill Trail where the Hedlund House Museum now stands and stayed (*see* Appendix A, The Smoky Hill Trail). The Willow Springs station is now the site of the Lincoln County Fairgrounds located in Hugo.

The Kansas Pacific Railroad reached the watering stop near the stage station on July 5, 1870. Hill followed the railroad construction crews westward. He had stopped at Abilene, Hays City, and other points in Kansas.

Hill and his partner, Clifford Rogers, operated a general store and trading post serving the new rail line. The two men filed a homestead claim in 1875, and homesteaded the half section that is now the town site of Hugo. It is unknown where Hill lived from 1870 to 1875.

In 1877, Hill married Josephine Hegg, who had come to Hugo in 1876. They had three children, George, Ida, and Lottie. Records are unclear as to when the house that is presently the museum was built. Perhaps a portion of this house or a different structure was erected in 1877. In any case, Hill and his family lived in the house from 1877 until 1886, when it was perhaps leased for two years.

In 1886, Hill also platted Hill's Addition, which was immediately adjacent to the original town site. He retained part of the addition to the end of his life. To keep out other merchants, he placed a clause in the deeds to the lots he sold that prohibited the buyer from using the property for mercantile purposes. The reserve clause was stricken out of at least one of these deeds in a case heard in 1918 after the lot had changed hands several times.

When Lincoln County was created in 1889, Hugo became the county seat. The Hills moved back to the house from 1889 to 1899. William served as secretary of the Hugo school board for many years.

Changing Hands

The house passed through several owners from 1899 to 1912, including Lincoln County's first sheriff, Frank Tompkins.

From 1912 until 1918, James Dostal owned and lived in the house. He was a longtime employee of the Union Pacific Railroad. He also farmed 480 acres in Cheyenne County, just east of Lincoln County. In 1916, he built another house in Hugo, just south of the present house museum.

In 1918, the Peter O. Hedlund family assumed ownership of the house, and for the next fifty-three years, it was home to three generations of Hedlunds.

The Hedlunds

Peter Olof (P. O.) Hedlund was born in 1856 in Sweden. He came to America with his family when he was one year old. They settled in Knox County, Illinois.

Ellen Anderson also grew up in Knox County. She was one of a family of eight girls. P. O. and Ellen met at some time while both families lived in Illinois. In 1876, P. O.'s family moved to Holdredge, Nebraska. He and Ellen were married in Wataga, Illinois. Both were twenty-four.

P. O. held numerous county and state offices in Nebraska before he and Ellen came to eastern Colorado in 1900. He was 44 when he settled on a farm in Cheyenne County. Farm life was not new to them; both had been raised on

Back row: Ellen, Clarence,
Mertle, Helen (Arthur's wife),
Arthur, and P. O.
Front row: Helen and Arthur's
children, Marlyne and Audrey.

Courtesy of Karen Hedlund Scott

farms in Illinois. They were the first to raise wheat in Cheyenne County in 1903. P. O. served as county commissioner. The couple had two sons, Arthur and Clarence.

In 1911, President Taft appointed P. O. registrar of the federal land office in Hugo. P. O. and Ellen moved to Hugo that year. In 1916, he was elected to the office of judge of Lincoln County and served until 1932. Ellen served as the clerk of the county court and as acting probation officer of the juvenile court.

Meanwhile, Clarence Hedlund met Mertle Clark (sometimes called Mertie) in Cheyenne Wells, Colorado. Mertle's family had come by train from Milan, Missouri, to homestead in Cheyenne Wells in the spring of 1900 when Mertle was sixteen. She attended Denver University and Greeley Teachers College. She taught six pupils in a small sod schoolhouse located twelve miles from her family's ranch in Cheyenne Wells. During the week, she slept at the ranch where the school was located. On weekends, she made the long ride back to the ranch on horseback, wearing a divided skirt.[1] In a letter to her grandfather, she reported that once home, "I don't have a minute's time at home to do anything, but read my letters that have come during the week, and do the work."[2]

Later, she taught in Limon and Cheyenne Wells before her marriage to Clarence in June 1910, when both were twenty-five. At the wedding, Clarence sang "I Love You Truly" to the bride.

Second Generation

At some point after their marriage, Clarence and Mertle moved to Boulder, Colorado, where their first son, Robert, was born. They then moved to Chicago, where Clarence worked for Sherwin-Williams Paint Company. A second son, Thomas, was born there.

Clarence, Mertle, and their two sons joined P. O. and Ellen in the house in Hugo around 1925. P. O. founded the Hedlund Abstract Company, which traced

land titles when property was bought or sold. Clarence continued to run the abstract company after his father's death two decades later, and the current owners in Hugo still call it the Hedlund Abstract Company.

Robert's daughter, Fran Hedlund Mitterer, later recalled, "The County Court House used to be across the corner from their home, which was certainly convenient. I remember P. O. performing weddings in the living room. Mertie and Ellen would whip up refreshments on these occasions."[3]

Mertle and Ellen each won many ribbons at the county fair for jams, jellies, quilts, and pies. They were always knitting and sewing.

"I especially remember her [Mertie's] great doughnuts," Fran said. "They were a heavy, potato doughnut which she always fried in a vat of bacon grease. They cooked up plump, the hole nearly closed. They were delicious dusted with powdered sugar or just plain, dunked in coffee. Each time I go into the house in Hugo, I expect to be greeted by the smell of freshly made doughnuts and my heart aches because that smell is no longer there.

"Mertie and Ellen always spent one day each week just baking. They made rye bread, white bread, cinnamon rolls, and doughnuts enough for the whole week."[4]

Fran continues, "When I was a child, they always kept chickens in a coop out back. Clarence would kill the chicken, and Mertie would dress it for cooking. I used to watch her singe the bird over the flames of the coal stove. Then I would sit on the drain board and watch her as she cleaned and cut up the chicken. I was always promised the drumstick at the meal. I was much older before I realized that this was because the grown-ups preferred the white meat. To this day, I always eat the drumstick and think of Mertie."[5]

Tale of Two Kitchens

The house served the two families, and each had their own kitchen. Mertle did the cooking in her kitchen, and the meals were served in Ellen's kitchen. This arrangement required the food to be carried through the bathroom in order to be served. All went well unless the bathroom was occupied. In that case, one had to detour through Clarence and Mertle's living room (there was a door between her kitchen and living room then), go up two steps, through a door, across the landing, pass through another door, and go down two steps into the other kitchen. After the meal, Ellen washed the dinnerware in her kitchen sink and Mertle washed the cookware in her kitchen.

Fran Mitterer stayed with her grandmother in Hugo while her mother and father (Betty and Robert) went east, where Robert was stationed during World War II. Fran recalled those days: "I attended first grade in Hugo. The early morning dash down the stairs to the warmth of Mertie's kitchen was a bracing

experience. Mertie would always have my long underwear warming on the oven door handle ready for me to hop into."[6]

"Both Ellen and Mertie did a great deal of hand work. They cut tiny squares of fabric from worn-out clothes or scraps, hand stitched them and sent them to Mertie's cousins in Missouri where they were hand-quilted.

"The rug in Mertie's living room was handmade by Mertie to fit the room. It took many years to complete. It was made from scraps of fabric from articles of clothing worn by members of the family. In fact, I can recognize some of the materials. For some time, my grandmother Mertie helped at the abstract office, and we helped move the project there, so that she could work on the rug when she wasn't busy with abstract work. By that time the rug was getting large and hard to handle.

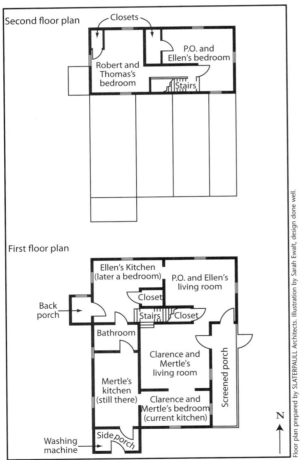

Floor plan showing original layout and later changes.

"Mertie willed the rug to me, but it is too large to fit in any room in our house (or any other family member's house). So I have loaned it to the museum and I do intend to leave it to the museum when I am gone. It was lovingly made for that room and that is where it should stay."[7]

In later years, the house was remodeled to accommodate just one family.

The current bedroom is located in Ellen's original kitchen, and the current kitchen was Mertle and Clarence's original bedroom. The new kitchen had modern gas and electric appliances. When Mertle cooked holiday meals, she continued to use the coal stove in her old kitchen. She never trusted important cooking to the newfangled appliances.

Both of Clarence and Mertle's sons were raised in Hugo and graduated from the Hugo schools. Thomas Hedlund lived in the house from about 1925 to 1939. His fondest memories include climbing a silver maple that stood in the front yard and doing his homework at a drop-leaf table in Mertle's kitchen. He also recalled sitting on the screened-in porch in the

evenings, where it was cool, and gathering with the family in P. O. and Ellen's living room to listen to "Amos and Andy" on the radio.

Thomas graduated from the Colorado School of Mines and worked as a mining engineer. He entered the Navy in May 1944 and trained in radio and radar, serving until the war ended. He went overseas as an air group and squadron radio/radar officer, and was discharged as a lieutenant junior grade in late 1946.

Robert graduated from Colorado University and was a metallurgical chemist. He joined the Marines and was killed in the Battle of Okinawa, the last campaign of the war. He is buried in Punchbowl Cemetery, the National Memorial Cemetery of the Pacific, in Hawaii.

P. O. died in 1943 at age eighty-seven. Ellen survived him by eight years.

Courtesy of Terry Blevins

The rug in the dining room was hand-braided by Mertle Hedlund especially for this room. It was made of scraps of family clothing and took many years to complete.

Becoming a House Museum

After Clarence passed away in 1971, Mertle Hedlund donated the home and property to the town of Hugo to be used as a museum. In August 1972, the Lincoln County Historical Society dedicated the museum. Officially named The Lincoln County Museum, it has been known casually as the Hedlund House since its inception.

Mertle died in 1972.

About the Hedlund House Museum

Address: 617 Third Avenue, Hugo, Colorado 80821

Phone: (719) 743-2233

Hours: Memorial Day through Labor Day, Friday 4:00–7:00 p.m., Saturday 1:00–7:00 p.m., Sunday 1:00–4:00 p.m. Or by appointment

Admission: Free; donations accepted

Driving directions: I-70 to Exit 363 toward Hugo/Kit Carson. Drive 0.3 mile. Turn south on U.S. 40. Drive 12.9 miles. U.S. 40 becomes Fourth Street. Drive 0.3 mile. Turn left on Third Avenue. Go 0.2 mile.

Parking: Free on the street

Web site: www.ourjourney.info/MyJourneyDestinations/LincolnCountyMuseum.asp

15 Hiwan Homestead Museum

The house grew to seventeen rooms with seven fireplaces, seven bedrooms, and seven bathrooms.

Courtesy of Jefferson County Historical Society

Mary Neosho Williams became a widow when her husband, Brigadier General Thomas Williams, was killed at the Battle of Baton Rouge in the Civil War. Mary and her grown daughter, Josepha, came west. Josepha enrolled in Denver's Gross Medical School. When she graduated in 1889, she became one of Colorado's first female doctors. People called her Dr. Jo.

In 1891, Mary, Dr. Jo, and Dr. Madelaine Marquette established the Marquette-Williams Sanitarium in Denver for tubercular patients. One year later, they added what was probably the first nurses' training school in Colorado.

Hiwan Homestead House. A seventeen-room rustic log lodge. Hand-hewn timbers, massive rock fireplaces, built-in cabinets, leaded glass in several upstairs windows, overhanging roof with dormers.

Evergreen

Mary's brother had a cabin in the present-day Evergreen area. In 1893, Dr. Jo bought 40 acres of Evergreen land from Jefferson County by paying back taxes.

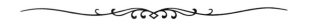

An unfinished hay barn on the property was converted into a one-room cabin by local carpenter Jock Spence.

Dr. Jo set Jock to work building an octagonal, two-story, tower like structure attached to the original cabin, which was converted to a large dining room. This room also served as living room, music room, and social gathering area. Mary was the oldest daughter in a family of twelve children, so this place became a favorite vacation spot for many of her relatives.

The first floor of the tower was Mary's sitting room and library. When she wanted privacy, a Navajo blanket hung in the doorway between the octagonal room and the original room of the cabin. People knew they were welcome to visit her if the blanket was pulled back.

Mary's bedroom occupied the second floor of the tower. The interior wood, pine and fir, was harvested nearby.

Guests slept outside in sturdily constructed wood-floor tents in a grove. The tents had furniture and their own wood stoves. She called the place Camp Neosho, after her middle name. It took a stagecoach or wagon two days to travel the rudimentary roads from Denver to the camp.

The Douglases

In 1896, Josepha married Charles Winfred Douglas, a young Episcopalian clergyman. Though they made their home in Denver, they joined the campers at Neosho when they visited Mary. When their son, Eric, was born the following year, Jock Spence was hired again—this time to build a second house behind the main lodge. The Baby House was used by Eric and his nanny whenever the Douglases visited Camp Neosho.

The rustic camp was a chance to get away from the grinding work of caring for patients during a hectic week. But the temporary nature of the small cabin changed now that Dr. Jo was married. Charles—a composer who wrote many hymns—brought a love of music and art into the home. He was music editor of the 1940 hymnal for the Episcopal Church.

The family enthusiastically gathered items from the natural world around them—pelts from coyotes and twigs and branches—and fashioned them into furniture and baskets. Rocks and antlers picked up during hikes reflect the curiosity of these original owners. The out-of-doors was to be both enjoyed and studied. In homage to nature, Dr. Jo asked the carpenter to build around the trees rather than cut them down. Giant stone benches circle what was once a fishpond, and the outdoor seating provided an opportunity to sit around a campfire and watch the stars.

Electric lights were installed in the house in 1913.

Another Addition

When Mary died in 1914, the Douglases moved into the main house. Jock Spence began another eleven-room addition. The present dining room was added. He built window seats with storage under each. Bookcases were built in at each end of the room, as was a hutch in the side wall.

The long dining table flanked by hickory chairs seats a crowd. Giant rock fireplaces dominate the larger rooms. Building a fire, even in the summer, must have been commonplace.

Spence added seven stone fireplaces throughout the house to provide warmth. He added a second octagonal tower to the north end. Upstairs, he built a small chapel, finished in 1918, which seated only a handful. There, the Reverend Douglas held services for family and friends. The stunning joinery in the chapel ceiling reflects Spence's heritage from the Scottish Orkney Islands, famous for shipbuilding.

Small eyebrow windows peer through a circular roofline. Verandas and porches accommodate bent or crooked tree limbs.

Next Generation

Eric grew up and married a beautiful Philadelphia socialite, Freda Gillespie, in 1926. They adopted three children, so Jock Spence added more rooms to the Baby House to provide Eric's family with a home. Today, this house serves as the museum offices.

Eric and Freda named Jock Spence godfather of the children. He was so proud of this honor that he built the children a stone building on the other side of the creek to be used as a playhouse.

Eric embraced his father's interests in Native American arts and collected Indian artifacts. He painted Indian designs directly on the dining room walls, which remain untouched. His collection later became the nucleus of the Native American Arts collection at Chappell House, the forerunner of the Denver Art Museum. He eventually served as curator for the Native American Arts Department at Denver Art Museum.

The Buchanans

In 1938, Dr. Jo died. Charles and Eric decided to rent out Camp Neosho the following summer. The delighted renters were the Darst Buchanan family. Buchanan was a Tulsa oilman. The Buchanan daughters had spent many happy summers in Evergreen and persuaded their father to buy the property as a retirement ranch.

Buchanan's wife renamed the place Hiwan Ranch. *Hiwan* is Anglo-Saxon

meaning "members of a family household."

The Buchanans acquired additional land for a cattle ranching business that spread to 15,000 acres and extended as far as Central City. Their Herefords won prizes at stock shows. Hereford hide still covers the dining room chairs.

The Buchanans' three daughters all married husbands active in Evergreen businesses. Mrs. Joan Landy was the last to raise her family on the property. She raised six children in a modernized version of the homestead. A third floor increased the number of rooms to seventeen, with seven bathrooms and a large modern kitchen. She stayed on the property until 1973.

Becoming a House Museum

In the early 1970s, the property was bought by a developer. By 1973, most of the land had been sold for housing. Fearful that Hiwan would be demolished, Jefferson County Open Space bought it in 1974. The museum operates through a partnership between the county Open Space Department and Jefferson County Historical Society.

The several outbuildings built by Jock Spence over the years, give the appearance of a compound. These include a housekeeper's cabin, woodworking shop, and gift shop.

Today, the remnants of the gigantic ranch include Hiwan Hills, the Hiwan Country Club, Hiwan Broadmoor, and the Ridge at Hiwan.

About the Hiwan Homestead Museum

Hours: June–August: Tuesday–Sunday, 11 a.m.–5 p.m. September–May: Tuesday–Sunday, Noon–5 p.m.

Admission: Free

Address: 4208 South Timbervale Drive, Evergreen, Colorado 80439

Phone: (720) 497-7650

Driving directions: I-70 to Exit 252, Evergreen Parkway. From the stoplight at the bottom of the ramp, go 6.3 miles. Turn left on Douglas Park Road. Go 0.3 mile. Bear left onto Meadow Drive. The road is unmarked, but there is a brown historical marker. Go 0.2 mile. Turn left into parking lot.

Parking: Free

Web sites: www.frontrangeliving.com/architecture/Hiwanhomestead.htm and www.co.jefferson.co.us/openspace/openspace_T56_R137.htm

16 Humphrey Memorial Park and Museum

As the first known commuter from Evergreen, Lee Humphrey made the daily commute to Denver over Lookout Mountain in a Model T. In more than thirty years of commuting, he missed only three days of work because of snow.

Courtesy of James Werner

J. J. Clarke began to homestead the present museum property in 1878. He was a miner and supply store proprietor from Central City, and he later served as state senator.

Under terms of the Homestead Act, Clarke was required to "prove up" the land—build a home, make improvements, and live on the homestead at least three months of the year. He built a small log cabin and lived on the claim during the summers. The main house was built in 1883. In 1912, when J. J. Clarke died and the Clark family moved out, the house was rented to loggers.

In 1920, J. J. Clarke's widow sold more than 350 acres and the house to Lee and Hazel H. Humphrey.

Humphrey House
Fifteen-room rustic log house built of hand-hewn logs felled from the property. A sawmill set up at a nearby spring was used to cut lumber and make roof shingles. The front yard is modeled on British gardens with stone-lined paths, a croquet court, and restored stone walls.

The Humphreys

Hazel Harry Hammer was the daughter of D. Harry Hammer, a wealthy Chicago judge. He wanted a child to carry his name. Because he and his wife had married in 1874 and did not have a child until 1881, he feared they might not have any more children and named the baby girl Hazel Harry.

Hazel Harry Hammer, 1890

Courtesy of Humphrey Memorial Park and Museum

Hazel H. could trace her ancestors back to England in 1630. Her mother, Mary Amaryllis Hammer, was a well-known Chicago socialite who traveled all over the world collecting art, textiles, china, porcelain, furniture, and other curiosities. She gave her daughter many collectibles from these trips, and many of those pieces can be seen in the present house museum.

Hazel H. was educated at English boarding schools and traveled extensively with her mother.

In 1898, the Federated Women's Clubs of America held a convention in Colorado Springs. As president of the Chicago chapter, Mary Amaryllis attended the convention with her daughter, who was 17 years old. At that convention Hazel H. met Carl Paddock, a newspaperman from Denver. They married in 1901 and had two sons. After Carl's death in 1914, Hazel H. married Lucius (Lee) Humphrey, another Denver newspaperman, in 1916. Their only child, Hazel Lou, was born in 1917.

Lee Humphrey was twenty-seven when he moved to Denver in 1910. He worked for several small newspapers before joining the *Rocky Mountain News*.

Commuting in a Model T

Though Lee Humphrey worked for newspapers in Denver, he wanted the Clarke ranch to be his family home. Lee moved the original Clarke "prove up" cabin to the main house in 1921. In the present house museum, the original cabin serves as the main bedroom.

The Humphrey family expanded the home, adding a guest room in 1927 and sun porch in 1935. For the remainder of the twentieth century, the Humphreys lived and ranched there. They raised horses, burros, Tagenberg goats, and other small animals.

Lee was the city desk editor for the *Rocky Mountain News* for nearly twenty-three years, and he was at the *Denver Post* for more than eleven years. As the first known commuter from Evergreen, he made the two-and-one-half hour, one-way, daily

commute to Denver over Lookout Mountain in a Model T that he named Mary Ann. He missed only three days of work because of snow—those during a storm in 1934.

The Humphreys were vegetarians and great entertainers. At their frequent dinner parties, they used one of their twenty-three sets of dishes. They also entertained on horseback, offering dinner from a wagon. Lee made wine from currants grown on the property.

A band of Utes sometime camped near the ranch house, sometimes coming to beg for some of the freshly baked bread they smelled. When the Utes saw that Hazel Lou was the only little girl in the house, they brought some of their children to play. As a result, Hazel Lou had many life-long friendships among the Utes.

Hazel Lou

Hazel Lou Humphrey began her education at a one-room school in Soda Creek Valley. After two years at the school, her mother hired a former schoolteacher to teach Hazel Lou at home. The teacher had left her position in the public school when she married. The restrictions of hiring married teachers did not stop the Humphreys. (*See* Chapter 13, Healy House.) The Humphreys built a cabin to be used as the school building.

After her formal education ended, Hazel Lou continued to read, study, and take classes, particularly in art. She made jewelry, trademarked with the ranch brand of a teepee and the letter *H*.

Hazel Lou was an accomplished horsewoman. Her horse, Cheyenne, was more pet than mount, and she taught him many tricks during the seventeen years she had him, including lying down with his head in her lap.

Courtesy of Humphrey Memorial Park and Museum

Hazel Lou Humphrey

Hazel Lou was also civic minded, participating in many clubs and organizations. She and her mother were very supportive of the Evergreen Players Club, and she appeared in at least one play when the club was first organized.

After her mother's death in 1972, Hazel Lou remained active in community affairs. She was one of the three founders of the Jefferson County Historical Society whose main purpose was preservation of the Hiwan Homestead Museum through Jefferson County Open Space. The society provides tour

guides and carries out special events and exhibits. (*See* Chapter 15, Hiwan Homestead Museum).

Hazel H. left many scrapbooks that she carefully put together in her own handwriting. The scrapbooks document the many guests to the ranch and contain photos of Hazel Lou.

Becoming a House Museum

Lee Humphrey died in 1946 at age 63.

Hazel Lou envisioned that her ranch and home would someday be a museum. She left a trust fund and a will creating what is now the Humphrey Memorial Park and Museum. It is full of collections the family gathered during world travels as well as Native American artifacts from many tribes.

The ranch buildings were granted national historic designation in the 1970s. The house museum contains nothing that did not belong to the Humphreys. Since the Humphreys were avid collectors, the museum is filled to overflowing with valuable artifacts as well as interesting nostalgia items such as rows of mason jars canned with strawberry and cherry jelly. The house is preserved as it was when Hazel Lou died in 1995 at age seventy-eight.

A board of directors owns and manages the museum and estate as there are no heirs.

About Humphrey Memorial Park and Museum

Address: P.O. Box 2122, 620 S. Soda Creek Road, Evergreen, CO 80437

Phone: 303-674-5429

Hours: Monday—Friday by appointment only. House museum tours last about one and one half hours. Add one-half hour for tour of the grounds. Children over 12 accompanied by a parent are welcome.

Admission: $5 per person donation is requested.

Driving directions: I-70 to Exit 252 Evergreen Parkway (Highway 74). Pass through one stop light at the El Rancho intersection. Continue on Highway 74 up the hill to the next stop light at Bergen Park. Turn right (north) onto Bergen Parkway and follow around the front of Fillius Park. Take the first left onto Soda Creek Road. Do not turn onto Humphrey Drive. The museum is about a mile down the road on the right side.

Parking: Free

Web site: www.hmpm.org

17 Jack Dempsey Museum and Park

A school chum wrapped a bullet in a wad of paper and handed it to Jack, encouraging him to throw it into the school stove. When the shell exploded, Jack received a willowing from the teacher. He in turn thrashed his classmate.

Courtesy of James Werner

Manassa, Colorado, was settled by Mormons in 1878. Two years after the initial group arrived, Jack Dempsey's parents came from Logan County, West Virginia, where they had been converted to the Church of Latter Day Saints.

Hyrum Dempsey and his wife, Celia, and their two children drove a prairie schooner through dust storms and prairies scarce in water in search of a better life in Colorado. Hyrum built an undistinguished little stucco shack and surrounded it with a tattered picket fence. The logs now on the cabin were not added until after the house became a museum. The original location was at the northwest lot at the intersection of 7th Street and Morgan Street within town limits.

Jack Dempsey Cabin, Manassa, Colorado.
One-room stucco with log facing. The log house has a side gable and stone fireplace. A stone well stands in back of the cabin.

Hyrum accepted the Mormon faith but believed he was too weak to follow it. In Manassa he took various jobs as laborer, mill attendant, and farmhand. He moved from job to job. Celia was ambitious, loving, hard working, and religious. Her Cherokee, and Hyrum's Choctaw lineage, gave their son Jack his high cheekbones and cinder-black hair.

Jack Dempsey was born June 24, 1895, and was named William Harrison Dempsey, after President William Henry Harrison. As a boy, he was called Harry or Willy; but when he reached his teens and began to box, he took the name Jack.

Dempsey weighed 11 pounds at birth. The Dempsey family already had eight other children. There would be 11 Dempsey children in all, and two would die in infancy. The family was poor, and the children played with scraps of wood as substitute toys. The Church Relief Society made sure they had food.

Jack learned to ride a horse almost before he could walk. He spent summers at a swimming hole on the nearby Conejos River called Dead Man's Gulch. In the winter he hung around Haynie Store or Rogers' Blacksmith Shop. Celia believed in letting her kids play outside in the wet and rain, and they were seldom sick.

Learning to Fight

His brother Bern, who was nearly twenty years older, taught Jack to box. He made sure the boy learned that the thumb belonged on the outside of the hand, not stuck inside.

Once a school chum wrapped a bullet in a wad of paper and handed it to Jack, encouraging him to throw it into the school stove. When the shell exploded, Dempsey received a willowing from the teacher. He in turn thrashed his classmate.

On another occasion, when he got into a fight with a boy named Fred Daniels, a crowd gathered to watch the fight. The senior Daniels yelled out, "Bite him, Fred!" When Fred paused to look at his father, Dempsey landed a crunching blow to the boy's chin. Young Fred had to be revived by the local veterinarian.

But Jack wasn't always fighting. He also liked to hunt birds' nests and was thought of as a bit of a mama's boy.

Leaving Manassa

The Dempseys spent twenty-five years along the Conejos River in the 26-by-18-foot stucco house. In 1905, when Jack was ten years old, Hyrum grew restless. He sold everything, packed the family into a wagon, and moved eighty-

five miles west to Creede. Celia pooled the family resources and opened a boardinghouse.

Bern Dempsey was now a struggling amateur fighter. He continued to teach Jack what he knew including how to stand and how to lead. He introduced Jack to Andy Malloy, another prizefighter who came to Creede now and then. Malloy would later accompany Dempsey, billed as Kid Blackie, across Colorado for boxing exhibitions.

By the time he was 11, he was chewing the gum from pine trees to toughen his jaw. When he was a teenager, he would walk into saloons and challenge the toughest men to fight for a dollar. He had as many as 200 such fights and rarely lost. At this time, he began calling himself "Jack," after a famous fighter named Jack Dempsey from the late 1800s.

When Jack beat Jess Willard for the heavyweight championship world title in 1919, the *Antonito Ledger* put the story on page five. But Manassa was quick to claim him. The "Manassa Mauler" was heavyweight champion from 1919 until 1926.

Dempsey returned to Manassa in 1966 for a Pioneer Days Celebration that honored the opening of his boyhood home as a museum. More than 5,000 people turned out for the festivities. It was the last time he would be there. When asked about his playmate, Fred Daniels' brother, Mooney Daniels, Dempsey commented, "Mooney Daniels was the only boy in Manassa I was never able to lick."[1]

Becoming a House Museum

In the 1960s, the town board acquired the house where Jack Dempsey was born, made repairs, and moved it to its present location. The exterior log façade was added at this time.

About Jack Dempsey Museum and Park

Address: 412 Main Street, Manassa, CO 81141

Phone: (719) 843-5207

Hours: Memorial Day Weekend—Labor Day Weekend, Tuesday—Saturday 10:00 a.m—5:00 p.m.

Admission: Free. Donations are appreciated.

Driving directions: I-25 to Exit 52 toward Walsenburg on U.S. 160. Go 2.4 miles. U.S. 160 becomes Main Street in Walsenburg. Turn right on 7th Street (U.S. 160). [The author highly recommends Andy's Smokehouse BBQ just past this turn at the far side of Safeway parking lot.] Continue West U.S. 160 for 71.4 miles. In Alamosa, turn left on West Avenue (U.S. 285). Go 21.1 miles. At Romeo, turn left onto Main Street. Go 2.8 miles. Note: From Alamosa to Romeo there are no road signs for mileage to Manassa. But after the turn at Romeo, there is an indication that Manassa is ahead.

Parking: Free on street

Web site: www.museumtrail.org/JackDempseyMuseum.asp

18 John Gully Homestead

For decades, the Gully family held rodeos to raise money to sustain the ranch.

Courtesy of James Werner

John Gully was born in Neanagh, Tipperary, Ireland, in 1850 to Thomas and Temperance (Powell) Gully. Besides John, the Gullys had six other children. Due in part to the lingering effects of the Great Famine, the family traveled in steerage below decks to America. From New York, they traveled west in 1862 by wagon train across the Great Plains. Thomas was sixty years old, Temperance fifty. Daughter Bridget, her husband, John DeLaney, and infant daughter Molly traveled with the Gullys.

The family reached Colorado and lived off the land, working for pay when they had the chance. Shortly after their arrival, they headed to the gold diggings in the mountains. Their

John Gully Homestead.
Oldest surviving dwelling in Aurora. Frame structure. Clapboard on the front and board and batten on the sides and around the kitchen. Wood shingle roof with three working chimneys and one fake chimney arising from the loft. Formal façade with central door and symmetrically placed window on each side of the door. East and west gable ends contain loft windows. A large front porch spans the front of the house. Wood columns are detailed with caps and bases.

cousins, the Powells, had settled in Central City. John went to school in Silver Plume, Blackhawk, and Central City as the family moved from place to place. In 1866, when John was 16, the family moved to Tollgate, in what is now the city of Aurora, where they worked their own ranch.

In 1871, John Gully homesteaded 160 acres in Arapahoe County near Tollgate Creek, when that part of the territory was unbroken wilderness. He built, or brought to the site, a one-room frame structure that can be seen as the back part of the current house museum. He carried on **dry land farming** and raised horses to sell to local delivery businesses, including the Daniels and Fisher Department Store and Denver Dry Goods.

Sometime in the mid-1870s, he built a one-and-a-half story addition to the earlier one-room house. This is the front part of the current house museum. The new house contained a living room and a bedroom. An enclosed central stair led to a loft room. The attached older house became the kitchen. As the years passed, John continued to add to his property until he had accumulated 1,120 acres.

In September 1892, John married Elizabeth Clifford. Elizabeth was born in Iowa in 1866 and was educated there. She obtained a teacher's certificate and taught in Iowa for two years. She taught in Colorado at Tollgate's one-room schoolhouse until her marriage to John.

John and Elizabeth (Clifford) Gully

Courtesy of Aurora History Museum

John and Elizabeth Gully had seven children. Five survived: Mary Frances, James Edward, John Thomas, William Anthony, and Elizabeth Alphonse. All the children went to Tollgate School.

Mary Frances Gully later recalled that there were Indians in the area before 1900. In an oral history, she recalled, "I remember hearing about how they would walk off with our bright tin pans for milk. They never harmed any of us and we thought a few pans as a peace offering were a bargain."[1]

Mary Frances also pointed out that settlers in those days had very little money. They made most of their own recipes for treating coughs and various ailments. Many of these old-time remedies are the basis for best-selling remedies today. Out of her Grandfather Gully's notebook comes, "Red Pepper Rub for arthritis: alcohol plus cayenne pepper applied freely to affected joints— external only."[2]

John Gully was active in Democratic Party politics and was offered nomination to public office several times. He always declined, preferring to put his attention on business affairs and farming.

Mother Cabrini, head of the Queen of Heaven Orphanage, used to ride out to the end of the streetcar line and head for the Gully Ranch. John would have Mary Frances hitch up a team to take Mother Cabrini to visit the various ranches.

When he was approaching death, John requested that he be buried at Fairmont Cemetery because the long drive to Mount Olivet in Wheat Ridge would be too hard on the horses. He died in May 1915 at age 65. Elizabeth died in 1927 at age 61.

Courtesy of Aurora History Museum

Mary Gully with her class in front of Tollgate School.

Courtesy of Aurora History Museum

Gully family rodeo, 1920s

Rodeos

Mary Frances married John O'Brien in 1925. Their sons, John Jr. and Jim, lived on the home place. From the 1920s to the 1950s, the Gully family held widely attended rodeos on the ranch to raise money needed to sustain the ranch.

The house was occupied until the death of John Gully Jr.'s son, William, in 1962.

Becoming a House Museum

In 1976, the grandchildren of John and Elizabeth Gully offered the house to the city of Aurora. In 1978, real estate development company Medema Homes again offered it to Aurora. The homestead was located in a one-hundred-year flood plain and directly in the center of a proposed runoff canal. The city of Aurora purchased the house and associated outbuildings in 1982. The house was moved to its present location at Alameda Avenue and Chambers Road in 1983. Moving the house cost $4,000 and restoration began following the move.

About the John Gully Homestead

Address: 200 S. Chambers Rd. Aurora, Colorado 80017

Phone: 303-739-6667 to schedule a tour.

Hours: February–October, by appointment only

Admission: Price information available at time of reservation.

Driving directions: Driving arrangements are made when the tour is arranged.

Parking: Free at DeLaney Farm Historic District parking lot, 170 South Chambers Road.

Memberships: Membership in the Aurora Museum Foundation are available at various levels of support. Contact the Foundation at (303) 739-6705 or www.aurora-museum.org

Web site: www.aurora-museum.org or www.auroragov.org/AuroraGov/ Departments/LibraryRecreationandCulturalServices/CulturalServices

19 Justina Ford House

The lady doctor was often paid in groceries and poultry for delivering babies.

Justina Laurena Warren was born on January 22, 1871, in Knoxville, Illinois. Her mother was a nurse. Justina was allowed to assist her mother as she made rounds caring for the sick.

In 1873, the family moved to Galesburg, just a few miles from Knoxville where Justina grew up. In 1884, her father died.

In an interview later in life, Justina said, "I wouldn't play with the others unless we played hospital, and I wouldn't play even that unless they let me be the doctor. I didn't know the names of any medicines, so I had one standard prescription: tobacco pills. I didn't know the names of any sicknesses, so I invented names. I remember that I used to like to dress chickens for dinner so I could get in there and see what the insides were like."[1]

In 1890, she graduated from high school and enrolled at Hering Medical College in Chicago. In those days, students often entered medical school following high school. An undergraduate college degree was not required. Hering

Courtesy of Joyce B. Lohse

Justina Ford House.
The two-story brick Italianate house in its present location on California Street in Denver.
The Justina Ford House is the property of Black American West Museum.

accepted women equally with men, and women could be on the teaching staff. The school also welcomed students from all ethnic groups. School was hard work. It required lectures, lab work, and attendance at hospital or dispensary clinics.

In 1892, just a month before her twenty-second birthday, Justina married the Reverend Dr. John Elijah Ford, who was nearly ten years her senior. He was a well-known minister, educator, scholar, and businessman.

Justina graduated in 1899, and the state of Illinois awarded her a medical license. She set up practice in Chicago but was soon invited to assist in the building of a hospital at the State Normal and Agricultural College in Normal-Huntsville, Alabama, and to serve as its director. She accepted with the understanding that she would not stay in Alabama more than two years.

Life in Alabama was a cultural shock to Dr. Ford. In Illinois, life for blacks was not as restrictive as it was in the South. When her two years in Alabama were up, she moved to Denver where her husband served as pastor of the Zion Baptist Church. She hoped there would be more opportunity for a black woman doctor in the West.

Two Strikes Against Her

Dr. Ford served briefly in a hospital in St. Louis before rejoining her husband in Denver. While attitudes toward blacks in Denver were better than those in Alabama, Dr. Ford quickly discovered that Denver had its own obstacles. Upon applying for her license to practice medicine, the licensing examiner said, "Ma'am, I'd feel dishonest taking a fee from you. You've got two strikes against you to begin with. First off, you're a lady. Second, you're colored."[2]

Dr. Ford often referred to the double barrier that she struggled against all her life. She was not only aware of the prejudice, but, as she said in later years, "I fought like a tiger against those things."[3]

In spite of the warning from the licensing examiner in Denver, she received her Colorado medical license on October 7, 1902. She was one of only a very small number of black female doctors in the United States. And, she was the first one in Colorado.

Home Practice

In 1911, Dr. Ford purchased her nine-room home at 2335 Arapahoe Street in the Curtis Park area of

Dr. Justina Ford

Denver Public Library, Western History Collection, Z-8947

northeast Denver. It served as her home and her medical office for forty-three years. She did not own a car, but a streetcar served the area. One of the streetcar lines ended in a section of town where Welton Street, Twenty-seventh Street, Washington Street, and East Twenty-sixth Avenue met, forming a five-pointed intersection. The streetcar company was unable to list all these street names on their sign to show the destination, so it was shortened to Five Points.

Dr. Ford offered services in obstetrics, gynecology, and pediatrics in her home. She also took care of patients in their homes. When she received a phone call or message that a patient needed her, she called the cab company. As soon as she said it was Dr. Ford, a cab was dispatched with haste. They usually did not charge her for the ride.

In Denver, she found that the Mexicans, Spaniards, Greeks, Koreans, Hindus, Japanese, and Bohemians preferred that a woman physician be in attendance at childbirth rather than a man. Many of these groups could not afford hospital care during childbirth, and most Denver physicians would not deliver babies in a home. So people came to her. She treated whites as well as blacks. Many of her clients lived in surrounding counties, accessible only by rugged mountain roads. She learned enough of at least seven languages to diagnose an illness, prescribe medications, and write dosage directions in her patients' native tongues. Her care persisted for many days after the delivery, as she was prone to making surprise visits to mother and child to check on them.

Justina's husband served as minister of the Zion Baptist Church for seven years. He was a good manager and helped the church pay its debts and increase its treasury. He also invested successfully in the Golden Chest Mining, Milling and Tunneling Company with other African-American investors from the church community. He was vice president of the mining company and served on its board of directors.

In 1907, Reverend Ford received a call to be the minister of Bethel Baptist Institutional Church in Jacksonville, Florida. Justina did not want to leave her medical practice in Denver. In July 1915, after 23 years of marriage, the couple divorced.

Career Challenges

Being black and female, Dr. Ford was not allowed to be a member of the Colorado Medical Society or the American Medical Association. And because she was not a member of those organizations, she could not use Denver's hospitals. After she had practiced for thirty-three years, Denver General Hospital granted her a faculty position. However, that position did not give her privileges to admit and treat her patients in the hospital.

Like other physicians of the time, Dr. Ford also faced the challenges of irregular hours, irregular pay, and the need to be on the go all the time. She often didn't sleep for two days. She never pressured patients who could not pay. Some paid in goods rather than cash—groceries, poultry, and the like. One woman didn't pay for her baby's birth until the child was thirteen years old.

Around 1920, Dr. Ford married Alfred Allen, who was eighteen years younger than she. He owned a farm in north Denver, where he raised chickens, rabbits, guinea pigs, and mushrooms. He was a professional woodworker as well. He took care of the household and acted as his wife's chauffeur. They also rented out a room to boarders, which brought in needed extra income. Justina kept the name Ford, by which she was known professionally and which was on her medical license. She loved children but never had any of her own.

One time, a little boy came to Dr. Ford's home office with his mama. He was looking around as if he was looking for something. Finally, Justina asked him what he wanted. "Well," the boy said, "where do you keep all those babies?" It took a lot of explaining to make him understand that although she delivered them, she wasn't allowed to keep them.[4]

Dr. Ford once estimated that in the fifty years she practiced in Denver, she delivered more than 7,000 babies. She was also extremely generous. Often she bought groceries for patients who needed them. And she helped many young people financially with their education.

She also liked to ride ninety miles an hour in an ambulance. "That to me is good fun," she once said.[5]

In 1950, Dr. Ford was finally allowed to join the Colorado Medical Society and the American Medical Association—at the age of seventy-nine. She continued her practice and worked until two weeks before her death in 1952 at age 81.

Petra Lopez-Torres tells of a conversation she had with Dr. Ford four months before her death. Dr. Ford said, "Well this one," pointing to the crib, "will be of a generation that will really see opportunity. I won't see the day, you may, and this one certainly will...When all the fears, hate, and even some death is over, we will really be brothers as God intended us to be in this land. This I believe. For this, I have worked all my life."[6]

Honors

Dr. Justina Ford was honored with a Human Relations Award from the Cosmopolitan Club of Denver in 1951. The Ford-Warren Branch of the Denver Public Library was named for her in 1975. In 1987, a group of black health professionals at the University of Colorado Health Sciences Center organized the Justina Ford Medical Society. This group offered medical services and

provided medical education on a volunteer basis to ethnic minorities and to those who could not afford medical care.

She was inducted into the Colorado Women's Hall of Fame in 1985. In 1989, the Colorado Medical Society named her a Colorado Medical Pioneer, thirty-seven years after her death.

Becoming a House Museum

The Justina Ford House, the present house museum, stood for ninety-four years at 2335 Arapahoe Street. In the summer of 1983, local residents learned that the entire block on which the house stood was being cleared by a private developer to make room for parking and possible future development. Historian Paul Stewart, City Councilman Hiawatha Davis, and other officials won an initial seventy-two-hour reprieve for the house, though that wasn't the end of the threat. The president of Used Brick Inc. had seven men, three trucks, and a loader on the site. He had all the permits he needed to tear the building down. He complained that it was costing him $1,000 an hour because his crew got paid whether they worked or stood around arguing about it.

Hearing a rumor that a demolition specialist was on his way to the site, supporters rushed over. The wrecker arrived, but the driver said he wasn't there to do any work. By that time, the Ford House was the only building still standing on the block. The operations manager for East-West Investment Partnerships agreed to not demolish the building.

In early 1984, the Ford House and lot were purchased by the Black American West Museum at a cost of $22,500. Subsequently, Historic Denver, Inc. moved the 200-ton property thirteen blocks to 3091 California Street, where the present

Courtesy of Historic Denver, Inc.

The 200-ton house was moved through the streets of Denver to 3091 California Street in 1984.

house museum now stands. Every line and cable along the streets had to be taken down as the house moved through. The house was restored in 1988.

Salvaged instruments

After Dr. Ford passed away, Alfred lived in the house for a few years before selling it to Albert Radetsky. The house stood in disrepair for many years, until it was sold again to developers. When Radetsky owned it, he made periodic inspections. On one occasion, he noticed homeless people had taken up residence and were cooking there. He decided that this was a fire danger and checked to see what of the home's contents could be saved from possible vandalism, theft, fire, or other disaster.

In one corner of the house, he found Dr. Ford's medical instruments and decided to keep them as souvenirs. He stuffed them into a pillowcase and took them home. They remained in a corner of his basement for years. When he heard about Dr. Ford's home being moved, he decided that the instruments might be of interest. On the day of the dedication ceremony, he presented the instruments to the museum—still in the pillowcase.

About the Justina Ford House

Address: 3091 California Street, Denver, Colorado 80205

Phone: (303) 292-2566

Hours: Call to confirm. June 1–August 31: 10 a.m.–5 p.m., Tuesday – Saturday. September 1–May 31: 10 a.m.– 2 p.m., Tuesday – Saturday

Admission: Adults $8, Seniors $7 (65 and over), Children $6

Driving directions: I-25 to Exit 210A, Colfax Avenue/US 40 E. Go east on Colfax Avenue 1.1 miles. Turn left on Kalamath Street. Go 0.1 mile. Kalamath Street becomes Stout Street. Go 1.9 miles. Turn right onto 31st Street. Turn right onto California Street. Turn left into parking lot.

Parking: Free in museum lot

Memberships: Memberships in the Black American West Museum are available at various levels of support

Web site: www.blackamericanwestmuseum.org

20 Lula Myers Ranch House

Lula liked to drive an old red truck. She sometimes drove right into the irrigation ditch and had to be pulled out.

Lula Orsburn was born in 1881 to William and Susan Orsburn and grew up as one of eight children on a homestead ranch seven miles north of Elizabeth, Colorado, near the Castle Rock area. William served as the local postmaster and ran sheep with local herders. When Lula was a child, her father was caught in an irrigation ditch cave-in—he saved his men but suffocated. Her mother, a southerner from Virginia, struggled to cope with running the ranch.

Lula passed the exam for a teacher's certificate. When a position in Frisco came vacant, she got the job, along with a new schoolhouse that was roomy enough for growing classes. This log structure still stands today on Frisco's main street. Her eight-month term began in September 1902. She had twenty-six students, ranging in age from five to sixteen.

Lula Myers Ranch House.
Log house 16-by-24 feet, with open room downstairs that served as sitting room, dining area, and office. An addition at rear, now gone, became the kitchen with adjacent glassed sun parlor. Narrow stairway leads to single bedroom upstairs.

Fired

Suddenly, in December 1902, she was fired. Apparently, two of the three old bachelors on the Frisco school board were in love with Lula. At the same time, Lula was being courted by James Havens "Dimp" Myers Jr. In 1902, Dimp was general superintendent of Ophir Mountain's Mint Mining Company, southeast of Frisco. He was complimented on his industry in many issues of the *Summit County Journal*. He had a good reputation for personal integrity and was well-liked. His father, Colonel James H. Myers, was a successful mining promoter.

Possibly the two men on the school board who were in love with Lula resented Dimp's courtship, because miners were not well-regarded in Frisco. The bachelors nailed boards across the school to bar Lula from entering. She escaped to her mother's ranch near Elizabeth for the Christmas holidays.

Lula filed suit against Summit School District No. 9 in Frisco in February 1903. Powerful local residents squashed the suit.

Romance

Dimp and Lula's romance blossomed quietly over the next few months. They were married at the Elizabeth ranch in June 1903 and set up housekeeping in Frisco. Dimp eventually took over mine management at the King Solomon mine.

Lula gave birth to a baby girl, Lucy, in April 1904. In May 1905, Dimp was elected to the Frisco School Board. He hired Lula's younger sister for an eight-month term beginning in September.

Dimp and Lula left Frisco around 1907. They lived for a time in one of the cabins near Lenawee Mill in Montezuma, one of Dimp's father's mining projects. From there, they moved to Old Dillon, where Dimp ran a freight wagon line.

As little Lucy grew up, her musical talent began to flourish from the piano lessons her mother gave her. Lucy played jazz tunes and dance melodies by ear and performed at many local dances.

Meanwhile, Dimp was busy promoting the 1920 improvement of the Loveland Pass Road, which had been constructed in 1879.

Dimp's wedding photo

The Delker Ranch

Lula's mother died around 1922, leaving each of her children $1,000. Dimp and Lula purchased the Delker Ranch for $1,200 from the Delker heirs in June 1924.

This two-story, 16-by-24-foot log house had been built in 1885 by Dutch millwright, miner, metalsmith, and inventor Charles Delker under the Federal Homestead Act. Delker had come to Colorado from Iowa. He earned his homestead patent in 1919. The house was located near the bank of the Snake River near Keystone. The logs were cut by hand and chinked with sticks, rocks, clay and rags. Newspapers covered the interior walls for insulation.

The Myers added a lean-to kitchen to the original cabin and a sun parlor, glassed on three sides, where the family had their meals.

Many parties and social events were held in this house. Kitchen paraphernalia and a handsome cook stove used then are now on display in the museum. A comfortable, cozy atmosphere pervades the house.

Dimp continued his work at the Hunkidori Mine and the Marlin, both above Montezuma. He also acquired other mine interests. Colonel Myers, Dimp's father, died in 1923.

Courtesy of Summit County Historical Society

Lula's wedding photo

Later Years

The Myers lived in the house for more than forty years. When Lula was in her mid-sixties, she drove an old red truck. But her driving skills were questionable. "She would come flying in, turn into the yard and drive right into the irrigation ditch."[1] Someone would have to pull her out.

Dimp died in 1954. Lula subdivided and sold some of her ranch property in the late 1950s. She remained at the Myers Ranch until 1966, then moved to Aurora. She passed away in 1973 at age ninety-one.

Becoming a House Museum

Originally located next to the Snake River near the present-day Skyway Gondola and Keystone Resort's River Run Plaza, the house was moved to its present site in 1976.

It was donated to the Summit Historical Society by the Arapahoe Basin ski area. It was opened as part of the museum in 1981, commemorating the 100th anniversary of Lula's birth.

About the Lula Myers Ranch House

Address: 403 LaBonte Street, Dillon, Colorado 80435

Phone: (970) 468-2207

Hours: Summer, Tuesday–Saturday 1:00–4:00 p.m.

Admission: Free; donations accepted

Driving directions: I-70 to Exit 205, U.S. 6. Turn toward Dillon/Silverthorne. Drive 0.3 mile. Turn left onto Blue River Parkway/U.S. 6 East. Drive 0.5 mile. Turn right onto Dillon Dam Road. Go 0.1 mile. Turn left at West LaBonte Street. Go 0.8 mile. Located behind the Dillon Schoolhouse Museum.

Parking: Free in parking lot

Memberships: Membership in the Summit Historical Society is available at varying levels of support. Call (970) 468-2207.

Web site: www.summithistorical.org

21 MacGregor Ranch

Clara Heeney MacGregor's paintings hang in the house museum today.

Courtesy of James Werner

Alexander MacGregor was born in 1846 in Milwaukee. As a young man, he was publisher of the *LaBelle Mirror* newspaper Oconomowoc, Wisconsin for a year . At age twenty-six, he came to Colorado and, in 1872, was working as clerk of Arapahoe County Court in Denver.

Clara Heeney was born 1852, also in Wisconsin. At age fourteen, she went to normal preparatory college at the University of Wisconsin in Madison. She attended the new teacher training college at the university until she was eighteen but did not graduate. During the summer of 1870, she taught a three-month school at Stoner's Prairie, Wisconsin. The next year, she studied at the Chicago Academy of

MacGregor Ranch house.

Turn-of-the-century log and vernacular wood frame construction ranch house with native stone foundation. Original furnishings and personal memorabilia of three generations of MacGregors. Forty-two outbuildings ranging from log construction to wood frame construction, many with native stone foundations. Sidings vary from clapboard to shiplap siding. Roofing ranges from tin to sawn wood shingle. Many of the buildings are constructed of timber milled at Alexander MacGregor's 1876 water-powered sawmill.

Courtesy of MacGregor Ranch Museum

Alexander MacGregor

Design under Henry Crawford Ford. (This academy later became the Art Institute of Chicago.)

In the spring of 1872, Clara came to the Colorado Territory on a sketching party conducted by her art teacher, H. C. Ford. Clara's widowed mother, Georgianna Heeney, chaperoned the group.

Alex and Clara probably met that year, either in Estes Park or in Denver. They were married in Black Earth, Wisconsin, on Christmas Day 1873. They returned to Colorado Territory and claimed a homestead in the Black Canyon area of Estes Park facing Longs Peak. They lived in Estes Park and Denver.

Clara's mother sold her large Wisconsin farm and also came west to stake land claims in Estes Park. Under the Preemption Act, she purchased land near the present-day location of the Stanley Hotel for $1.25 an acre. Later, she traded that property for land adjacent to her daughter and son-in-law's land on Black Canyon Creek.

Serving the Community

Clara was commissioned the first postmistress in the park in 1876 and 1877. However in March 1877, Clara wrote in her diary that "Mrs. (Griff) Evans came over and presented her commission as postmaster of Estes Park and demanded the key."[1] The next day, the post office was moved to the Evans ranch.

Clara and Alex also ran a general store from the ranch and sold eggs, produce, dairy, and other merchandise. They also accommodated tourists. Visitors could get room, meals, and washing for $7 per week. Stabling a horse was 50 cents a day without feed.

"The great rivalry seems to be in the matter of camp fires, each party strives to create the largest blaze...The white tents and wide awnings gleam through the dark pines, and the blaze of the crackling camp fire throws into bold relief the rustic seats and picturesque groups of men, women, and children."[2]

Many of the buildings on the ranch were built with log, but MacGregor also operated a sawmill. By 1876, lumber was sawed for the ranch and also for sale.

Many of Clara's paintings adorn the house today. Clara also left journals and a handwritten cookbook dated 1865. The cookbook included recipes for medicinal use of herbs and plants.

Clara and Alex had three sons, George, Donald, and Halbert. The family built the three main houses on the ranch, the last one being the current museum, which was built around 1896.

The Homestead Act

The Homestead Act of 1862 encouraged western expansion by opening America's public lands to agricultural settlement. Under the Homestead Act, more than one million families received title to more than 248 million acres of public land across the western states and territories.

To qualify, an applicant had to be a United States citizen or intend to become one. He or she had to be older than 21 years of age, the head of a household, and own fewer than 160 acres of land.

The applicant had to "prove up" the land, meaning that the homesteader had to dig a well, put a fence around part of the land, plow ten acres, and build a house on it within five years. The land had to be occupied at least six months of each year. A typical homestead was 160 acres. After six-months, the land could be purchased for $1.25 per acre. If the homestead was managed for five years, the title only cost the filing fee of $15.

The majority of the homesteaders failed the five-year residency requirement to gain full title to the property. The program ended in 1976 in all states except Alaska, which ended its program in 1986.[3]

The Preemption Act

The U.S. Congress passed the Preemption Act in 1841, in response to the demands of western states that squatters be allowed to preempt lands. That is, be given the right to purchase lands ahead of others. Pioneer squatters often settled on public lands before they could be surveyed and auctioned by the U.S. government. In 1830, Congress passed the first of a series of temporary preemption laws.

A permanent Preemption Act was passed only after the eastern states had been placated by the promise that the proceeds of the government land sales would be distributed among all the states in the Union based on their representation in Congress.

The act of 1841 permitted settlers to stake a claim of 160 acres, and after living on it for fourteen months, they could purchase it from the government for as little as $1.25 an acre before it was offered for public sale. After the passage of the Homestead Act in 1862, preemption became a tool for speculators. Congress repealed the Preemption Act in 1891.[4]

The Infamous Toll Road

With $10,000 from Clara's mother and exclusive right to collect tolls for ten years granted by the territorial government, Alex built a toll road from Glen Evans (north of Lyons) to Estes Park in 1874 and 1875. Some of the road followed the present Highway 36.

Much of the toll of $1.00 a team each way was spent on maintaining the road. Heavy storms washed out roadway and bridges, and vandals broke the tollgate and cut the fence. After rain damaged the road almost beyond repair, it was sold in 1882 and discontinued in 1885.

At age thirty-seven, Alex served as Larimer County judge, from 1883 to 1885. He spent winters in Fort Collins, where he practiced law for some years before moving back to Denver. But he always spent summers in Estes Park.

In 1896, Alex and son George were struck by lightning on Trail Ridge Road, near Fall River Pass. George survived. Alex was killed. He was fifty years old.

Donald and Maude

Alex and Clara's middle son, Donald, was sixteen when his father died. He and his brother George took over the responsibility for managing the MacGregor holdings.

He leased out the ranch for seven years to Charles and Edward Johnson, and took a job with Hendrie and Bolthoff Manufacturing and Supply Company in Denver. He advanced rapidly in his job, married Minnie Maude Koontz, and settled down in the family home in Denver. After the seven year lease on the ranch had terminated, he raised money to buy out his brothers and returned to the ranch.

Donald, Maude, and their only child, Muriel, moved to the ranch around 1910. The ranch flourished and prospered. Crops of hay, oats, and vegetables did well. Donald also raised Aberdeen Angus cattle. Donald increased his land holdings to nearly 4,000 acres of land in the Estes Park valley by the time he died.

Besides doing the household chores of cooking, cleaning, and sewing, Maude tended the garden, did some sketching, and ran the sales of produce and dairy products including butter, cream, milk, and eggs on the ranch. Records show that local and summer customers purchased wood products, hay, oats, straw, ice, milk, skimmed milk, cream, butter, eggs, chickens, turkeys, produce, potatoes, and cattle from Maude.

Donald MacGregor

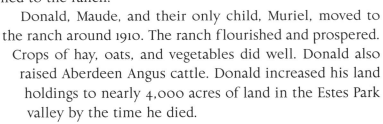

They also rented cabins to summer visitors. Donald boarded horses, rented pasture, and rented his hay baler for income. They even rented their cows if someone had a need such as milk for a new baby. Hotels and businesses purchased milk, cream, butter, vegetables, and hay from the MacGregor Ranch.

When the town of Estes Park was incorporated in 1917, Donald served on the Estes Park School Board, serving as board president in 1921.

Donald suffered from asthma for several years and died at his home in 1950 at the age of seventy. He left an estate of $86,222, which was divided equally between Maude and Muriel. The 4,000-acre ranch was appraised at $66,000.

Maude Koontz MacGregor

Muriel

Muriel was born in 1904 in Denver. As a child, she enjoyed ranch life and playing with her dog, Tiger. She was imaginative, intelligent, and creative. She was an excellent student and rarely missed a day of class. In 1911, Muriel described a day at school in a handwritten note now on display in the museum, "Dear Father and Mother, I am getting along fine at school. Rita struck Maurine with a stick."

She loved animals and became an accomplished horsewoman. In 1910, her father gave her a pony, probably the black pony, Zephyr, that Muriel is sitting on in the museum's pictures.

Muriel helped her dad with chores each day, tending the cattle, poultry, and hay crop. She rode Zephyr down what is now MacGregor Avenue to the schoolhouse, where the First National Bank now stands in Estes Park. She also helped her mother with domestic chores in the house and garden.

Some of the shells in the museum's bookcase may have came from a trip to New Orleans, Panama, Guatemala, and Cuba with her parents in 1921.

Muriel enjoyed reading and writing stories. In April 1921, she won third prize in a creative writing contest in the local newspaper. One of her stories, "Pioneer Days," was written in 1935, when she was thirty-one years old. It focused on her grandparents' days as settlers in early Estes Park. She also played the piano and wrote music. One song, "The Ups and Downs of It" was copyrighted in 1929; a copy is on display in the museum.

Muriel obtained three higher education degrees. The first was a bachelor of arts degree in math from Colorado College in 1925; she was class valedictorian.

Muriel entered college again in 1930. She kept in close contact with her parents. She wrote almost daily, called weekly, and came home on the holidays. When she was in graduate school, she had her own car and would come home on the weekends.

She earned a masters degree in history from the University of Colorado in 1931 and a law degree from the University of Denver in 1934. She was one of two women to take the bar examination in 1934 and was admitted to practice law in 1936.

Muriel practiced law without leaving the ranch. She used her legal skills much like her grandfather had, helping with family matters and assisting a few local people. Much of her legal work dealt with disputes over water rights at Black Canyon Ranch.

Muriel MacGregor in graduation garb

Becoming a House Museum

After Donald and Maude died in 1950, Muriel assumed sole responsibility of the ranch. During her father's waning years, the ranch had begun to decline, and Muriel had to sell some of her land.

She was unable to cultivate the land as her father had done, and she had to purchase hay and grain for winter feed. She also discontinued raising garden crops and quit raising chickens and dairy cows.

In the mid-1960s, the herd of Black Angus cattle was reduced to less than 130 head. She continued to sell calves and rent cabins as a source of income. She soon had to borrow just to carry on the minimum operations. The large barn in the meadow was burned by an arsonist.

Muriel died land rich and cash poor in 1970 at the age of sixty-six. The ranch had about 3,085 acres at the time. Two weeks before her death, she had written her will and then a codicil.

> It is my will that my ranch shall be maintained and retained insofar as is possible, and that the new proceeds of the production of my ranch and cattle herd be used for charitable and educational purposes.

Because distant relatives contested the will, the settlement took three years. In the end, the ranch was reduced to 2,710 acres.

There were no funds to operate the ranch. In 1976, the National Park Service purchased 400 acres of the ranch, which had been within the boundaries of

Rocky Mountain National Park since 1917. But it took another seven years for the Muriel L. MacGregor Charitable Trust to execute a conservation easement with the Park Service. The easement agreement protects the property from development and preserves the land for future generations.

The Park Service paid the trust $3,935,000 and guaranteed that it would allow the MacGregor Ranch to operate with only minimal restrictions. Formal closing ceremonies were held on October 13, 1983. The MacGregor Trust retains ownership, and the family's legacy lives on as a 1,200-acre cattle ranch and museum.

About the MacGregor Ranch Museum

Address: 180 MacGregor Lane, Estes Park, Colorado 80517

Phone: (970) 586-3749

Hours: June–August Tuesday–Friday 10 a.m.–4 p.m. Self-guided tours of the museum, milk house, smokehouse, blacksmith shop, and horse-drawn machinery exhibits.

Admission: Adults $3, Children under 18 free

Driving directions: I-25 to Exit 243 toward Lyons on CO 66. Go 16 miles west on CO 66 to Lyons. Turn right onto U.S. 36 and go 16 miles to Estes Park. From downtown Estes Park on Elkhorn Avenue, drive north on MacGregor Avenue (Devil's Gulch Road) to the ranch entrance, where the road curves sharply to the right. Enter the main ranch gate. Follow the road and museum entrance signs. Drive slowly and watch for horses.

Parking: Free near the entrance to the ranch house and buildings

Web site: www.macgregorranch.org

22 Mayer House and South Park City

Frank Mayer claimed to be the last surviving Civil War veteran.

Denver Public Library, Western History Collection, X-8361

Mayer House on Main Street in South Park City in 1958, four years after Frank Mayer's death. Five-room frame yellow house. One of more than thirty historic buildings that make up South Park City

Frank Mayer was born in 1850 in Louisiana to a French mother and a Prussian father. At the age of thirteen, Frank enlisted as a drummer boy in the Union army during the Civil War. He saw the battles of Gettysburg and Gainesville, and he was present when Lee surrendered at Appomattox.

After the war, Mayer earned degrees at Goettingen and Jena engineering colleges in Germany. While in Europe, he also picked up several languages. Upon returning to the United States, he worked for the Pennsylvania and Reading Coal and Iron Company. But soon he satisfied his taste for adventure by taking a job as a mining engineer in Mexico. He married Marjorie Monroe of Pennsylvania, with whom he shared adventures for fifty-four years.

Back in the army in the 1870s and 1880s, Mayer rose from the ranks to lieutenant colonel. Colonel Mayer was known to his Indian friends as Walking Arrow. This name proved to be prophetic. Around 1870, the colonel was hit in

the shoulder by a chipped flint arrowhead in an Indian fight near Fort Apache in the Arizona Territory. The arrowhead remained embedded in his shoulder for eighty years. When he was 101 years old, the arrowhead broke in two and became painful, so it was finally removed. But, Mayer said, the Indian didn't live to tell the story.

Buffalo Running

When he met Bob McRea, the best-known buffalo runner on the western plains of America, Mayer's life changed. In 1872, buffalo hides were worth $2 to $3 each, which was a lot of money in those days. Young men, veterans of the Civil War like Mayer were at loose ends, wanting adventure and needing to make their fortunes. Mayer was twenty-two. He could shoot, and he liked to hunt.

Mayer claims that the U.S. government connived to kill the buffalo herds. In his book, *The Buffalo Harvest*, which he co-authored with Charles B. Roth, he writes, "Army officers in charge of plains operations encouraged the slaughter of buffalo in every possible way. Part of this encouragement...consisted of ammunition, free ammunition, all you could use, all you wanted, more than you needed. All you had to do to get it was apply at any frontier army post and say you were short of ammunition, and plenty would be given you."[1]

The rationale behind this generosity was that the Indians were dependent on the buffalo. By slaughtering the animals, the Indians would be conquered.

First Hunting License

In 1873, near what was to become Moran, Wyoming, Chief Medicine Arrow gave Colonel Mayer a tanned piece of buffalo hide cut in an oval shape with several Indian drawings. The drawings on the hide indicated where Mayer could hunt. He had permission to hunt "southward as far as a horse can run in three suns and westward as far as an eagle can fly in one moon and one sun."[2] It was his first hunting license, given in exchange for blankets and silver, and it was to be in force "as long as the sun shines and the river runs."[3]

Moving On

Mayer was a buffalo runner for nine of his 104 years. "When I finally sold out and quit, I had less than $5,000 on deposit, to show for nine years of hard work and sweat."[4]

He continued, "I wasn't sorry when I headed my wagons westward toward the Rockies and what I was sure would be the good life it promised to be. I didn't have my million, but I still had youth, and strength, and ambition, and

experience by now, so I thought I could cope with almost any situation."[5]

He hunted deer, antelope, elk, mountain sheep, and bear for the mining camp markets of Colorado. When not hunting, he guided sportsmen. Occasionally, he would return to the plains to hunt buffalo, but he would hire others to do the hunting and gathering of bones.

While homesteading in Routt County in northwestern Colorado, Mayer once broke his leg. He snapped the bone back into place by tying his foot to the bedstead, grasping the headboard with his hands, and pulling. He then set the leg in a cast of plaster of Paris he had bought for building purposes.

In 1893, he owned a ranch near Tensleep in the Wyoming Big Horns.

Later Years

In 1910, Moffat Yard & Company published his first book, *The Song of the Wolf*, which sold 37,000 copies. He then wrote *The Unmuzzled Ox*. Many of his short stories were published in *Field and Stream* magazine.

Courtesy of South Park Historical Foundation, Inc

Frank Mayer lived in the house in Fairplay for the last ten years of his life.

When his wife passed away in 1921 in California, he came to Fairplay. In 1931, he moved out to the Briscoe Ranch, where he stayed for ten years. He wrote poems, articles, short stories, and novels about the Old West, and regaled others with tales of his adventures. In 1941, he returned to town living in Fairplay and, for the last ten years of his life, resided in the yellow house that now sits in the South Park City Museum.

Mayer was insulted when a photo magazine published an article about a man in Minnesota who, the magazine claimed, was the last surviving member of the Union army. "It's a damn lie," Mayer said. "I'm still here."[6] The reason for the oversight, he claimed, was that he never applied for a federal pension. "I've never asked any man for anything I didn't earn. When I was mustered out of the army, I was given a tract of land and some scrip. That was enough."[7]

Mayer said he always followed his father's advice, "Keep your word good. Keep your credit good."[8]

The Other Side of the Mountain

Mayer traveled every country in the world, except Siberia and Tibet. He survived three earthquakes, including the 1906 quake in San Francisco, and three fires, including the one in Chicago in 1871. He was twice buried under

snow-slides and was lost at sea three times. He never stayed long in one place. He surveyed all over the mountains in Colorado and some in other parts of the world. He hunted big game in Alaska and built railroads in Brazil.

"Always wondered what was on the other side of the mountain," Mayer said in 1953. "That's what I'm wondering now. I know I am on my last lap. But I have lived a full life. I haven't a single regret...If I go somewhere after death, I'll not be afraid. It'll just be another wonderful experience."[9]

He was 104 when he died in 1954.

Becoming a House Museum

The Mayer House in South Park City, Fairplay, was home to Frank Mayer during his final days. The tiny, four-room frame house stood on the site of present-day South Park City, which was built around it. Mayer left no will, so the property went to probate. Lucy Roth, the wife of Mayer's friend and biographer Charles Roth, outbid the South Park City Historical Foundation and owned the house for nearly thirty years. The public was not allowed inside.

Finally, in 1985, the house was purchased from Mrs. Roth's heirs and made part of the museum. The house's period furnishings represent Mayer's lifestyle.

About Mayer House Museum

Address: 100 4th Street, Fairplay, Colorado 80440

Phone: (719) 836-2387

Hours: May 15–October 16: Daily 9 a.m.–7 p.m. Before Memorial Day and after Labor Day 9 a.m.–5 p.m.

Admission: Adults $7.50, Seniors (62 and over) $6.00. Children (6–12) $4.00, Children (under 6) free

Driving directions: From Denver: C-470 to Exit for U.S. 285 South. Take U.S. 285 South toward Fairplay. Go 67.2 miles. Turn right on Highway 9. Go 0.9 mile. CO 9 is Main Street in Fairplay. Turn left into South Park Museum parking area at Fourth Street.

From Colorado Springs: Take U.S. 24 West. Go 65.3 miles. Turn right (north) onto CO 9 toward Fairplay. Go 17.2 miles. CO 9 is Main Street in Fairplay. Turn left into South Park Museum parking area at Fourth Street.

Parking: Free

Memberships: Membership in the South Park City Museum is available at varying levels of support. Call (719) 836-2387 or write to: South Park Historical Foundation, Inc., P.O. Box 634, Fairplay, Colorado 80440.

Web site: www.southparkcity.org

23 McAllister House Museum

The McAllisters were entertaining Governor A. C. Hunt when Indians surrounded the house and flattened their faces against the windows to see inside.

Henry McAllister was born in Delaware in 1836. He moved with his family to Philadelphia at an early age. There he attended public school until he was eighteen. He then worked in a wholesale mercantile house for two years. For the next five years, he owned a general mercantile business in Delaware County.

When the Civil War broke out, he closed his business and enlisted in the Union army as a private. He was twenty-six years old. He was mustered into a regiment that had been organized by Captain William J. Palmer. From this time until McAllister's death, the lives of the two men would be closely intertwined. Both had Quaker backgrounds, so enlisting in the war effort must not have been easy for either of them.

McAllister House
Brick and limestone Gothic-style cottage. Original marble fireplaces and floor-to-ceiling pocket windows that slide up into the walls, making nice doorways to the verandas.

In 1863, McAllister was promoted to first lieutenant. Two years later, when Palmer was promoted to general, McAllister was commissioned as a major on Palmer's staff. After the war, he returned to Philadelphia. Like many Civil War veterans, McAllister used his military title for the rest of his life.

Elizabeth Cooper was born in 1836 to a prominent Quaker family in Darby, Pennsylvania. She and Henry McAllister were married in 1866.

After the war, McAllister became secretary of the American Iron and Steel Association of Philadelphia. Then General Palmer hired him as president of the National Land and Improvement Company. Palmer's railroad was to run close to the foothills along the front range of the Colorado Rockies. From the company's Philadelphia office, McAllister worked to promote the area to attract settlers and investors.

Colorado Springs Company

Palmer organized the Denver and Rio Grande (D&RG) Railroad to reach El Paso, Texas, and eventually extend into Mexico. The D&RG's subsidiary, the Colorado Springs Company, laid out a new town at the foot of Pikes Peak. In 1872, Palmer traveled extensively in Mexico. He asked McAllister to leave Philadelphia and come to the new settlement to act as superintendent and director in his absence.

McAllister left his wife and infant son in Philadelphia and traveled to Denver. On the way, he was delayed for several days because of blizzards east of Denver. Once in Denver, he rode the D&RG to Colorado Springs. "The night was very damp and cold, and my first impression of Colorado Springs was not favorable. At that time there were about twenty buildings in Colorado Springs and perhaps from 200 to 250 inhabitants."[1]

McAllister's April visit was brief. He returned to Philadelphia to close his affairs and make plans to move west.

He returned in October to assume the duties as executive director of the Colorado Springs Company, a position he held until 1879. McAllister also served as the second manager of the town. He was elected a member of the Board of Town Trustees, and served as president of the board from 1875 to 1877.

Henry's House

Crop failure and financial crisis brought hardship to the Colorado Springs Company in the early years. Some residents feared that the company might liquidate its interests. But the *El Paso County News* hushed the rumor by reporting:

"The foundations of a brick and stone villa, for Major McAllister, are already laid in the center of half a block on Cascade Avenue. Some of our candidates for

office have been trying to catch a vote or two by reporting that the Colorado Springs Company will soon sell out all their interests here. It scarcely looks like it when the Executive Director is just entering upon the work of building himself a costly residence."[2]

On his second trip to the Springs, McAllister purchased the northeast half of the 400 block of North Cascade Avenue and hired the Colorado Springs Company's architect, George Summers, to draw plans for the house. Summers also designed General Palmer's Glen Eyrie residence and Grace Episcopal Church.

McAllister wanted his home to withstand the worst of the elements. He had the outer walls built 20 inches thick, and the roof anchored into the masonry with thick iron rods. The McAllister House is one of the few homes surviving from the early days of Colorado Springs. It was built of rosy-red bricks with sandstone corner blocks and a dark gray shingle roof. McAllister sent to Philadelphia for the brick.

White marble mantelpieces were brought from Philadelphia. Unique pocket windows were built into the walls like pocket doors. Carpentry work was done by W. S. Stratton, later of Cripple Creek mining fame.

Visitors

In 1874, a large number of Ute Indians were encamped north of town. McAllister was entertaining Governor A. C. Hunt at lunch when thirty to fifty Indians surrounded the house and flattened their faces against the windows to see inside. The family was worried, until they learned that the Indians wanted to talk to the governor. He went out, shook hands with each one and distributed a few coins. When Governor Hunt asked them to return to camp, they immediately left.

Pioneer families in covered wagons that had crossed the Great Plains often camped across the street. Elizabeth McAllister was very kind to them, inviting them to draw water from her well and passing out loaves of bread.

Like others in town, the McAllisters kept a cow so their three children would have fresh milk. The town cowboy came each morning to gather the cows from along Cascade and Nevada Avenues and Tejon Street to drive them to the pastures. It is said that each cow knew where she lived, for when the cows were brought home in the afternoon, each one turned in at the proper address.

Politics, Business, and Community Service

In 1874, McAllister organized an expedition to Colorado Springs for the legislators who were in session in Denver. A D&RG private car brought the lawmakers to the Springs in the morning. They dined at the Colorado Springs Hotel, then toured the streets of the new town and the Garden of the Gods.

When the editor of the first newspaper in Colorado Springs died in 1875, McAllister temporarily took charge of the paper. When the Colorado Conference of Congregational Churches was considering founding a college in Colorado Territory, McAllister offered the spacious and beautiful track of land that had been set aside for a college. The Conference agreed to the location, and The Colorado College was founded. McAllister was elected to the school's board of trustees.

He often stumped the state for his favorite Republican candidates and was elected a delegate to the Republican National Convention in Cincinnati in 1876. He also attended a two-day convention of the Colorado Woman's Suffrage Association held in Denver in 1877 and was elected to the Executive Committee of the Suffrage Association.

In 1878, while he was deeply involved in the management of the D&RG Railroad, McAllister became president of a new enterprise near El Moro, Colorado. The project, funded by the Southern Colorado Coal and Town Company, was set up to support the business of manufacturing coke for smelting purposes. He was also elected president of the newly established Pueblo School Board.

Children

Henry Jr. (Harry) attended Swarthmore College, a Quaker school near Philadelphia. He later studied law with Judge Horace Lunt in Colorado Springs. He lived most of his life in Denver, where he was regarded as one of Colorado's most eminent attorneys. He served as general counsel for and as a member of the board of directors for the D&RG. He also served on the board of trustees of The Colorado College and the El Pomar Foundation.

McAllister's daughters, Mary and Matilda, taught school in the community. Mary taught at Colorado Springs High School, now Palmer High School. She married George Taylor and moved to his sister's home on Tejon Street. Matilda (Tillie) taught at Miss Henry's private school, later known as the San Luis School. Tillie lived with her father until his death in 1921.

McAllister passed away at age eighty-five. He is buried on a slope overlooking the town he helped found. Elizabeth died in 1912 at age seventy-six.

Becoming a House Museum

In 1960, the National Society of the Colonial Dames of America in Colorado, with the help of the El Pomar Foundation and Shepard's Citations, rescued the house from destruction and has owned and operated it as a museum since then.

About the McAllister House Museum

Address: 423 North Cascade Avenue, Colorado Springs, Colorado 80903

Phone: (719) 635-7925

Hours: May through August: Wednesday — Saturday 10:00 a.m.–4:00 p.m., Sunday Noon–4:00 p.m. September through April: Thursday — Saturday 10:00 a.m.–4:00 p.m. Closed in January

Admission: Adults $5, Seniors $4, Children ages 6–12 $3

Driving directions: I-25 to Exit142, Bijou Street. Turn left on Bijou Street. Go 0.2 mile. Continue on W. Kiowa Street for 0.2 mile. Turn left onto North Cascade Avenue. Go 0.3 mile. The museum is on the right side of the street.

Parking: The parking lot behind the museum can be accessed from the alley off St. Vrain, which is the cross street north of the museum.

Memberships: Membership in the Friends of McAllister House Museum is available at varying levels of support. Call (719) 635-7925 or visit www.mcallisterhouse.org/become-involved.

Web site: www.mcallisterhouse.org

24 Meeker Home Museum

Ute Massacre survivor Josephine Meeker enjoyed telling her story on stage.

Meeker Home in the 1880s. Two-story adobe brick.

Nathan Meeker was born in 1817 in Ohio. At seventeen, he visited New Orleans and found work as a copy boy for newspapers in towns along the Mississippi River. Meeker moved across many states between 1835 and 1843, supporting himself at various times as a newspaperman, traveling salesman, and teacher. When his health declined in 1843, he returned to Ohio.

He began reading a French philosopher named Fourier whose ideas sparked Meeker's interest in becoming part of a utopian type of community, where people live together and work toward a common goal.

He courted and married Arvilla Delight Smith, and they moved to a utopian community in Ohio called the Trumbull Phalanx. During their time at Trumbull, sons Ralph and George were born.

After the break up of the Trumbull community, the Meekers moved to several Ohio towns, trying unsuccessfully to run different types of stores. In 1850, their first daughter, Rozene, was born. Two more babies arrived—Mary, in 1854, and Josephine, in 1857. During the Civil War, Meeker worked as a war

correspondent. After the war, the family moved to New York, where Meeker worked for Horace Greeley, publisher of the *New York Tribune*, eventually becoming the agriculture editor.

The *New York Tribune* was America's largest newspaper. Greeley was a great proponent of the Homestead Act. (*see* sidebars on the Homesteading Act and the Preemption Act in Chapter 21, MacGregor Ranch). Greeley sent Meeker west to write about the possibilities for agriculture in the new territories. He visited Colorado Territory and wrote about the Rocky Mountain Front Range area, encouraging settlers to go west.

Nathan C. Meeker

The Union Colony

On his way home to New York in October 1869, Meeker thought again of his ideas of a utopian community. He brought these ideas to Greeley, who issued an invitation in the *Tribune* to join a utopian community settling in the West. All applicants had to promise to abstain from alcohol. Greeley and Meeker called the agricultural community the Union Colony of Colorado. They were overwhelmed by the response—they heard from more than 1,000 people in the first month. Three hundred families were selected to be a part of an initial joint stock venture. Each family put in $155.

The committee chose the location between the Cache la Poudre and the South Platte rivers. This site would have water for irrigation, and it was located on the railroad line about halfway between Denver and Cheyenne.

In the spring of 1870, the committee bought 12,000 acres of land from railroad easements and local ranchers and farmers and homesteaded the rest for the settlers to move to and develop.

The first colonists arrived in the spring of 1870. By the end of 1870, more than a thousand people resided in the community.

Meeker and his son George came with the first wave of colonists. George had suffered with tuberculosis from an early age. He had hoped for a cure in the dry air and high altitude. While Nathan was in the East arranging to bring a second group of colonists, George died.

The townspeople named the colony after Horace Greeley. Greeley visited the town for the first and only time in October 1870.

Corner Lot

Meeker knew from reading that clay soil could be mixed with manure, straw, and water and baked dry to create adobe bricks (*see* Chapter 4, Baca House, and Chapter 27, Museo House). Meeker spent all his savings, $6,000, and then borrowed money to purchase a large corner lot on the outskirts of town and built an adobe house.

The new residence, which is the present house museum, had two parlors, a kitchen, and three bedrooms. Later, Meeker built a small adobe office building in downtown Greeley for his new business, *The Greeley Tribune* newspaper.

By 1877, Meeker was deeply in debt to Horace Greeley and others. When Greeley died, his lawyers called in all of his debts, and Meeker was forced to find employment.

White River Ute Agency

Nathan Meeker was appointed Indian agent at the White River Ute Agency in northwestern Colorado in 1878 at the age of sixty-one. Arvilla managed the agency store, and daughter Josephine became the agency's schoolteacher.

Miss Josephine Meeker

Eight agents had come and gone by the time Meeker arrived. He was determined to run the agency fairly, and he instituted reforms that he hoped would satisfy both the U.S. government and the Utes. He felt that if the 700 Ute Indians adopted modern farming methods and education they would become self-sufficient and assimilated. The Ute people had very different views of land use and education. The differences were irreconcilable, partly due to Meeker's intense idealism.

In 1879, after a year of disagreements and poor communication between vastly differing cultures, Meeker took a firm stand and had a pasture where the natives grazed their ponies tilled and commanded an end to horse racing.

On September 29, 1879, thirty or so Utes at the agency fired on the white men working there. Nathan Meeker and the male employees were all killed. Arvilla, Josephine, Mrs. Flora Ellen Price, and her children, Johnnie and May, were taken captive by the Utes who fled from the agency.

Captivity and Release

The women and children were held for twenty-three days in the White River Ute camp. During that time, the women baked, sewed, doctored the ill, and kept busy. They made clothes for themselves as well as the younger Indians. Josephine made a dress out of a blanket given to her. This dress is on exhibit in the Meeker Home Museum.

Shawsheen, sister of Ute Chief Ouray, was instrumental in negotiating the hostages' safe release. General Charles Adams, a longtime friend of Chief Ouray, eventually escorted Mrs. Meeker, Josephine, and Mrs. Price and her two children back to Denver.

Upon hearing of the difficulties suffered by the Meeker family, Horace Greeley's daughters immediately forgave Nathan Meeker's debt to the Greeley estate.

When the Meeker women returned to Greeley, they rented out rooms, sold produce from their garden and homemade jams and jellies to help make ends meet.

Josephine stayed only a short while, then moved to Washington, D.C., to take a job as a secretary, working for legislators. She died there of pneumonia at age twenty-five.

THE UTE MASSACRE!

Brave Miss Meeker's Captivity!

HER OWN ACCOUNT OF IT.

ALSO,

The Narratives of Her Mother and Mrs. Price.

TO WHICH IS ADDED

FURTHER THRILLING AND INTENSELY INTERESTING DETAILS, NOT HITHERTO PUBLISHED, OF THE BRAVERY AND FRIGHTFUL SUFFERINGS ENDURED BY MRS. MEEKER, MRS. PRICE AND HER TWO CHILDREN, AND

BY MISS JOSEPHINE MEEKER.

PUBLISHED BY

THE OLD FRANKLIN PUBLISHING HOUSE, PHILADELPHIA, PA.

Entered, according to Act of Congress, in the year 1879, by the OLD FRANKLIN PUBLISHING HOUSE, in the office of the Librarian of Congress, at Washington, D. C.

Colorado Historical Society # 10036433

The Ute Massacre poster

Later Years

In 1884, Mrs. Meeker added a two-story brick addition onto the adobe Meeker House, doubling its size. She and her daughter Rozene lived in the house for thirty years, until Arvilla was ninety. That year, she went to live with her son Ralph in New York, where she died in 1905.

The Meeker Children

Ralph, the eldest son, was working for the *New York Times* when the family went west with the Union Colony. After the massacre, he returned to Greeley to write a story about the history of Greeley. When he died, Rozene would not

allow him to be buried in the family plot.

George died of tuberculosis in 1870, the first year of the Union Colony settlement.

Rozene, the eldest daughter, was talented and quite eccentric. She was married for a short time but had no children. Rozene lived in the Meeker House until 1910. She died in 1935, outliving all of her siblings.

Mary married a rancher named Fullerton and had two children. She died in the Meeker home shortly after giving birth to her second child. Mr. Fullerton moved with the children to California.

Josephine was thirteen when the Meeker family moved to Greeley. Josephine was an independent spirit. For instance, she refused to ride a horse sidesaddle. One of the city fathers wrote to *The Greeley Tribune*, complaining of her unladylike behavior, riding astride in trousers. After high school, Josephine attended business college in Denver. She followed her mother's ideals and was a fervent advocate for the rights of women and Native Americans.

Nathan, Arvilla, George, Rozene, Mary, and Josephine are all buried in Greeley at Linn Grove Cemetery.

Becoming a House Museum

In 1910, the house was sold for back taxes. It had two other owners between 1910 and 1927.

In 1927, the City of Greeley bought the home. It was opened as a museum in 1929. To help defray the cost, the upstairs rooms were rented out to boarders. Maude Meeker Gilliland, Nathan's brother's daughter, was the first curator.

In 1959, the brick addition and the porches were removed, returning the home to its original 1870 appearance. The house was again renovated in 1995. Approximately one-third of the artifacts are traceable to the family.

About the Meeker Home Museum

Address: 1324 Ninth Avenue, Greeley, Colorado 80631

Phone: (970) 350-9220

Hours: Open to walk-in visitors sporadically, May to October. Call (970) 350-9220 for information or to schedule a tour.

Admission: Charged for groups of ten or more. Free to individuals.

Driving directions: I-25 to Exit 257A, US 34 East. Turn right on US 34 East. Go 10.3 miles. Turn right at 11th Avenue. Go 0.3 mile. Take the 3rd left onto 13th Street. Go 0.2 mile. Turn right onto 9th Avenue.

Parking: Free on street.

Web site: www.greeleygov.com/Museums/MeekerHome.aspx

25 Miramont Castle

A mysterious priest built this mansion for his mother, then disappeared for twenty years.

Courtesy of James Werner

Miramont Castle
Elements of English Tudor, Elizabethan, Romanesque, Byzantine, and Moorish styles. Battlements on one section of the roof.

"Miramont castle was built last year by Father Francolon after months of deep study of which style of architecture should be adopted as better suited to the locality. Romanesque alone was found too uniform, Ionic too classic for romantic Manitou, Gothic too pious for a residence, Moorish too pagan for a clergyman and Colonial out of place in a mountain region. So it was decided by the reverend clergyman to take some of the Romanesque, Gothic, Moorish and Middle Ages style and blend them so artistically together as to give at once satisfaction to the eyes and make it appear as though built on the border of France and Spain, countries in which Father Francolon traces far back his ancestors. No architects were employed, as it was feared few would understand exactly what was wanted. The plans were drawn by Father Francolon himself, every detail given ear and attention, and the work superintended by him alone from the beginning to the end."[1]

It's true. According to the daughter of one of the contractors, Father Francolon spent countless hours drawing up the plans for contractors Angus and Archie Gillis. using ideas collected during his years of travel with his diplomat father.

How It All Started

Father Jean Baptiste Francolon was born in 1854 in the Clermont region of France. In 1878, he came to the United States and served as secretary to the Archbishop of Santa Fe. In 1880, he became chancellor of the Archdiocese of Santa Fe, in charge of an area in which the church was developing missions. He assisted the Denver and Rio Grande Railroad to negotiate arrangements to pass through Mexican and Indian territories.

Father Francolon

The French government then called upon him to visit Venezuela and Guatemala on diplomatic missions. Following that, his health declined.

Father Francolon and his mother, Marie, purchased several lots in Manitou beginning in October 1890. In late 1892, he finished a cottage on Capitol Hill. He was assigned the pastorate of Our Lady of Perpetual Help in Manitou Springs in 1892.

He designed and built the Miramont Castle from 1892 to 1895. the *Manitou Springs Journal* proclaimed it to be "one of the handsomest and most artistic buildings in Colorado."[2]

Marie Francolon

The House

Miramont means "look at the mountain." It was built on four levels, following the line of the hillside and covered 14,000 square feet. Each story had at least one exit to level ground. Few of the 46 rooms are square. One room has eight sides and another has sixteen.

There are eight fireplaces, one of which extends back eight feet into the side of the mountain. Electricity had become available in the 1880s, and the castle had both

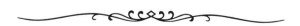

electricity and running water. An addition, built sometime after 1896, included the chapel, grand staircase, and solarium.

All cooking was done in the sanitarium just up the hill and across the street. Three tunnels were used to bring meals to the house. The tunnels are now collapsed.

In the end, the Gillis brothers had to take Father Francolon to court to obtain payment. He took out a loan on the property in order to pay them.

The Ball

Some reports say that Father Francolon was rarely seen outside the castle except when he took his mother driving or walked his two huge dogs. Others said that he shared his talents at the piano at social gatherings.

He did open his home on February 22, 1897, for a gala charity event to raise funds to purchase land for the public library in Manitou. On this occasion, 300 people paid admission to come in colonial costumes. If you didn't want to dress up, you could pay a dollar to come as a spectator.

The *Gazette Telegraph* reported the event this way:

> General and Martha Washington, Miles Standish, Mr. and Mrs. John Adams, Mr. and Mrs. Gov. Winthrop, Gen. Lafayette, Gen. Rochambeau, Mr. and Mrs. James Madison and many other men and women of the old and quaint days of America were represented.
>
> As the ninth hour was pealing the reception party assembled in the picture gallery and marched to the receiving room as the orchestra rendered 'Columbia'.
>
> Two minuets were danced by four couples each, followed by general dances participated in by all the historical characters. Most graciously and stately they tripped to and fro in unison to the music.
>
> Those who did not fancy a dance enjoyed themselves in the library or drawing room where various games and other pleasures were indulged in. Refreshments were served in the room off the ballroom. The table was prettily laid and was bedecked with roses and smilax.[3]

Another charity ball was held August 24, 1897, which was also a smashing success.

Sudden Disappearance

It is unclear how long Father Francolon served the parish. He left town suddenly around 1900. After 1900, his business affairs were handled by George

Renn, who had his power of attorney.

He went back to France, and his mother followed sometime before March 1900. She died soon after her return to France. Father Francolon returned to the United States, but never to Colorado. He died in New York City in 1922.

Sisters of Mercy

When Father Francolon and Marie moved into Miramont, they donated their cottage home to the Sisters of Mercy to use as a sanitarium. The new sanitarium, called *Montcalme*, was soon overflowing with patients, and two more cottages were added. Tents were also erected on the hillside.

In December 1898, the sisters agreed to cook for Father Francolon and his mother. For unclear reasons, the Sisters also borrowed $3,000 from him the same year.

In 1902, after Father Francolon had left the area, General William Palmer, founder of the Denver and Rio Grande Railroad, donated $1,000 to help relieve the debt. But when a fire destroyed the furnace room of Montcalme, the sisters purchased the then-vacant Miramont Castle and renamed it Montcalme.

In spite of financial hardships, the sisters ran the sanitarium until 1928. From 1928 until 1946, the castle was used by sisters from other parishes for vacations and rest.

In 1946, the castle was converted into ten apartments. Under the ownership of Mrs. Cora Wood, the name was changed back to Miramont. By then, the famous landmark was partially hidden by houses built along Ruxton Avenue.

Nine other owners followed in twenty-two years. Some of the tenants respected the historical background. Others burned parts of it for firewood.

Becoming a House Museum

When the Manitou Springs Historical Society was formed in 1971, it sought to

Haunted Castle

Many claim that Miramont Castle is haunted. On one occasion, the museum president's son looked in a mirror and saw a woman in Victorian dress looking back.

On another occasion, museum president Kathy Thomson was standing by the butler's kitchen looking toward the grand staircase. She saw a man in a frock coat and a woman in a bustle dress wearing an old style hat coming down the stairs. She could see right through them.

Another incident occurred at closing time when the sun had already gone behind the mountains. As board member Bee Busch began to walk from the front counter in the gift shop to the rear hallway, she looked up. She saw a headless woman in an ankle-length, cream-colored dress with long sleeves, high collar, and laced bib front coming toward her. Whoever or whatever it was turned toward Bee, then disappeared into the Christmas room.

acquire a building to preserve and display Manitou's Victorian heritage. Miramont Castle was purchased by the society on February 17, 1976. With assistance of a matching grant from the Centennial-Bicentennial Commission, the work of restoration began.

The Castle was added to the National Register of Historic Places in 1977. More than 40,000 people visit the Castle annually.

About Miramont Castle

Address: 9 Capitol Hill Avenue, Manitou Springs, Colorado 80829

Phone: (719) 685-1011

Hours: Memorial Day–Labor Day, 9 a.m.–5 p.m. daily. Winter hours: Tuesday–Saturday 10 a.m.–4 p.m., Sunday Noon–4 p.m.

Admission: Adults 16–59 $6.00, Seniors (60+) $5.50, Children (6–15) $2.00, Children (5 and under) Free, Active Duty Military Free

Driving directions: I-25 to Exit 141, Cimarron Street/U.S. 24 West. Turn left at the light at the end of the ramp. Continue to follow U.S. 24 West for 3.9 miles. Take the Manitou Avenue exit. Keep right at the fork to go on Manitou Avenue. Go 1.4 miles. Turn left onto Ruxton Avenue. Go 0.2 miles. Turn right onto Capitol Hill Avenue.

Parking: Follow signs up the winding road to the parking lot above and behind the castle.

Web site: www.miramontcastle.org

26 Molly Brown House

"I am a daughter of adventure. That's my arc, as the astrologers would say. It's a good one too, for a person who had rather make a snap-out than a fade-out of life."

Courtesy of Jeff Padrick of Klug Studios

Margaret Tobin Brown's life was far more interesting than any of the myths spun by storytellers or by the movie, *The Unsinkable Molly Brown*, that made her a household name. She was born in 1867 in Hannibal, Missouri, to John and Johanna Tobin. They called her Maggie, but as an adult, she preferred to be called Margaret. She had an older brother, Daniel, and a younger sister, Helen. John and Johanna each had a daughter from previous marriages. Margaret's older half sisters were Mary Ann and Catherine.

Molly Brown House, also known as the House of Lions.

Dove-colored rhyolite and smooth red sandstone. Balusters, capstones, steps and trim also of sandstone, probably quarried in Manitou Springs. Terra cotta roof with cupola on main house. House and carriage house are built from Castle Rock rhyolite with sandstone trim. A stone retaining wall stretches across the front of the site.

The Tobin home was perched on a hill a few blocks from the Mississippi River. Maggie attended a grammar school run by her aunt, Johanna's sister, Mary O'Leary. Mrs. O'Leary eventually turned classes over to her daughter, another Margaret. Margaret Tobin and Margaret O'Leary were close cousins. At age thirteen, Maggie went to work at Garth's tobacco company, where Irish girls with few choices worked.

Margaret Tobin Brown poses in a wicker rickshaw in Palm Beach, Florida.

Going to Leadville

A young man named Jack Landrigan fell in love with and married Margaret's half-sister, Mary Ann. A blacksmith by trade, Jack persuaded Mary Ann that opportunities waited in Colorado. In 1883, Jack, Mary Ann, and Daniel, boarded a train for Leadville. The Landrigans stayed. Daniel liked what he saw in Leadville, but returned to Hannibal to run a newspaper and become a railroad contractor for a while.

Late in 1885, Daniel was ready to return to Leadville. He bought train tickets for Maggie and Helen. Maggie, who was eighteen, hated leaving her family, but she longed to be rich enough to give her father a home so he would not have to work.

Leadville was a full-fledged mining camp. Tradesmen, miners, prospectors, freight wagons, burro trains, and horse-drawn carriages crowded the streets. Maggie took a job at the dry-goods firm of Daniels, Fisher, & Smith, where she worked in the carpet and drapery department.

Helen returned to her parents' home in Hannibal. But Daniel stayed and worked ten- and twelve-hour days at the mines. Maggie stayed as well and dreamed of marrying a wealthy man who could help her family.

J. J. Brown

James Joseph Brown was born in 1854 in Wayne County, Pennsylvania, and was thirteen years Margaret's senior. He was the son of immigrant parents and

wanted to someday live in his parents' home country of Ireland.

J. J. was schooled by his mother and eventually attended St. John's Academy in Pittston, Pennsylvania. He left the state at twenty-three to pursue mining, working for a while on a farm in Nebraska before finding work in the placer mines in the Black Hills of the Dakotas. Two years in the mines gave him experience, but it took a toll on his health. He spent time in several Colorado towns, and in Aspen established an important network of mining contacts. In 1882, he headed to Leadville. He worked as a day miner and studied geology books at night. He eventually landed a job as shift manager for the conglomerate of mines owned by David Moffat and Eben Smith.

Over the course of the next few years, J. J. was promoted to superintendent of the Maid and Henriette Mine, one of the largest mineral producers. He worked with Moffat and Smith for fourteen years, developing some of their most important properties.

J. J. and Maggie met in late May or early June 1886 at a picnic sponsored by the Catholic church in Leadville. J. J. was personable, charming, and had many friends. He wasn't wealthy, but he had a steady job.

He squired her to the Tabor Hotel and the opera house, and they both loved to dance. Maggie had wanted a rich man, but now she wanted Jim Brown. She decided she would be better off with a poor man if she loved him. They married in 1886.

J. J. and Margaret wanted to better their educations. Margaret hired a tutor to help with her studies which included music, piano, and singing. She gave birth to Lawrence in 1887 and Helen in 1889. Margaret also became active in politics, helping to improve the area schools. The Browns were not in the highest echelons of the silver barons in the 1880s, but they did enjoy modest success in the booming town.

The silver boom was not to last. In October 1893, the Sherman Silver Purchase Act was repealed. Gold was now the standard, and the price of silver dropped. Banks, mining operations, and businesses came to a standstill. Ninety percent of Leadville's labor force was out of work.

However, J. J.'s luck held. He was appointed superintendent of the Little Johnny Mine, owned by the Ibex Mining Company, of which he was a partner. The mine was just up the hill from Harrison Avenue. The Little Johnny was mined for gold, not silver, and on October 29, 1893, the *Leadville Herald Democrat* reported that the Little Johnny was shipping 135 tons of gold ore per day.

When Ibex Mining paid $1 million in dividends to shareholders, the Browns were rich and celebrated by touring the state and visiting family. They could now afford to divide their time between the social circles in Denver and

summertime in Leadville. On April 6, 1894, J. J. purchased the modest-sized but elegant house designed by architect William Lang at 1340 Pennsylvania Avenue. They called it the House of Lions. After a spring snow, the Browns drove a sleigh up and down Pennsylvania and Colfax Avenues, singing Irish songs at the top of their lungs to celebrate.

J. J. and Margaret were prominent in Denver business and social circles from the first. They were welcomed into the homes of millionaires, and Margaret was quick to take up social causes.

J. J.'s Chickens

Wanting a rural home for the children to play freely and for entertaining on a grand scale, J. J. purchased the C. F. Reed farm nine miles from Denver on Bear Creek. Majestic maple trees served as property lines. The rushing waters of Bear Creek created a natural irrigation system through Pioneer Union Ditch, which entered the farm on the northwest, and the Simonton Ditch, which brought fresh water from the west. On the northwest corner of the farm was an artesian well, and on the south a fresh spring. Margaret named the property that cascaded with water "Avoca," after a poem by her favorite Irish-born poet, Sir Thomas Moore.

There in 1897, they built a foursquare Victorian home and a large brick barn that had a hardwood floor in the loft for dancing. There was even a pond for fishing. For nearly ten years, the Browns welcomed visitors at their summer farm. Margaret entertained volunteers for her charity projects with sumptuous luncheons and a chance to wander in the fresh country air. Helen and Lawrence could run and play and ride their ponies there.

In addition to tending to thoroughbred horses, J. J. was determined to raise natural or "pure" chickens. He built a chicken village, where the birds could eat the best diet and get the best care. J. J. sold his chicken to restaurants where they were a popular menu item.

Different Pages

Their fortunes still rising, the Browns toured Europe. Lawrence was eight, Helen was six. Back home, they enjoyed the benefits of the Denver Country Club, and Margaret continued her philanthropic work, hosting a lavish Catholic fund-raising bazaar. The Denver newspapers praised her organization skills.

However, by this time, J. J. and Margaret were on different paths. J. J.'s health was declining, and he was ready to settle down. Margaret, on the other hand, was in her prime, ready to use her many talents and abilities to the fullest in public and social settings.

Because of J. J.'s poor health, he and Margaret moved to Ireland, while

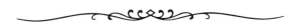

Photographer, Pat Werner; Courtesy James Werner

Helen attended school in Paris. However, J. J. felt too removed from his mining interests and returned after only a year. Margaret continued to study and travel, enrolling in literature and drama classes at the Margaret Morrison Carnegie School for Women in Pittsburgh. She spent the year 1900 studying at Carnegie and traveling briefly with her cousin Margaret O'Leary. Lawrence was enrolled in the Pennsylvania Military College in Chester in 1902, and Helen now attended school in New York.

After again spending fall semester 1902 at Carnegie, Margaret returned to Denver in time for Christmas and an unhappy surprise.

Molly Brown Summer House
Two-story dipped brick construction with sandstone foundation, window lintels, and eyebrow windows in the attic. Three corbelled brick chimneys and several "dragon back" crowns. The foundation, sills, lintels, and porch supports are cut with sandstone from Lyons, Colorado. A frame porch with triple columns at the entryway and a Chinoiserie patterned rail extends around two sides of the house. The west facade has a gabled roof above the porch steps topped with a hip finial (ball in crown).

J. J. was being sued for $50,000 by Harry D. Call, the stenographer of Colorado silver baron W. S. Stratton, for alienation of his wife's affections. Apparently Maude Morton Call had met J. J. at a health resort in Pueblo and, because of him, decided to leave her husband and three-year-old son.

The case made the news and was eventually settled out of court. The Browns rented out the house on Pennsylvania Avenue, withdrew from society, and embarked on an around-the-world trip together. They were gone for nearly

a year, with Margaret's sister, Helen, looking after the children. Margaret came back with silk kimonos and astonished her friends with a Japanese-style coiffure and unusual clothing. She wrote a lengthy article on life in India, though she was deeply disturbed by the caste system.

Mrs. Crawford Hill

At this time, Mrs. Crawford Hill set about to change the make up of Denver society. She created new rules regarding what determined social standing. She created a list that was known as "The Sacred Thirty-Six"—those whom she invited to her own parties. Many of those excluded were miffed, and newspapers had a field day.

Though J. J. and Margaret were listed in Denver's social register, they were not among the thirty-six. The Browns were Irish, Roman Catholic, and "new money." Mrs. Hill was a staunch member of the Daughters of the American Revolution, and Margaret did not qualify for DAR membership. In spite of this, the two ladies served on many of the same committees. Often, Mrs. Brown and Mrs. Hill tried to out dress each other.

Family

Meanwhile, Helen and Lawrence were struggling to establish their own lives in the shadow of their famous parents. Lawrence's relationship with his father had been strained ever since he had been evicted from the expensive military school in Pennsylvania after a spree with some boys while on the way back to Denver. Lawrence had to explain himself to J. J., who was displeased.

Now Lawrence wanted to marry Eileen Horton. Margaret approved of the girl, but J. J. wanted his son to settle into a career before starting a family. The couple married in January 1911 against his parents' wishes; neither J. J. nor Margaret attended the ceremony. J. J. apparently cut off Lawrence from the family fortune. The young couple moved to Victor, Colorado, and Lawrence took a job as a day miner.

J. J. spent time in Arizona and New Mexico, where the warmer climate helped him recoup his health. Lawrence changed jobs again and again, struggling to build a career. Margaret often stayed with friends in New York, Newport, and Paris. J. J. resented the notoriety that Margaret received in the Denver newspapers. But her opinions and activities regarding women and children's rights had grown stronger and were of interest to newspapers.

In spite of her social successes, the press carried headlines that the Browns were separated. J. J. was no longer supportive of his wife's drive and accomplishments, and he preferred the rough life of the mining camps instead.

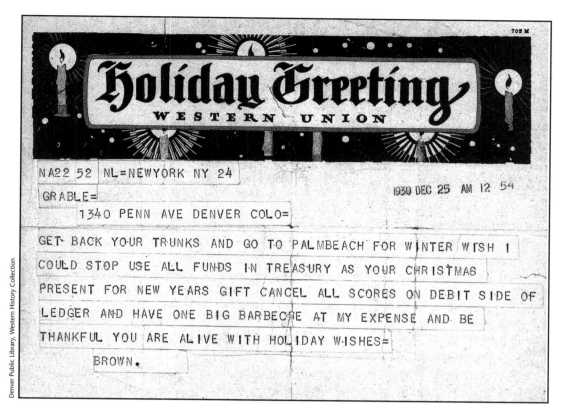

NA22 52 NL=NEWYORK NY 24
GRABLE=
    1340 PENN AVE DENVER COLO=

1930 DEC 25 AM 12 54

GET BACK YOUR TRUNKS AND GO TO PALMBEACH FOR WINTER WISH I
COULD STOP USE ALL FUNDS IN TREASURY AS YOUR CHRISTMAS
PRESENT FOR NEW YEARS GIFT CANCEL ALL SCORES ON DEBIT SIDE OF
LEDGER AND HAVE ONE BIG BARBECUE AT MY EXPENSE AND BE
THANKFUL YOU ARE ALIVE WITH HOLIDAY WISHES=
    BROWN.

Denver Public Library, Western History Collection

Margaret signed a separation agreement that caused financial problems in later years. She retained ownership of the House of Lions and its furnishings, though her resources were substantially reduced.

Telegram from Margaret Brown to her housekeeper, Ella Grable

Doing Her Duty

Margaret was a close friend of three generations of the Astor family. In 1912, she accompanied them on a trip through northern Africa and Egypt. Helen took time off from her studies at the Sorbonne to accompany her mother.

On the return trip, they stopped in Rome, where Margaret bought some busts and models to bring back to the Denver Art Museum. When Margaret and Helen returned to the Ritz Hotel in Paris, Margaret received a telegram from Lawrence saying that his baby was ill. She booked passage on the *Titanic* with the Astor party. Helen remained in Paris.

Margaret's heroism in Lifeboat Six is well-documented, but it is her heroism following the rescue by the *Carpathia* that goes largely unsung.

Once rescued by the *Carpathia*, Margaret returned again and again to the

ship's wireless room to send messages for friends as well as poorer survivors who could not afford to pay for telegrams to their loved ones. She distributed supplies to women and children sleeping in the corridors and dining rooms. She ignored the ship's doctor who tried to keep her from helping the poorer women. She and other women scoured the ship for all the necessities that these people would need once they got off the ship.

Some of the wealthier passengers aboard the *Carpathia* hesitated to donate funds that would allow the poorer immigrants to get off the boat once it docked in New York. Undaunted, Margaret formed a committee and started a subscription list. She posted the list at the foot of the stairs, where social pressure encouraged contributions. By the time they reached New York, $10,000 had been pledged.

The media was in a frenzy. But Margaret kept her cool, refusing to leave the boat until everyone she had watched over was safely taken care of. She wrote down the destination of each survivor and only after giving the list to the shipping line's agents did she meet her brother, Daniel.

She delayed her return to Denver, setting up headquarters in New York City at the Ritz Carlton. There she and Daniel directed foreign-born survivors to various consuls in New York, helping them contact friends and relatives and sending a flurry of telegrams. They also tried to ensure that the donations of cash got to those who needed it most.

Margaret held the position of chair of the Survivors' Committee until her death, eighteen years later. When J. J. learned that she had been saved, he evidently quipped to a friend, "She's too mean to sink."[1]

the *Denver Times* quoted Margaret as saying, "I simply did my duty as I saw it. I knew that I was healthy and strong and was able to nurse the suffering. I am sure that there was nothing I did throughout the whole affair that anyone else wouldn't have done. That I did help some, I am thankful and my only regret is that I could not have assisted more."[2] Back in Denver, Mrs. Crawford Hill hosted a luncheon in Margaret's honor.

Political Accomplishments

In 1914, Margaret began to think about political office and considered running for the U.S. Senate. The *New York Times* thought she had a good chance of winning, as did Colorado supporters. She was favored by the Progressives and the Democrats.

Two things kept her from entering the primaries. One was that there was already a female, pro-suffrage candidate, Helen Ring Robinson. The suffrage movement had split into two camps, and Robinson was with the National American Woman Suffrage Association (NAWSA)—a rival to the organization

founded by Margaret's good friend Alva Belmont. Dr. Anna Shaw, who served as president of NAWSA from 1904 to 1915, opposed the idea of two women who supported suffrage running against each other. Shaw felt that splitting the support between them would be detrimental.

The second reason was that Margaret's sister was married to Baron Von Reitzenstein, a German. When World War I broke out, Helen's husband was called to serve on the staff of Emperor William of Germany. Helen had to remain in Berlin. Political advisers told Margaret she would never win with her sister in such a position.

Margaret concurred. She wired Robinson that she would not attend the congressional primaries. She made it known that although she was postponing her bid, she hoped in two years to unseat U. S. Senator Charles S. Thomas. Robinson herself stated her support for Margaret to succeed Thomas.

Margaret never ran for that office. Instead, she helped establish medical relief facilities in France. She also developed a series of lectures on human rights, suffrage, the life and writings of Mark Twain, and her travels in Europe and India. She was a popular and colorful speaker.

In Paris, she assisted the American ambulance system and earned the French Legion of Honor award for her war efforts there. She was appointed a director of the American Committee for Devastated France, where she worked with government officials and local villagers to rebuild and refurnish houses and to distribute food, clothing, household linens, and tools.

Final Years

Margaret leased out the House of Lions and spent time at Newport, where she had found acceptance and friendship among wealthy and powerful families. She visited Hannibal once a year. When she returned to Egypt, she brought back two sphinx-headed lionesses for the House of Lions.

Meanwhile, J. J. was now in his sixties and began to pine for Leadville. He telegraphed Helen to come to Los Angeles, where he had been hospitalized. After a stop in Leadville, where Helen worried that he might not be able to breathe in the high altitude, they traveled back to her home in New York. He died September 5, 1922, at age sixty-eight.

Margaret died in her sleep on October 26, 1932, at the Barbizon Hotel in New York from a brain tumor. She was buried in Holy Rood Cemetery next to J. J., the man she loved despite all their differences. There was little left of her wealth. At the height of the Great Depression, the House of Lions was worth only a fraction of the original price. Her other belongings were worth about $20,000.

"I am a daughter of adventure," she once wrote. "This means I never experience a dull moment and must be prepared for any eventuality. I never know when I may go up in an airplane and come down with a crash, or go motoring and climb a pole, or go off for a walk in the twilight and return all mussed up in an ambulance. That's my arc, as the astrologers would say. It's a good one too, for a person who had rather make a snap-out than a fade-out of life."[3]

Reactions to the Legend

Lawrence was aware of how strong and successful a figure his mother was, and he abhorred the Hollywood version of her life. The Lawrence Brown and Helen Brown Benzinger families were averse to publicity and so remained silent for many years. Lawrence once wrote a letter to his sister's husband saying he wanted to deliver a good thrashing to the author of one particularly wacky account of his mother's life. But he feared the assaults and lawsuits and so did nothing. It was true that some of the liberal causes for which she fought ruffled a few feathers. And she was eccentric enough to have propelled some of her own myths into the limelight.

Helen Brown did not agree with her mother's liberal policies and married into a dignified and sophisticated family. The folklore that grew up was embarrassing and painful to her. She vowed to squelch any Hollywood attempt to adapt her mother's story and threatened to publish her own documented biography.

Recent research has proven that Margaret Brown was revered and respected in mainstream Denver society. Poisoned pens attacked some of her antics and J. J.'s competitive mining business, but one thing is clear: Margaret Tobin Brown was always true to herself.

Becoming a House Museum

In 1898, the title of the house had been transferred to Margaret, though neither she nor other family members lived there continuously. In 1902, while the Browns were traveling around the world, the house was rented to Governor and Mrs. James Orman, making it the governor's mansion for that year. After Margaret and J. J.'s separation in 1909, she spent less time in Denver. When she did return, she often took a suite at the Brown Palace Hotel.

To help bolster her finances, she rented out rooms in the House of Lions. She first rented the entire house to the well-to-do Cosgriff family until their own mansion was built at 800 Grant Street. In 1920, the house was leased to the Keiser family. In 1926, Margaret took legal action to evict Lucille Hubbel, who was subletting rooms. At that point, Margaret converted the home into a

rooming house under the supervision of her housekeeper, Ella Grable. It was never a boardinghouse, though, as there was no central kitchen serving meals.

A friend of the family who visited the house at that time reported that the rooms were not modern enough, and, as the neighborhood had declined, the fashionable were moving south and east.

Subsequent owners altered the house over the next thirty-eight years, making space for more than twelve separate roomers. In 1958, the home was bought by Art Leisenring, who operated it as a gentlemen's boardinghouse.

In the late 1960s, it was leased as a home for wayward girls. It was a far cry from the Victorian showplace it had once been. Finally in 1970, through the efforts of Historic Denver and others, restoration began. In a spirit of community that affected the neighborhood in a positive way, many volunteers pulled together to restore the first floor.

About the Molly Brown House Museum

Address: 1340 Pennsylvania Street, Denver, Colorado 80203

Phone: (303) 832-4092

Hours: Tuesday–Saturday, 10–4 p.m. Last tour starts at 3:30. Sunday, noon–4 p.m. Last tour starts at 3:30

Admission: Adults $6.50, Seniors (65+) $5.00, Children (6–12) $3.00; under 6 free

Driving directions: I-25 to Exit 210A, Colfax Avenue/US 40. Go east on Colfax Avenue for 1.8 miles. Turn right on Pennsylvania Street. Go 0.2 mile.

Parking: Paid parking lots within two blocks of the museum; limited free parking on street near house

Memberships: Membership is available for the Molly Brown House at varying levels of support. Visit http://www.mollybrown.org/get-involved/

Web site: www.mollybrown.org

About the Molly Brown Summer House

Address: 2690 South Wadsworth Boulevard, Denver, Colorado 80227

Phone: (303) 989-6639 or (800) 971-6639

Hours: Call for tour appointment.

Admission: No charge for tours, however donations are accepted. All donations are used to maintain the Molly Brown Summer House and grounds.

Driving directions: I-25 to Exit 201, Hampden Avenue/U.S. 285. Go west on Hampden Avenue for 8.7 miles. Take Wadsworth Boulevard/CO 121 exit from US 285. Turn right (north) onto South Wadsworth Boulevard. Go 1.0 miles. The house is on the northeast corner of Yale and Wadsworth.

Parking: Free parking lot

Web site: www.mollybrownsummerhousehistory.org

27 Museo de las Tres Colonias

John Romero made adobe to build the house using clay from the backyard.

Museo de las Tres Colonias
Adobe brick structure.

John Romero was born in Santa Fe, New Mexico, in 1897, and moved to Fort Collins to work for the Colorado and Southern Railroad in 1922 at age twenty-five.

Inez Rivera Romero's family came from northern New Mexico to Fort Collins in 1917. Inez's mother was a *curandera*, a practitioner of herbal folk medicine. John and Inez married in 1925. For the first two years of their marriage, they lived in a boxcar provided by the railroad.

Between 1927 and 1935, John built the three-room adobe structure that is the present house museum, using straw and clay dug from the backyard for the adobe bricks. Inez put wallpaper on the walls and made the house a home. John and Inez raised seven children in this house: Johnnie, Charlie, Frances,

George, Arthur, Juliet, and Antoinette (Toni). A midwife helped deliver all but two of the babies at home; Toni and Juliet were delivered in the Poudre Valley Hospital. Two more children died in infancy and are buried in Belleview Cemetery.

One room in the house served as a living room and the parents' bedroom. The second room had two beds, one for the boys and one for the girls. The children slept crosswise on the beds to fit better. When company came, the kids slept on the floor. A frame addition was added to the house during the 1950s.

The Romero children considered themselves well off. Their 24-inch-thick adobe walls kept them warm in the winter and cool in summer. They raised chickens, rabbits, and pigs; and had all the food they needed. Water was delivered and dumped into a cistern on the north side of the house. An icebox held perishables. Inez's father, Frederico, lived next door,

John Romero making adobe bricks in the lot where he built his house

Courtesy of Juliet Romero Chavez

where Arthur grew a garden of zucchini and other squash. The children picked wild spinach and asparagus by the stockyards east of the house.

Education

John Romero had only a third-grade education, but he read extensively. He educated himself and became a notary public and legal adviser to the Hispanic community. He was also one of the first welfare investigators. All his life, education remained important to him, and he encouraged his children to get good educations.

In 1932, John started to work for the Great Western Sugar Company in the beet factory. During the three- or four-month beet harvest, he worked construction during the day, came home for a while, and then worked the second shift at the factory as a line foreman. Charlie and Arthur brought him dinner.

During the Depression, when there was no work, John worked in the Civilian Conservation Corps (CCC). The corps lived in tents at a camp in Estes Park, under the charge of military officers, fixing bridges and doing other conservation and construction projects.

Life at Home

John and Inez spoke Spanish to each other, but spoke only English to the children. A teacher had told them that the children had to know English when they entered school, so the children did not learn Spanish until later.

Everyone had to be on time for meals if they wanted anything to eat. Inez did all the cooking on the coal- and wood-burning Majestic stove, which was also the only heat source in the house. To feed the stove, John brought leftover lumber from the construction sites where he worked. The kids also remember that a coal train passed near the house at night, and men on the train would drop coal from the train as it passed through because they knew that the poorer people needed coal would collect it.

A special treat was when John brought home a round steak on Saturdays, which Inez used in her special chili. She baked bread every Wednesday. Her baked buns were particularly popular. The kids were not allowed to help with the cooking.

Inez was handy with home remedies. Potato soaked in vinegar and wrapped in a cloth was used on the forehead for fever. A honey mixture with onions was used for coughs. Inez also had an aloe plant in the window that she used to treat burns.

Every evening, the family gathered in the house at seven o'clock to pray the rosary. After prayers, the children could play for another hour. John often sat reading his newspaper after supper, but he sometimes fell asleep. The newspaper kept the kids from knowing he was not awake.

Kids Work and Play

A favorite outing was to go cherry picking. Many people picked cherries for a living, but for the Romero kids, this was a chance to play. A neighbor loaded workers along with the kids into his truck at five o'clock in the morning and drove an hour north to the cherry orchard. Everyone was assigned a tree, and they were supposed to pick the whole tree. But sometimes the kids snuck around and picked the bottoms of the trees to fill their buckets. George liked to climb the highest ladder, where he was dared to jump off.

Inez packed their lunch pails with potatoes and fried *taquitos* rolled with potted meat. John didn't like for his kids to work in the fields—he didn't want it to look like he could not provide for his family.

When he was older, Charlie had a store on the corner of the Romero lot in an old shed. Neighbors bought pop from him to give to Toni and Juliet.

Johnnie served four years in the military, starting at age sixteen. He became an aerial photographer and a lightweight boxing champion.

At fifteen, Arthur went to work in the lumberyard. He also worked occasionally in the pickle factory, where he was sometimes given five-gallon cans of pickles. He stayed in school until he was seventeen and then went into the military.

George worked at the lumber company, got married at age seventeen, and went to California to work for the Ford Motor Company.

Juliet worked at Woolworth for eleven years, beginning as a senior in high school. Toni worked in a laundromat at age fifteen. Frances left school at fourteen, got married at eighteen, and raised a family.

When injuries forced John to retire from construction work, he worked as a sheepherder with his two herding dogs, Tuffy and Scottie. He rode horseback to the herd and stayed in a cozy trailer with the dogs. Tuffy and Scottie were fed cooked meat scraps from the store and hot broth. John's grandchildren loved to visit him in the trailer because they would get a ride on his horse. When he retired from that job, he refused offers from other sheepherders for his dogs. When he retired, so did the dogs.

Facing Discrimination

Life was far from easy for Hispanics in Fort Collins. The developers of Great Western Sugar Company had taken care to situate the sugar factory company towns of Buckingham, Andersonville, and Alta Vista so that workers could walk to the plant and the sugar beet fields. But they secluded these communities from Fort Collins across the Cache la Poudre River. Roads were not paved. There were no sewer lines.

The Hispanic families forged a strong, vibrant community. But on the other side of the river, store windows displayed signs that read "No Dogs or Mexicans Allowed." Many Anglos considered all Hispanics to be immigrants from Mexico, even if their ancestors had lived for more than four centuries in what became the American Southwest.

The Romero children remember that their father taught them to respect others. They kept close to home for the most part, learned good morals, and did not know a lot about discrimination. It was part of life, but John taught them to just be themselves and to walk away from trouble.

John Romero was a leader in the Democratic Party. He helped organize the Hispanic community politically and conducted voter registration drives. He was

one of a generation of leaders who sought to improve conditions and create new opportunities. As the only Hispanic notary public, he was a friend of the officials in Fort Collins.

Adobe

Adobe buildings are aptly suited to the semiarid and treeless landscape of the high prairies. Museo House was one of the first adobe homes built in Andersonville. The house demonstrates John Romero's skill and the expediency and adaptability of adobe as an inexpensive but sound construction material. Wooden additions were added between the 1950s and the 1980s.

The naming of Romero Street and Romero Park after John Romero serves as a tribute to his leadership in the community.

Becoming a House Museum

The house was home to members of the Romero family until May 2001. In 2002, the City of Fort Collins accepted the donation of the house from Mark Goldberg and Fort Collins Partners I, LLC, who purchased it because a group of individuals wanted to turn it into a house museum. The city leases the house to the Poudre Landmarks Foundation, which maintains it.

The house is a representative dwelling in the so-called sugar factory company towns of Buckingham, Andersonville, and Alta Vista (which were collectively called Spanish Colonies), all now part of greater Fort Collins. The Museo de las Tres Colonias reflects the intention to represent the contributions of Hispanics in the three neighborhoods. Many oral histories have been collected from residents of these neighborhoods.

When rain fell on the grand opening of the museum, Romero family members said, "Mom and Dad are crying tears of joy seeing this today."

About the Museo de las Tres Colonias

Address: 425 10th Street, Fort Collins, Colorado 80524

Phone: (970) 221-0533

Hours: Third Saturday of each month, 12:30–3:00 p.m., and by appointment

Admission: Free

Driving directions: I-25 to Exit 269B (CO 14/E. Mulberry Street). Go west on Mulberry Street 3.1 mi. to LeMay Street (traffic light). Turn right on LeMay. The street curves and becomes 9th Street. Go 0.8 mi. At the flashing speed light, turn right onto Romero Street. Proceed to 10th Street. House is on the southwest corner.

Parking: Free on the street

Memberships: Membership in the Poudre Landmarks Foundation is available at varying levels of support. Call (970) 221-0533.

Web site: www.poudrelandmarks.com/plf_museo.shtml

28 Old Homestead House Museum

Pearl DeVere's sister told the undertaker, "This harlot is no sister of mine."

Victorian women organized their housekeeping duties according to the day (*see* "Household Tasks" sidebar in Chapter 6, Bloom Mansion). Wash day often fell on Monday. In Cripple Creek, Monday was also the day the girls from The Row (the red-light district) were allowed downtown to shop. We don't know for sure, but this arrangement could have been put in place because the respectable women were safely at home washing and would not have to rub shoulders with these girls.

Old Homestead Museum in 1969. Two-story, flat-roof painted brick with bay window and open porch. The stone columns supporting the porch have now been restored to wooden columns as on the original structure.

Few American prostitutes in the 19th century left diaries, letters, or other primary sources. Except for some of the more famous madams, we know little of their lives—why they took up the profession or how they felt about what they did. Pearl DeVere is one of several madams who operated in Cripple Creek.

Little is known about Isabelle Martin, who went by the name Pearl DeVere after opening the Old Homestead in 1896. It is thought that she came from Evansville, Indiana, and married twice before arriving in Cripple Creek. Accurate records are lacking.

Nor do we know why she set out for Cripple Creek, but she may have arrived there in 1893. She married Charles B. Flynn, a sawmill owner, around 1895. When his sawmill was ruined in the 1896 fires, he took a job smelting iron and steel in Monterey, Mexico. Pearl, who was already in business as a madam, declined to accompany him.

Her parlor house at 327 Myers Avenue burned, too, in 1896. But as the rest of Cripple Creek rebuilt, so did she—this time, in brick. The new parlor house was spared nothing. It had electric lights, running water, a telephone, and a bathroom in an era where most houses had a privy out back. She imported wallpaper and brass fixtures from London.

The 12th Census of Population, 1900, Colorado, Precinct 16, Cripple Creek, June 13, 1900.

Entries in the 1900 census show Hazel Vernon as head of household, Inda Allen as boarder, and the rest of the girls as lodgers.

The downstairs consisted of three elaborately furnished parlors, a wine cabinet, dining room, and kitchen. The three parlors were used for card games, singing, and dancing. Upstairs were five comfortable bedrooms. Pearl's bedroom was elegantly furnished with an oak bedstead, a writing desk, sofa, rocking chairs, and wardrobe. She held a lavish grand opening, the likes of which had never been seen in Cripple Creek.

Pearl's girls were in their late teens or early twenties. They were known to be beautiful and of a much higher class than other prostitutes. They were

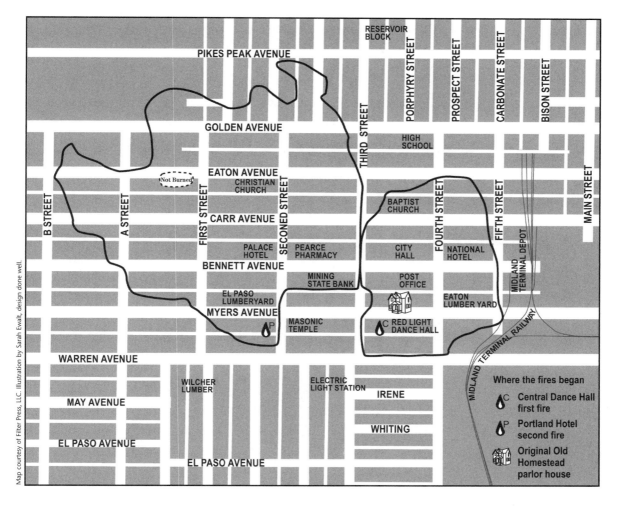

Map courtesy of Filter Press, LLC. Illustration by Sarah Ewalt, design done well.

expected to entertain five guests per night at $50 each and were allowed to keep 40 percent of the total. A girl could earn $100 per night. Though the girls paid for their own clothing, Pearl fed them well and made sure they visited the doctor regularly.

The two fires in April 1896 burned 27 blocks, including the first Old Homestead

From city directories, we have the names of some of Pearl's employees. Lola Livingston became madam of the Mikado until 1900. Nell McClusky is thought to have opened her own parlor house in Cripple Creek later. As for Wellie Boudine, Ella Dickenson, Ida Grey, Flora Hastings, Mable White, and Mayme Wellington, except for the time they worked for Pearl, their lives are largely lost to history. Pearl also employed a black cook, America "Mary" Samuels, and a twenty-five-year-old housekeeper of English descent, Inda Allen.

The $50 fee for a trick or $250 for all night included a fine dinner, wine,

and entertainment. Only the wealthy with good credit could make a reservation. Pearl scrupulously checked the gentleman's credit, and the fee was collected in advance.

Gentlemen could view their prospective partners for the evening by watching them parade through a viewing room upstairs. This closet with its glass window is preserved in the Old Homestead Museum.

Madam DeVere cut a striking figure riding around town in a carriage with red wheels, pulled with a matching pair of black horses. She might take a new girl in the carriage to show off the new arrival.

Death of Pearl DeVere

On Saturday night, June 4, 1897, the thirty-six-year-old Pearl had been partying. The *Denver Republican* tells us what happened next. "This morning, after a night's carousal, she went to bed at 7 o'clock, saying to a girl of the house that she would take some morphine to make her sleep. She was restless and asked the girl to sleep with her. At 11 o'clock the girl was awakened by the heavy breathing of her companion, and becoming alarmed, made an ineffectual attempt to arouse her. Dr. Hereford was sent for and applied all known remedies to revive his patient, but without success, and at 3:30 o'clock life was extinct."[1]

An article from the files of the *Cripple Creek Gold Rush* tells us, "There is no evidence that the act was intentional, and it is the opinion of all her friends that in taking a sleeping potion she had carelessly taken too much of the drug."[2]

A deputy sheriff had all the girls move out, taking only their personal possessions, and a guard was placed at the house. Pearl's husband, Charles Flynn, was notified in Mexico, but he did not return.

The Plot Thickens

In the meantime, Pearl's mother and sister back in Indiana thought that Pearl was working as a milliner or dress designer. When the sister arrived to claim the body, she was shocked to learn the truth.

Author Mabel Barbee Lee claims to have visited the mortuary where Pearl was laid out and overheard the sister tell the undertaker, "This harlot is no sister of mine," slamming the door on the way out so hard that the calendar on the wall fell to the floor.[3]

Who would pay for Pearl's funeral? The girls from the house didn't have the $210.25 required by the undertakers, Fairley & Lampman Brothers. While debating whether to auction off Pearl's $800 Parisian gown, allegedly given to her by an admirer, an anonymous donor from Denver furnished $1,000 for the funeral, asking only that Pearl be buried in the Parisian dress.

The town turned out to pay their respects to this much-admired lady. No one tells the story better than Lee in her book *Cripple Creek Days*:

> I watched from the top of a barrel in front of Roberts' Grocery. Somebody claimed he saw ladies from up on the hill sitting in the shadows of upstairs office windows. The Elks Band headed by Joe Moore led the procession, playing the 'Death March.' Then came the heavily draped hearse with the lavender casket almost hidden by a blanket of red and white roses. Just behind, a man walked solemnly beside the empty rig with the shiny red wheels, driving the span of restive black horses. A large cross of shell-pink carnations lay on the seat.
>
> My throat ached; I swallowed hard to choke back the tears. Now four mounted police were coming down the avenue, pushing back the crowd to make way for all the lodge members in brilliant regalia trying to keep in step. The sight of their red fezzes, feathered helmets and gold braided scabbards sent thrills of ecstasy through me. Bringing up the rear were buggies filled with thickly veiled women who, a man said, were Pearl's friends from the row.

After the procession wound its way to Mount Pisgah graveyard and gathered round the grave, the casket was lowered. Joe Moore's cornet played "Good-bye, Little Girl, Good-bye." Mabel Barbee buried her face in her coat and sobbed.

> When I looked up again, the long line of carriages and men had begun to file through the cemetery gate and down the slope back to camp. But the order had been reversed. The women, coming first, had thrown the veils off their faces and were laughing merrily as the trotting horses kicked up dust. Lodge members hurried willy-nilly ... The driver of the buggy with the shiny red wheels had jumped on the seat and the frisky steeds galloped wildly while he held the reins with one hand and pulled for a bottle from under the seat with the other. Even the hearse had picked up speed and the wheels rattled clumsily over the stones. [Then Joe Moore] trilled the whistle, the snare drums rolled and the whole band burst into 'There'll Be a Hot Time in the Old Town Tonight!'[4]

Pearl's Estate

From her property, mining shares, household furnishings, clothing, and jewelry, Pearl was worth more than $7,000 at her death. The estate took a year and a half to settle. Orinda Strail, who had loaned Pearl $3,100 in 1896 to rebuild

after the fires, was awarded the house, furnishings, glassware, and crockery.

In early 1900, Strail sold the house to O. A. Rowe, who sold it to twenty-three-year-old Hazel Vernon the same day he purchased it and made $1,000 in the deal.

Pearl's girls had moved on, so Hazel had to find new employees. Among them were Gladys Gray, Edith Green, and Lillian Hill. Inda Allen and Mary Samuels continued on Hazel's staff, as well as a butler, chambermaid, musician, and porter. Hazel retired to California in 1902 to take care of her mother.

In 1905, the house passed to Phil DeWilde. Allen, who had been housekeeper there since 1896, became the next madam until about 1907. Samuels remained as cook. City directories list the names of the girls who worked there. But of their lives, only a line or two at most is recorded.

After 1910, red-light districts began to be closed down. Moral reform, Prohibition, regulations, and the boomtown bust took their toll. In *Her Life as an American Madam*, Nell Kimball suggests that in the first years of the century, "there was a kind of breakdown of the conventional ways of doing things; you might say the morality was getting loose and slipping."[5]

By 1915, the Old Homestead no longer appears in the Cripple Creek City Directory. In 1935, Mrs. W. F. Peterie purchased the house for back taxes.

Modern Times

Pat and Fred Mentzer came to Colorado in the 1950s to visit relatives in Colorado Springs. When Fred retired, the couple decided to make their home in Cripple Creek. After buying the notorious house, friends were captivated by its history. Tourists would stop by and ask to go through the house. The Mentzers decided to restore it. They interviewed old-timers and some of the former occupants of the house, though not the girls who had lived there; none of these interviews is known to have been recorded. Some of the original furniture was stored in the home, and the Mentzers completed furnishing the house based on descriptions from the old timers who had visited the place.

From then until now, the public has been able to visit the Old Homestead and revel in its authenticity. Piece by piece as much history as possible has been reconstructed. Charlotte Bumgarner, manager of the Old Homestead Museum, said that in addition to the primary sources, "I think Pearl is still here, and she slips me information once in a while."

About the Old Homestead House Museum

Address: 353 Myers Avenue, Cripple Creek, Colorado 80813, (The original address was 327 Myers Avenue. The street numbers have changed, but the lots remain the same.)

Phone: (719) 689-9090

Hours: Open daily from Memorial Day weekend through mid-October, 11 a.m.–5 p.m.

Admission: Adults $4, Children 10–13 $3, Children under 10 free, Seniors and military $3. Group rates available (will open anytime for group of six or more).

Driving directions: I-25 to Exit 141, U.S. 24/Cimarron Street in Colorado Springs. Turn left at the light at the end of the ramp. Follow U.S. 24 23 miles to Divide. Turn left on Colorado 67. Go 18 miles. In Cripple Creek, turn left on 5th Street. Go 0.1 mile. 5th Street becomes Myers Avenue. Go less than 0.1 mile.

Parking: Allowed in casino parking lot next to the museum, or park on the street

Web site: www.cripple-creek.org/Old_Homestead/homestead_house.html

29 Orum House

Emma Schmidt Orum left her estate, which included the historic house, to her attorney.

Orum House
Three-room frame bungalow with attic.

Thomas Sloan owned land west of Denver near present-day Sloan's Lake. While trying to irrigate for farming in 1861, he hit an artesian well that overflowed and created a lake that covered 200 acres. People rode out from Denver to see Farmer Sloan's lake. Native Americans came down from the hills and camped on the northwest edge of the lake.

With his farm now under water, Sloan needed another way to make a living. He cut ice in the wintertime, stored it in sawdust, and shipped it to local breweries.

Cattail swampland stretched from present-day 20th to 17th avenues and from Sloan's Lake to Depew Street. The area west of the lake was known as Edgewater.

A dusty stage route and sometime cattle trail eventually developed as a route to Fort Sheridan, which was subsequently known as Fort Logan. The route later became Sheridan Boulevard and was the dividing line between Jefferson County and Arapahoe County (later Denver County).

The Schmidts Arrive

Edgewater was platted in 1889. The present house museum was built in 1889 by A. C. Pattee. The original three-room house is believed to be the second dwelling built in Edgewater.

Frank and Elsie Rink Schmidt moved to Edgewater in 1891 and built a home at West 22nd and Ames Street. That home was located on a fifty-acre farm tract. Two children were born in the house—Emma in 1893 and Louis in 1894.

Frank was a commercial fisherman. Elsie made nets for him and strung them from the trees. He put in two ponds, which he filled with fish that he brought down from the mountains in water-filled barrels. He sold the fish at his Colfax Avenue fish market.

Manhattan Beach

Adam Graff was a German immigrant who cut ice in the winter on Sloan's Lake. In 1889, he approached Robert and Ernest Steinke with a proposal to build an amusement park on the north side of the lake. When Manhattan Beach Amusement Park opened in 1891, it was the largest amusement park west of the Mississippi River.

People traveled by streetcars and horse-drawn buggies to the gala opening. The park originally consisted of a bandstand, gardens, and picnic grounds. Later there was a zoo, dance pavilion, roller coaster, skating rink, concessions, and a theater with an 80-foot observatory. The theater seated 3,000.

Fountains at the entrance to the park shot 100 feet into the air, and ostriches pulled a Cinderella coach around the park. Five hundred tons of sand were brought in to create a beach. At Manhattan Beach, one could witness a hot-air balloon ascension, see a lady shot from a cannon, watch magic acts, swim, and hear bands playing. Adding to the beauty were 10,000 trees and shrubs and 500 potted palms.

In 1890, a fire destroyed the dance pavilion, the surrounding concession stands, and several Edgewater saloons. And in 1908, the theater burned to the ground along with a few other outbuildings. The heat was so intense it buckled shop windows along Sheridan Boulevard and terrified Edgewater residents.

But Edgewater survived and set its sights on the future.[1]

The Schmidt Family Moves

Upon Frank Schmidt's death around 1910, Elsie bought the present house museum. She and the two children moved in. Emma was seventeen, and Louis was sixteen. Plumbing was installed in the 1930s by Edgewater plumber Sam Marine.

The family lived in the house until Elsie died. Then the house passed to Louis. Louis never married. He was the first Edgewater fireman to sustain an injury while fighting a fire when fell from a ladder and broke an ankle.

Louis deeded the house to Emma in 1961. Emma married twice but had no children. Her second marriage was to Severin (Chris) Orum. He preceded her in death. She resided in the house until her death in 1980 at age eighty-seven. She left her estate to her attorney.

Becoming a House Museum

Orum House remained empty until 1983, when the City of Edgewater secured the property.

In 1984, the house moved five feet onto a new foundation. This was done to correct an erroneous property line.

Many of the furnishings and articles in the home are original to the time that Emma lived here, including the wood-burning cook stove in the kitchen. The house has never been remodeled.

Orum House is owned and maintained by the City of Edgewater. The Orum House Community Garden is a project sponsored by the City of Edgewater and supported by Denver Urban Gardens.

About Orum House

Address: 2444 Depew Street, Edgewater, Colorado 80214

Phone: (303) 238-7803

Hours: By appointment only and on certain holidays

Admission: Free

Driving directions: I-25 to Exit 209B 6th Avenue west toward Lakewood. Go 1.8 miles on 6th Avenue Freeway to Sheridan Boulevard exit. Turn right on Sheridan Boulevard. Go 1.8 miles. From Sheridan Boulevard, turn west on West 25th Avenue. Go 0.3 mile. Turn left on Depew Street. Go 0.1 mile. House is in the middle of the block on the left.

Parking: Free on the street

Web site: www.edgewaterco.com

30 Rock Ledge Ranch Historic Site

On the trip west from Pennsylvania, Robert Chambers carried $10,000 in cash. He also carried a pistol but arrived in Denver without having to draw the gun.

Courtesy of James Werner

Rock Ledge House.
Built from fieldstone quarried on the land. Long wooden structure served as original ranch house.

Robert Chambers brought his ailing, pregnant wife, Elsie, west in 1874 hoping the mountain air would help her with her tuberculosis. Robert, his sister Nettie, his daughter Eleanor, his son Ben (by a first marriage), and Elsie left Pennsylvania by train.

Nettie had raised Ben since his own mother died at his birth. He was now seven years old. The family thought Nettie was not strong enough for life in the Wild West. They decided she would go to live with her sister in Wisconsin,

and Ben would stay with his father. This must have been a painful parting for Nettie and Ben.

On the trip, Robert Chambers carried $10,000 in a roll of cash—from the sale of his wheat crop as well as the sale of Aunt Nettie's farm. To protect them all, he carried a small pistol. The family bid farewell to Nettie in Wisconsin and arrived safely in Denver without Robert ever drawing the gun.

Though they intended to settle in Denver, Chambers was looking for a place with enough water for a fruit ranch. He fell in love with Colorado Springs, which had a population of only a few hundred people. He bought a house in town for the family and a 160-acre ranch with water rights for $1,700 that had been homesteaded by Walter Galloway. Elsie named it Rock Ledge Ranch.

Chambers built a long, wooden house on the ranch property, and the family moved into it. Then they started work on the stone house using fieldstone from the quarry on the land. The new house was finished in time for daughter Mary to be born in the main bedroom in 1875. The wooden portion continued to serve as a kitchen.

When a band of Indians passing through the valley stopped to beg, Elsie was frightened because of stories her friends from the East had told her about the dangers of life in the West. The encounter was peaceful and not the last.

During the sporadic grasshopper scourges when produce and fruit crops were decimated, Chambers bought milk cows and ran a dairy. Because the grasshoppers ate every blade of grass, he had to buy feed for the cows.

Ben helped build a dam for a reservoir and an irrigation ditch to get additional water for the ranch. Eventually, the family had a successful produce farm, providing fruits and vegetables to the settlers of the young city of Colorado Springs. One of the original apple trees still stands. Chambers also had six acres of asparagus, hundreds of cherry trees, and other fruit trees. They constructed two steam-heated greenhouses and sold out-of-season produce and Elsie's jams and jellies to the Antlers Hotel. It is possible Elsie also grew flowers in the greenhouses as she listed her occupation on the 1880 census as "florist."

Ben was an adventurous fellow who later in life told many tales to his daughter-in-law, Dorothy Chambers. One story told how he hauled a great wagonload of kinnikinnick (a vine-like plant with red berries similar to holly) from the mountains to the home of the famous novelist Helen Hunt Jackson to decorate her home for Christmas. According to Ben, she never paid him.

He also said he herded cattle up Pikes Peak and camped in the Cripple Creek area on the very spot where Bob Womack later discovered gold. Ben was also an entrepreneur. He invented a horseradish grinder for the horseradish he raised. He bottled the ground horseradish and sold it to customers as far away

as Pueblo. Ben also made a sauerkraut mill for shredding cabbage.

Ben attended Colorado Agricultural College for two years, paying his tuition by caring for and driving the horses belonging to the college president. When his father found out he was studying to be a mechanical engineer instead of a scientific farmer, that was the end of college. Ben married Madge Kinney in 1891, and their son, Robert, was born in a tent outside the ranch house in June 1895.

Other Family Activities

Elsie had taught school before her marriage. When her children were school age, she gathered children from surrounding farms and set up a classroom upstairs in the Chambers' house. Later, a little school was constructed across from the Chambers' land farther south in the Camp Creek Valley.

When Eleanor and Mary were ready for high school, the family spent winters in Colorado Springs. During the summer, they all returned to the ranch, which everyone considered their home. The Chambers also took in summer boarders, who were often tuberculosis patients from the East.

When Robert and Elsie retired in 1900, Colorado Springs had grown to a town of 30,000. Robert and Elsie traveled in the United States before settling in Pasadena, California, in 1903.

Orchard House

General William J. Palmer, the founder of Colorado Springs, was a friendly neighbor. He often rode horseback into town and stopped at the Chambers' home. When Robert and Elsie retired, Palmer bought the ranch along with the Hardwick and Neff farms in the same area to secure the water for his Glen Eyrie estate.

Palmer built a three-story residence in 1907 for Charlotte and William Sclater, his wife's half-sister and her husband. The Mission-style house, called the Orchard House, included indoor plumbing and steam heat. The Sclaters left the home and moved to England in 1909 following Palmer's death.

Becoming a House Museum

The Rock Ledge Ranch was placed on the National Register of Historic Places in 1979. It is privately supported by the Rock Ledge Ranch Living History Association. The City of Colorado Springs, Parks, Recreation, and Cultural Services Department manages the property.

Orchard House. The Mission-style suburban estate
included indoor plumbing and steam heat.

About Rock Ledge Ranch Historic Site

Address: 310 South Gateway Road, Colorado Springs, Colorado 80904

Phone: (719) 578-6777

Hours: June–August: Wednesday–Saturday, 10 a.m.–5 p.m. Sunday, noon–5 p.m.
Winter hours: www.rockledgeranch.com

Admission: Adults $6, Seniors and students $4, Children (6–12) $2. Tickets may
be purchased at the site or at Garden of the Gods Visitor Center.

Driving directions: I-25 to Exit 146, Garden of the Gods Road. Go west to 30th
Street. Drive 2.4 miles. Turn left on 30th Street. Drive 1.5 miles. Turn right on
Gateway Road. Drive less than 0.1 mile. Turn left into driveway.

Parking: Free in parking lot

Memberships: Membership in the Rock Ledge Ranch Living History Association is
available at varying levels of support. Call (719) 578-6777.

Web site: www.rockledgeranch.com

31 Rosemount Museum

The Thatcher brothers slept under the counter or in the mouth of the big chimney in their first general store.

This thirty-seven-room mansion was home to the John A. and Margaret Thatcher family. It was named for Mrs. Thatcher's favorite flower and remained a family residence for seventy-five years.

The rise of the Thatcher brothers—from selling goods out of a primitive log cabin, to entering the cattle business, to founding Pueblo's first bank, to making transcontinental investments—is the stuff of which western myths are made. We have much of the Thatcher brothers' history from their sister, Sarah, who was courted by (and later married) her brothers' employee, Frank Bloom (*see* Chapter 6, Bloom Mansion).

Rosemount Museum.
Richardsonian Romanesque with exterior of pink volcanic stone quarried in Castle Rock, Colorado. Stairs are red sandstone. The interior features oak, cherry, maple, and mahogany woodwork. The lighting system by Tiffany & Co., New York, used a combination of both electric and natural gas to power chandeliers and wall sconces.

Settlers first came to the confluence of the Arkansas River and Fountain Creek in the 1840s, establishing El Pueblo as a fortified trading post that was active from 1840 until 1854. Miners, ranchers, and shopkeepers arrived to settle in the 1860s. The town had been surveyed and laid out in 1860.

John Thatcher had worked as a schoolteacher, store clerk, and tannery employee before arriving in Denver, Colorado, and working in J. H. Voorheis's general store in 1862. One day, a man from Pueblo came in and suggested that Pueblo needed a general store. Voorheis decided to supply the goods for the store and have John run it. John had to walk 30 miles to obtain the services of a Frenchman and his oxen team to move the goods south. While the Frenchman obtained camp equipment for the trip, John walked the 30 miles back to Denver to get the inventory ready for the new store. Eight days later, after replacing the Frenchman's tender-footed oxen with studier ones, they arrived in Pueblo.

John sold merchandise practically as fast as it arrived. Few people had money, so bartering was the norm. John sold "food, fabric to make clothing, ready made clothes, medicines to cure a cold, or whiskey to forget the cold."[1] He also sold goods from a wagon, which he drove to outlying settlements. Family stories tell of how on a trip to Pennsylvania, he bought the entire stock of a bankrupt button factory. On the southern plains of Colorado, he sold the buttons to Native Americans.

Mahlon Thatcher was three years younger than John. Mahlon came west in 1865, traveling by railroad, ferry, and stage, seeing "a good many wild Indians and about a thousand buffalo a day."[2]

Future brother-in-law to the Thatchers, Frank Bloom, caught western fever in 1865. He was four years younger than Mahlon. In order to cut the costs of traveling to join the Thatcher brothers, Frank auditioned to drive a team of mules in the wagon train. For the audition, he had to drive the mules through mud where others had gotten stuck. He passed the test, then returned to help others get unstuck. It took thirty-two days to get from St. Joseph, Missouri, to Denver in his Studebaker prairie schooner, part of the wagon train. The previous year, Native Americans had burned all but three stage stations for a distance of 450 miles along the Platte River.

Frank and Mahlon slept on and under the counter or in the mouth of the chimney in Thatcher's General Store. Frank said, "When we hit the hay we were asleep, to rise at five, as there was some ranchman every night sleeping in the store."[3]

Sarah's letter of May 29, 1866, comments, "Your counter must be...serviceable. It is not very often that they are occupied by night as well as by day but I suppose your accommodations will be better after a while when brother gets to housekeeping."[4]

Wedding Bells

At the age of sixteen, Margaret Henry became the first public school teacher in Pueblo. She taught in an old soddie house during the school term of 1864–1865. Two years later, on April 17, 1866, she married John Thatcher. Frank Bloom was left in charge of the store while the wedding took place.

Evidently, sleeping arrangements improved greatly for Mahlon and Frank after the wedding. They bid farewell to the store counter when John and Margaret invited them to share their home.

Margaret gave up teaching when she married. She and John eventually had two daughters and three sons. From the arduous frontier life in rough-and-tumble Pueblo, Margaret would rise to become one of the town's most influential society women by the turn of the century.

Calvin Henry Thatcher (called Henry) joined the other brothers in Pueblo at an unknown date. Henry had graduated in law from Albany University in New York. In Pueblo, he began practicing law and joined the school board.

Families grew, and the Thatcher brothers' businesses diversified and thrived. They were well liked by the community, and known to be honest and fair. Sarah married Frank Bloom in 1869, after a five-year engagement (*see* Chapter 6, Bloom Mansion).

Mahlon married Luna A. Jordan on August 1, 1876. She had been courted by a Methodist minister, who was so distraught when Luna chose Mahlon that he left

Courtesy of Rosemount Museum

John Thatcher's residence is far left. Mahlon's residence is visible behind and the immediate right of Rosemount. The carriage house is on the far right

the area. The Methodist Church did not find him another appointment in a timely manner, so he became a Congregationalist minister.

By 1877, Pueblo had a population of 5,500. It had daily stages to Cucharas, Trinidad, and Santa Fe. The Colorado Business Directory of 1877 tells us "The Arkansas River furnishes first-class water power; and there are few better localities for woolen mills, foundries and machine shops. The various branches of trade are in the hands of active and energetic business men, who are pushing their enterprises in every direction."[5]

Millionaires

Mahlon's mansion was built first. In fact, it was Pueblo's first mansion, located at the top of a hill about a quarter of a mile north of town. Henry Hudson Holly, the architect, was known for his two books on architecture. Mahlon, Luna, and their two daughters moved into the mansion on July 1, 1882. Their only son was born there in November. Henry Thatcher's fourteen-year-old son also lived there, along with various servants.

Henry Thatcher passed away in 1884 at forty-two. His expertise as an attorney was missed as business continued to grow in complexity. Cattle companies were formed, cattle stolen, losses sustained, ranches sold. But this hardly made a dent in the Thatcher's fortunes. Banks, railroads, utility companies, and stocks in numerous other investments made up the Thatchers' portfolios. Banking was their primary business.

Both Margaret and Luna continued to lead civic activities and charities, including chapters of the Daughters of the American Revolution and the Wednesday Morning Club. The Wednesday Morning Club helped women learn public speaking. Each member had to stand and give a talk on a weekly assignment. Regular attendance was expected, and the ladies responded to roll call by giving a quotation, a historical fact, or a current event. Those who came unprepared were fined five cents.

Nearly a decade after Mahlon built his mansion, John built his. Plans for Rosemount were drawn in 1885, construction began in 1891, and in 1893 the family moved in. The mansion lay southeast of Mahlon and Luna's home. The floor plans alone are astonishing. In her book, *The Thatchers: Hard Work Won the West*, Joanne West Dodds comments on the designated sewing room. "A successful seamstress in the 1890s would move from family to family each year making everything from underwear and nightgowns to ball dresses. Margaret's seamstress must have been very pleased to have use of a special sewing room instead of working in one of the children's bedrooms as was often the case."[6]

Like many other mansions, the type of wood used in the family's side of the

house differed from that used in the servant's side—right down to the doors that divided them. The door on the family's side had fine wood such as oak and ornate doorknobs, while pine and plain doorknobs were used on the other side of the door.

But the magnificent mansion was not immune to robbery. On Saturday, February 3, 1912, while Margaret and John were entertaining, someone stole $10,000 worth of diamonds. It proved no easy matter to get rid of all those diamonds, so nearly six weeks later, the thief was caught.

The Thatcher Estates

When John Thatcher died in 1913, the Reverend C. W. Weyer pointed out that only two generations previously, "our schools taught that between the Missouri River and the Rocky Mountains was the great American desert. An empire of sand, alkali and sagebrush which would not support the white man."[7] Into this landscape, John Thatcher and a few others like him had ventured. They had a vision; they could see the future.

Courtesy of James Werner

Dining room at Christmas. Twenty people could be seated for dinner in this dining room. The French mural was painted on three walls after the house was built. The host or hostess pressed a buzzer underneath the table when service was required.

When John died, he was worth more than $4 million. He left Margaret half of the estate; the remainder was divided among the three surviving children, with smaller bequests to others.

John and Margaret lost their first daughter, Lenore, when she was twenty-three. Their second daughter, Lillian, married in 1915 at the age of forty-five. But she preferred life in Pueblo to the rougher mining life of her engineer husband in Arizona. After a few years of marriage, she divorced and returned to Rosemount in 1924.

Margaret lived for nine years after John's death. At age seventy-four, she purchased a custom-made Pierce Arrow automobile. She died in 1922 before she could ride in the chauffeur-driven black sedan, but Lillian used it. After Margaret's death, Lillian occupied her mother's part of the master suite.

Mahlon died in 1916 at age seventy-six, the same age as John when he died. Mahlon was worth nearly $9.3 million. He left Luna their home, his horses and carriages, his personal belongings, and $500,000.

Raymond was the youngest child of John and Margaret. Stories say that as a boy, he rode his Shetland pony across Rosemount's veranda occasionally. Raymond lived in the house until his death in 1968 at age eighty-three. He never married.

Becoming a House Museum

After Raymond Thatcher death in 1968, the heirs donated the house to the Pueblo Metropolitan Museum Association.

The 24,000-square-foot mansion was designed by noted New York architect Henry Hudson Holly was built at a cost of $60,750. Nearly all furnishings, accessories, decorative arts, paintings, custom paneling, and wall and window treatments are original to the home.

Margaret selected the furniture and the twenty-six hand-woven Persian, Turkish, and Oriental area rugs for the floors.

About Rosemount Museum

Address: 419 West 14th Street, Pueblo, Colorado 81003

Phone: (719) 545-5290

Hours: Tuesday–Saturday, 10 a.m.–4 p.m. Closed major holidays and the month of January

Admission: Adults $6, Senior (60+) $5, Youth (6–18) $4, Children under 6 free

Driving directions: I-25 to Exit 99B/13th Street/Santa Fe Avenue in Pueblo. Go west on 13th Street for four blocks to North Greenwood Street. Turn right on Greenwood and go one block.

Parking: Some street parking is free; most is two-hour monitored parking

Web site: www.rosemount.org

32 Streer-Peterson House

Dorothy Streer's father had a magnificent stud named Champagne. She was surprised to learn that champagne was a wine.

Courtesy of Lakewood's Heritage Center, City of Lakewood

The Streer-Peterson House that can be seen at Lakewood's Heritage Center originally stood in the foothills area known as the Morrison Hogback. It may have been built by a Civil War veteran who acquired the land through a land grant. Between 1870 and the mid-1980s, the house and its surrounding farmland changed ownership more than fifteen times. The present house museum focuses on the period when the Streer family owned the farm between 1918 and 1921.

Streer-Peterson House
American vernacular with gently gabled roof. Two-story frame construction with gingerbread trim. Original lathe and plaster and original wallpaper can be seen in the closet of a small office under the stairs.

Morris Streer was born in Kiev, Russia, in 1892. Sophia Deiner Streer was born in Kiev in 1896. They each came to America with their Orthodox Jewish parents, who fled Russia to escape pogroms. When the families emigrated, they brought with them their Sabbath candlesticks.

Morris's family entered America through Galveston, Texas, in 1898. The Hebrew Aid Society brought them first to Philadelphia around 1899, then to Denver, where there was a Jewish settlement. In Denver, Morris's father was employed at the Colorado Iron and Metal House.

Sophia's mother came to America as a widow with four children. Morris and Sophia met and married in Denver in 1913, when Sophia was only sixteen and Morris was twenty. They farmed in Westminster, Conifer, and Schaffer's Crossing before coming to the Lakewood house in 1918. They had three children, Dorothy, Ruth, and Sidney. Their youngest son, Leonard, was born after the family moved from the house.

Though Leonard never lived at the house that became a museum, he remembers stories about the family farming there. "Everything was labor intensive," he was told. "They had a lot of people working. My mother did all the cooking for the crew and relatives."[1] They did employ a seasonal cook to work in the cookhouse at harvest time, and there was a Japanese handyman.

Dorothy recalled that Morris was up at sunrise and never got back to the house until after sunset. Their parents worked very hard.

They called the farm in Lakewood the Morrison Farm Dairy. They milked Holstein and a few Jersey cows by hand at first. The family began using milking machines before they moved from the farm in 1921. Every day, they took their milk cans about a half-mile to the road, where the Windsor Dairy truck picked up the cans. The dairy processed the milk before delivering it to Denver homes.

The Streers also raised alfalfa and kept horses. Neighboring farmers brought mares to breed with their stud, Champagne. Dorothy later said Morris had "this magnificent stud by the name of Champagne, and I always thought champagne was a horse before I knew it was a wine."[2]

Morris loved to show his horses at the stock show. Dorothy said, "He would comb and curry his animals; no one touched them; and he'd braid their manes and tails, and that was such fun."[3]

They also had a pony named Trixie, chickens, a goat, barn cats, and a collie named Rover. Morris's parents, Peter and Zelda, helped work the farm, but Morris also hired seasonal workers to help with the harvest.

Family Heritage

Although they celebrated their heritage, neither Sophia nor Morris considered themselves Orthodox Jews. Sophia said a blessing over the candles every Friday night to usher in the Jewish Sabbath. They had a family mezuzah (a sacred parchment inside a case that is affixed to the door of a Jewish home), and they celebrated High Holidays. But they accepted invitations for Christmas

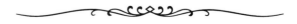

dinner with their neighbor Gertrude Almquist. And a friend of Sophia's in Denver kept presents on the tree for the Streer children. They traveled into Denver in their Model-T Ford to visit relatives and friends on special occasions.

Sophia had a talent for nursing, and many relatives came out to the farm to regain their health. She also knitted, crocheted, did needlework, and made the children's clothing. There was a vegetable garden behind the house, and an orchard produced fruit. Sophia's daughters remember that she made wonderful chokecherry jam and jelly because chokecherries grew wild in the area. Sophia also churned her own butter.

Ruth Streer Kobey of Denver told the *Intermountain Jewish News* that she remembered a lot of visitors to the farm during her childhood. Many were patients at the Jewish Consumptives Relief Society tubercu-

Courtesy of Lakewood's Heritage Center, City of Lakewood

Dorothy and Ruth Streer

losis sanitarium. Most of them wanted to purchase the farm's fresh milk, eggs, and cheese. Ruth recalled that the farm had no hot running water, and the electricity for lights was sporadic. They used kerosene lamps as well. Since there was no bathroom, only an outhouse, the Streers would haul out a folding rubber tub in which to bathe the children. Ruth wondered how her mother crammed all the relatives who visited into the tiny home.[4]

They hung their washing outside on a line between two trees. Sophia had to climb up on a chair to hang out her clothes. One day, they found the goat up on the chair, eating one of the sheets.

Sophia did have a few prize pieces of jewelry, which she kept in a buffet in the parlor. One time, lightning struck the roof, which caught on fire. Sophia ran to the parlor to get her jewelry. They put out the fire with minimal damage to the roof.

The Harley

Morris had a Harley-Davidson motorcycle during this time. "He was very proud of his Harley," Ruth said. "He used to drive it around the country there. He would run around with a little white spitz dog that we had."[5]

Every December, Morris went to the Montgomery Ward Catalog Store to get old catalogs that the family used for toilet paper. He also brought back a box of toys for the children. For vacations, they enjoyed taking trips to Estes Park.

Morris Streer

Since they had electricity for lights only, they used an icebox for food storage. The pantry kept food, pots and pans, and kerosene. A crank telephone was attached to one of the walls in the kitchen, and of course, the family was on a party line.

They also had a gramophone and Morris loved to listen to opera. His daughters recall that he loved to listen to Enrico Caruso and Amelita Galli-Curci. But he also enjoyed country music.

Though Dorothy and Sidney were too young to attend school when they lived at the Morrison Farm Dairy, Ruth went to Bear Creek Elementary. This was a one-room school where Miss Faith taught first through eighth grades, one grade per row. A neighbor girl came by on her horse every morning to take Ruth to school.

Leaving the Farm

Prohibition lasted from January 16, 1920 until December 5, 1933, when the 21st Amendment to the U.S. Constitution repealed it. During Prohibition, the Streers rented an outbuilding to moonshiners, who were eventually arrested.

After World War I, European farmers began to get their own farms back into production. This triggered an agricultural depression in the United States. In 1921, the Streer family was unable to meet their mortgage, and they lost the farm. They followed some cousins and Morris's parents to Detroit, Michigan. After seven years they returned to Colorado, first to Greeley and then to Denver to enter the poultry business.

The Petersons

The Peterson family owned and operated the dairy farm from 1939 to 1975, but they never occupied the house. Rather, they used it for storage and as quarters for farm workers.

Becoming a House Museum

In 1974, the area where the house originally sat was claimed by the federal government as part of a flood control project. This resulted in the creation of Bear Creek Lake on the western portion of the property and Bear Creek Lake Park. When the City of Lakewood built the Fox Hollow Golf Course at Bear Creek Lake Park in 1986, the house had to go.

The small farmhouse was donated to the City of Morrison, but the city was unable to find a suitable place for the structure. It was offered to the City of Lakewood. In 1986, the Army Corps of Engineers moved the house to its current site in the Lakewood's Heritage Center. Ruth Streer Kobey attended the dedication of her former home and felt it was "very much like it was, at least what I can remember."[6]

About Streer-Peterson House
Part of Lakewood's Heritage Center

Address: 801 South Yarrow Street, Lakewood, Colorado 80226

Phone: (303) 987-7850

Hours: Tuesday–Saturday 10 a.m.–4 p.m. Closed on holidays

Admission: Adults $5, Senior (65+) $4, Youth $2.50, Children 3 and under free

Driving directions: I-25 to Exit 209B. Take ramp onto U.S. 6 West. Go 3.9 miles. Take the Wadsworth Boulevard exit and turn south. Go 0.6 mile. Turn right on West Ohio Avenue. Go 0.1 mile. Turn left on South Yarrow Street. Go less than 0.1 mile.

Parking: Free in parking lot.

Web site: www.lakewood.org/ Click on the link to Visitors > History

33 *Tabor Home and the Matchless Mine Cabin*

Horace Tabor never said "Hang onto the Matchless Mine."

Courtesy of James Werner

Baby Doe's wooden one-room cabin
reconstructed at the Matchless Mine

Louisa Augusta Pierce was one of ten children born to building contractor William B. Pierce and Lucy Eaton Pierce. She was named after the capital of her native state of Maine, and always went by "Augusta".

She was not a healthy child and, therefore, was not charged with as many chores as most children growing up in those days. In fact, she never learned to cook.

Horace Austin Warner Tabor, a Vermont stonecutter, met Augusta's father in 1854. Horace, a young man of twenty-four, boarded with the large Pierce family. He and Augusta started courting right away. Sitting in the big backyard or strolling

down the slope to the garden and then the winding river below, Horace told Augusta of his dreams for the future.

When he proposed, they knew it would be two years before Horace would have enough money for them to marry. She hoped they could settle near her family. But Horace had read about gold in California, and his appetite was whetted. When he heard about the New England Emigrant Aid Company helping people go west, he followed his brother John, who had taken a homestead claim near Lawrence in Kansas Territory. Horace decided to go and establish a homestead claim as well, and after working it, he would return to marry Augusta.

Young Augusta Tabor

Free Versus Slave Territory

In the spring of 1855, Horace joined with Josiah Pillsbury and others for the trip west. Horace's claim was on Deep Creek in Riley County. The men helped each other build rude cabins. Horace's cabin was 12 feet by 16 feet and offered little protect from a freezing winter.

Not yet a state, Kansas was divided between free-state emigrants and slave owners already settled there. In December 1855, a pro-slavery faction prepared to attack the settlement of Lawrence. Horace walked more than 100 miles in three days to help defend the town. He gained a reputation for courage, intelligence, and initiative. He was elected as a representative of his district to the first Kansas Free State Legislature in Topeka. He was also a member of the County Board of Commissioners.

Horace returned to Maine, and on January 31, 1857, he and Augusta were married. Horace was twenty-six, and Augusta was twenty-three. According to the laws of the time, when she signed the marriage certificate, she became the "handmaid" to her husband. He would hold all property in his name alone, and money that either earned would be his.

The couple left for his homestead on Deep Creek. It was an arduous trip, made by train to St. Louis, then by steamboat up the Missouri River to Kansas City. There they purchased a yoke of oxen, a wagon, farming tools, and seeds for planting. Two friends from Maine, Nathaniel Maxcy and Samuel B. Kellog, accompanied them. When they reached the claim, and Augusta set eyes on the lonesome cabin on the wide prairie, she collapsed in tears.

Augusta soon pulled herself together. The same determination that helped her overcome her childhood illnesses now helped her do what needed to be done.

She found old copies of the *New York Tribune* under the bed. She made a paste of flour and water and plastered the black walnut logs with the paper, keeping the sheets upright. She rightly surmised that this would be the only reading material she would see for months.

Horace made some three-legged stools and a rough plank table. She covered the table with a linen tablecloth from home and prepared the first meal she had ever cooked in her life.

Salt pork and beans were served with sterling silver, and the men's hunger made them appreciative of her efforts. Nathaniel and Samuel agreed to board with the Tabors, and the money they paid for their board helped sustain Horace and Augusta.

In the spring of 1857, a pregnant Augusta joined her husband in the fields. However, drought robbed them of a decent harvest. With only the board money coming in, they needed more capital. Horace took a job at Fort Riley, about 18 miles from home. He had steady work there because most of the buildings were fashioned from stone. He stayed there most of the week, coming home for short weekends. Augusta worried that the baby would be born when he was not home.

Baby Maxcy

In October 1857, Augusta wrote in her diary that the baby "came to live with them." It is unclear whether Horace was at Fort Riley. If he wasn't there, Nathaniel Maxcy would either have delivered the baby himself or taken Augusta to a doctor in Manhattan, the nearest town. Either way, the first born was named Nathaniel Maxcy and called Maxcy.

In the spring of 1858, the Tabors seeded again. This time, the rains came, but an overabundance of crops in the region caused prices to drop. That winter, Augusta asked Horace to build a bigger house. He began working on a stone house, but they never lived in it. In early 1859, news came of the gold strikes in the Pikes Peak region of Kansas Territory. Horace wanted to seek his fortune in the goldfields. He returned to Fort Riley and saved his wages until they were able to go.

Moving On

Again, Nathaniel and Samuel accompanied them when they left. They took a few months' worth of supplies and necessities, cows, and several steers. Petty, the dog, rode with Augusta in the rear of the wagon.

There were few well-marked trails. The route they traveled was barren, with only a few scrubby cottonwood trees. While the men hunted for food, Augusta tried to keep a campfire alive, often with only buffalo chips for fuel. It took six weeks to make the trip, In addition to regular chores, she had to care for her year-

old son, who was fretful from teething. The animals in tow added to the work. Even with her slight, 90-pound frame, she would lend a hand when the wagon got stuck.

The sight of the Rocky Mountains lifted their spirits, and the party camped along the Platte River in Denver. There they remained until July to rest the footsore animals. Denver at the time boasted about a dozen buildings. Augusta estimated that she was the eleventh woman to arrive in this frontier outpost. Other estimates say that probably three dozen women in Denver before her. Either way, women were a rare sight in the region.

Horace first tried to prospect in fields close to Denver. But in the spring of 1860, he decided to try his luck farther inland, along the Arkansas River. To make it to the upper Arkansas Valley, they had to drag loaded wagons over steep, snowbound mountain passes. Provisions ran dangerously low, and the men supplied food by hunting and fishing. Augusta broiled for breakfast, fried for lunch, and boiled for supper, to try to provide some variety to the same food day after day.

She pounded clothes clean in icy streams, prepared meals from the barest of rations, took care of baby Maxcy, and guarded her own fragile health against the vagaries of spring in the high Rockies.

Augusta was the first white woman known to venture into the California Gulch gold camp area. The miners were so delighted with her presence that they erected a 12-by-14 foot cabin for her by nightfall. The Tabors slaughtered their oxen to share food with the community. Augusta endeared herself to the miners by becoming the camp's cook, laundress, postmistress, even banker, using the gold scales she and Horace had brought with them to weigh the gold dust. Horace helped organize the miners into the territory of Jefferson. They elected him as their representative to the state constitutional convention to be held in Denver. She and Horace ran a camp store, a pattern that they were to repeat in mining camps throughout the Rockies for the next twenty years.

At the end of that first summer season, the Tabors had accumulated $4,000 from their combined efforts. That winter, Augusta took Maxcy home to Maine. On the way, she stopped off to purchase an additional 160 acres of farmland adjoining their homestead at Deep Creek. Although she had helped to pay for both claims, only Horace's name appeared on the deeds.

Horace had given her $1,000 for the trip east, and to supplement that, she worked as a cook for the wagon train that carried her. Augusta kept an account of every penny. When Horace joined her in Maine their tales of adventure and success aroused much interest among Augusta's brothers and sisters.

Horace realized that supplying the needs of prospectors provided a steadier income than mining. They bought supplies to take back to the mining camp, using

the final $400 of the $1,000 that Augusta had brought home with her.

In the spring of 1861, they returned to Colorado, taking Augusta's sister, Lilly, and brother, Frank, with them. California Gulch had run its course. In August 1861, the Tabors packed their merchandise and household and headed over the Mosquito Range to a town called Buckskin Joe with Lilly, Frank, and four-year-old Maxcy. If Horace wasn't lucky with a mining claim, Augusta knew that their store and her cooking and washing would sustain them.

The seven years they lived at Buckskin Joe were good years. The store succeeded, and the family invested heavily in nearby mines. Augusta continued to do laundry for the miners, but she had faith that Horace would eventually make a big find. Horace was again active in community politics.

During 1862–1863, Samuel Leach, the mail carrier to Buckskin Joe, came to know the Tabors well. His letters reveal firsthand knowledge of the Tabors at that time. He recounts how Augusta scolded Horace for taking too much time off for fishing, hunting, and card playing, but there was no doubt she loved him.

When Buckskin Joe played out, they traveled back over the great Mosquito Range and eventually to the place called Oro City, just outside what was to become Leadville.

During the next ten years, Horace operated three stores in the area. Income from the stores made him one of the wealthiest men in the district. In 1872, he picked up a contract to cut and supply railroad ties to the Atchison, Topeka and the Santa Fe Railroad.

By spring of 1877, Maxcy was twenty and a capable partner in the business. The Tabors were well off, well liked, and well respected. In 1878, Horace was elected mayor of the mining camp, which was soon to be christened Leadville. Augusta was active in social and civic events, and still ran a boardinghouse that brought in excellent money.

In April 1878, two German immigrants, August Rische and George Hook, asked Horace to grubstake them as he had many miners in the past. Tabor provided tools, food for a week, and a jug of whiskey in exchange for one-third interest in their find. The two Germans named their mine the Little Pittsburg; the final "h" was left off because that spelling had been used on another claim.

Soon Rische and Hook came through with high-grade ore samples.

In fall 1878, each partner took out $10,000 in profit. At one point, the Little Pittsburg was producing $8,000 to $10,000 a day. Tabor began to buy other properties. He purchased the Matchless Mine for $117,000, and it produced an average of $2,000 a day in silver.

Tabor sold his share in the Little Pittsburg for $1 million just before it stopped producing.

He built Augusta a fine house on Harrison Avenue. He also bought her jewelry and fine furniture. But Augusta did not find it easy to change. It was natural for her to budget and live practically. She was no spendthrift. Augusta never forgot their humble, hardworking beginnings. But for Horace, the days of being tight with money were over.

In 1878, Horace was elected lieutenant governor of Colorado. Augusta was thrown into higher social arenas but never ignored her old friends. She criticized Horace's tendency to spend, drink, and gamble, and as they were now public figures, they became the subject of gossip.

In 1879, Horace decided to turn Leadville into a first-class city. He built the Tabor Opera House and the Clarendon Hotel. He also built the Leadville Gas Company at a total cost of $75,000. The Tabor home was moved up to East Fifth Street, where it stands as the present house museum.

At the dedication of the opera house, Horace turned to his architect and inquired whose picture adorned the keystone of the proscenium arch. The reply was, "Why Mr. Tabor don't you know who that is? Why that is the picture of Shakespeare." Tabor's response was, "Shakespeare, Shakespeare, who the Hell is Shakespeare, and what has he done for Leadville? Take his picture down, and put mine up."[1]

Horace and Augusta purchased a mansion at 17th and Broadway in Denver and moved there in 1880. They sold the Leadville house to Augusta's sister, Lucy Malvina Clark. Horace also built up Denver. At Sixteenth and Curtis, he built the Tabor Grand Opera House at a cost of $200,000. Tabor also bought the site at the corner of Arapahoe and Sixteenth Street and gave it to the government to build a post office.

Too Much Wealth

Differences between Augusta and Horace were exacerbated by the extreme wealth his mines brought. Augusta had no capacity for dealing with immense, unlimited resources. Her admonitions to save and spend carefully didn't sit well with a man who, now, literally made money faster than he could spend it.

Approaching fifty years old, Horace wanted to live it up after all the years of hard work. He felt it was his due. Augusta, on the other hand, took no such pleasure in their sudden riches and saw the wealth as the source of great distress between them.

Elizabeth Bonduel McCourt Doe

Elizabeth Bonduel McCourt was born in Oshkosh, Wisconsin, in 1854, one of fourteen children. She married a local boy, Harvey Doe, in 1877. They moved to

Horace Austin Warner Tabor, Colorado prospector, mine owner, and United States senator.

Elizabeth Bonduel McCourt "Baby Doe" Tabor, second wife of Horace Tabor.

Central City, Colorado, and worked a mine given to them by Elizabeth's father as a wedding present. At Central City, the miners dubbed her "Baby Doe." She was also known as Lizzie. Her husband often went away for two or three weeks at a time with his buddies, leaving Lizzie to work the mine with her own crew.

She divorced Harvey in 1880 and with the help of a friend, Jake Sands, traveled to Leadville. Baby Doe lived in a boardinghouse in Leadville at 115 East Fifth Street, directly across from the Tabor house, where Augusta's sister now lived.

Horace was forty-nine when he met twenty-five-year-old Baby Doe. Before long, Baby Doe was living in luxury in the Windsor Hotel in Denver owned by the Tabors and William Bush.

In January 1881, Augusta's husband of twenty-four years moved out of the Denver mansion and into the Windsor Hotel. Augusta would not grant him a divorce.

The Divorce

In April 1882, Augusta sued her husband for "maintenance and support," claiming desertion. She demanded $50,000 in alimony, although no suit for divorce was filed. She claimed that he had repeatedly offered her a portion of his fortune if she would grant him a divorce, but she refused.

In September 1882, Horace was secretly married to Baby Doe in St. Louis by a justice of the peace. That marriage was later ruled illegal.

Finally, in January 1883, Augusta was granted a divorce. Tabor's wealth was estimated to be $9 million. Augusta received $300,000 and the Denver mansion in the settlement.

Fortunes Not Shared

Soon after the divorce, Horace served as a U.S. senator for thirty days to fill a vacancy left when Henry Teller was appointed secretary of the interior. Horace legally married Baby Doe in Washington in 1883. He was

fifty-three, and Baby Doe was twenty-nine. Her wedding gown cost $7,000. His wedding gift to her was a $75,000 necklace containing the Isabella Diamond, which Queen Isabella of Spain supposedly had sold to raise money for Christopher Columbus's voyage to the New World.

President Chester Arthur and his cabinet attended the wedding. When the priest who married them discovered that both Horace and Baby Doe were divorcees, he returned his fee. The church contains no record of the wedding.

Horace bought Baby Doe a mansion in Denver, and they had two daughters, Lillie and Silver Dollar. Lillie's lace christening dress cost $15,000, and diamonds adorned the girls' hairpins.

The family enjoyed a wealthy lifestyle for ten years, until the 1890s when the price of silver started to drop. The repeal of the Sherman Silver Purchase Act and consequent Silver Crash of 1893 ended the boom in Leadville (*see* sidebar in Chapter 12, Hamill House). Poor investments, extended credit, and costly lawsuits took care of the rest of Tabor's fortunes.

Unexpectedly, Baby Doe stood by Horace in the bad times. She sold her jewels and fine clothing to help raise cash. He returned to Leadville for a while, where he worked for $3 a day in the Leadville smelters. He prospected for gold in Boulder. In 1897, Horace

Horace Tabor's fortune[2]

Horace Tabor's estate at the time of his divorce from Augusta consisted of the following:

Tabor Opera House Block	$ 800,000
The Tabor Block	250,000
Block 3 Brown's Addition	100,000
Dwelling on Welton Street	20,000
8 lots Block 98 East Denver	100,000
4 lots Block 107 East Denver	50,000
97 shares First National Bank	500,000
Bush Building Chestnut Street, Leadville	30,000
Coliseum Theater, Leadville	20,000
Bank in Gunnison City	70,000
Gas stock and loan to company	100,000
Matchless Mine	1,000,000
Tabor mill and telephone stock	75,000
Bank of Leadville capital and profits	100,000
Henrietta, Maid of Erin, and Waterlook mines	1,000,000
Breece-Iron	300,000
Chrysolite	50,000
Glass-Pendary	100,000
Smuggler, Lead Chief, and Denver City mines	500,000
Interest in Bull Domingo and Robinson	100,000
Polite and group	100,000
Mines in Summit County	200,000
Interest in Fibse Manufacturing Co. Old Mexico	50,000
Investment in lands and mortgage bonds near Chicago	500,000
275 acres of land near stockyards in Chicago	50,000
Lands in Kansas, Colorado lands in South Park, railroad stocks, shares in Denver Steam Heating Co., Durango Stage Line	120,000
Government bonds	200,000
23/48 Tam O'Shander mine	100,000
Moneys, loans, stocks, etc.	200,000
Diamonds and other jewels	100,000
Denver Utah and Pacific Construction Co.	10,000
Hibernia	100,000

and his family moved to Ward, Colorado. There they lived in a small house with a lean-to. The youngest daughter, Silver, enjoyed the wide-open spaces, the scenery, and the animals. But Tabor's mining venture did not succeed. The family moved back to Denver and lived in an inexpensive two-room suite at the Windsor Hotel.

Friends helped him secure an appointment as postmaster of Denver, a position he held for fifteen months, until an attack of appendicitis took his life. He died in 1899 at age sixty-eight. Lillie was fifteen, and Silver was nine.

He left Baby Doe, age forty-five, with only the Matchless Mine, where she lived for the last thirty years of her life.

The Children

Lillie moved back to the Midwest and eventually married her cousin. She never returned to Colorado, but she was in regular contact with Baby Doe and Silver. Her letters reveal that she cared very much for them.

Silver seemed to attract trouble. She had some success in a writing career but failed to pursue it when rejections disappointed her. She took jobs with road shows. In her letters she blames Baby Doe for her misfortunes. Baby Doe was obsessed with keeping Silver out of trouble. Baby Doe's brother, Peter McCourt, helped Silver financially for many years.

But neither Peter nor Baby Doe were able to help Silver. She continued to move from one unfortunate situation to another and died under mysterious circumstances in Chicago at age thirty-six.

Silver Dollar Tabor, daughter of Baby Doe and Horace Tabor

Baby Doe's Final Years

Baby Doe continued to live in the shack at the Matchless Mine where she died in March 1935 at the age of eighty-one. It is believed that she died of a heart attack during a blizzard. When the storm cleared, her frozen body was found by Sue Bonny.

When reporters called on Lillie after Baby Doe died, she refused to open the door. She said through the door that she was not Horace Tabor's daughter, but that her father was John Tabor, Horace's brother, and she wanted nothing to do with the Tabor legacy. There are no known descendents of either Silver or Lillie, though Lillie did have children.

Maxcy Tabor, son of Augusta
and H.A.W. Tabor

Augusta's Final Years

After their divorce, Augusta
lived for a while with Maxcy in
the Denver mansion that Horace
had built for her on 17th and
Broadway. She moved across
the street into the Brown Palace
Hotel shortly after it was built

Lillie Tabor, daughter of Horace and Baby Doe Tabor,
on Harper's Bazar cover

in 1892. Maxcy managed the hotel. During the last decade of her life, Augusta
devoted much of her time and fortune to the activities of the Pioneer Ladies' Aid
Society and the Unity Unitarian Church of Denver. She eventually sought out the
restorative climate of Southern California.

Final words

Horace's final words, "Hang onto the Matchless Mine," may never have been uttered.
Storyteller Caroline Bancroft claims that she made them up.[3] In 1932, author David Karsner
wrote that Tabor "had told [Baby Doe] over and over again to have faith in the Matchless
mine"[4] and that after he passed away, Baby Doe and her two daughters journeyed back to
Leadville "to hold on to the Matchless."[5] Duane Smith in his biography of Horace Tabor
points out that these and other accounts of Tabor's last days differ on minor points. However,
there is no mention in any of them that Horace said those famous words.

Augusta died in 1895 a wealthy woman and left her money to Maxcy. She is buried in Denver's Riverside Pioneer Cemetery. The back of her gravestone reads:

She came where there were no roads and left a path for us to follow.
She came to a wilderness and made it a place of settlement.
She fed the hungry and healed the sick giving generously of those
motherly gifts which gentled rough mining camps.
She came searching for gold and left behind the treasure of civilization.
She was above all the epitome of a pioneer.[6]

Augusta Tabor's Gravestone in Denver's Riverside Pioneer Cemetery. The headstone reads, "Tabor, Augusta L., Mar. 29, 1833, Jan. 30, 1895. A pioneering woman, wife and mother." The upright headstone was dedicated on March 18, 1995, by the Colorado State Historical Society because the original flat marker incorrectly lists her birth year as 1835.

Courtesy of Jason Roberts

Becoming a House Museum

The Tabor Home was built in 1877 at 512 Harrison Avenue. It was moved to its present location in 1879 when property on Harrison Avenue became too valuable for residential lots and was used for business buildings instead.

The home is owned by the City of Leadville. Restoration of the exterior was completed in 2006 through a grant from the Colorado State Historical Fund, and the museum. In 2009, the city agreed to lease the property to Colorado Mountain College whereby CMC historic preservation students operate the museum.

Baby Doe's cabin at the Matchless Mine was nearly demolished by vandals after her death but was reconstructed in 1953.

About the Tabor Home

Address: 116 East 5th Street, Leadville, Colorado 80461

Phone: (719) 486-3900

Hours: Memorial Day to Labor Day. Call for hours.

Admission: Adults $5, Seniors $3, Students $4, Children $2

Driving directions: I-70 to Exit 195, Colorado 91 South toward Leadville. Go 22.6 miles. Colorado 91 ends at the edge of Leadville and becomes U.S. 24. From there, go 1.1 mile. Turn left on Harrison Avenue. Go 0.2 mile. Turn left on 5th Street. Go 0.1 mile. The house is on the left.

Parking: Free on street

Web site: http://www.visitleadvilleco.com/history_tours

About the Matchless Mine Cabin

Address: 1¼ miles east on East 7th Street, Leadville, Colorado 80461

Phone: (719) 486-4918

Hours: Memorial Day to Labor Day, Daily 9 a.m.–4:45 p.m. Call for winter hours.

Admission: Adults $6, Children ages 6–12 $2, Ages 6 and under free

Driving directions: I-70 to Exit 195, onto Colorado 91 South toward Leadville. Go 22.6 miles. Colorado 91 ends at the edge of Leadville and becomes U.S. 24. From there, go 1.1 mile. Turn left on Harrison Avenue. Go 0.2 mile. Turn left on 7th Street. Go 1.2 miles.

Parking: Free in parking lot

Web site: www.matchlessmine.com or http://www.visitleadvilleco.com/history_tours

34 Thomas House Museum

A tunnel led from a foyer in the Thomas home directly into the mine behind the house.

Thomas House
Frame Greek Revival. Renaissance
features include the Doric columns,
entablature, and pediment windows.
The patio is terraced with a Cornish
mortarless rock wall.

When George and Gertrude Billings arrived in Colorado, they discovered there was a need for wood trim, doors, and furniture in the growing city of Denver that had been settled along Cherry Creek. They founded the Billings Millwork factory on Blake Street in Denver. It furnished needed materials for the expanding town, and the family prospered. Their daughter Marcia was born in 1865.

Benjamin Prosser Thomas was the son of Morris Thomas, who had emigrated from Wales in 1853.

In 1892, Marcia Billings married Ben Thomas. Their wedding gift was a home on Eureka Street in the mining town of Central City that is now the Thomas House Museum. Central City had been a booming gold mining town, but many

of the mines had been vacated by the time the Thomases moved there.

The house, except for the kitchen and upstairs balcony, was built in 1874. The most interesting feature is the tunnel leading from a foyer directly into the mine behind the house. After the mine was sealed off, a portion of the passage remained and was used as a root cellar. It can be seen on house tours today. The current dining room was apparently the original one-room miner's cabin.

Ben was vice president of Sauer-McShane Mercantile Company, an important general store in Central City. Advertising art and salesman's samples were framed and still hang in the house. Marcia was a talented artist, and the house is filled with her paintings and drawings. She was an honorary member of the Tuesday Reading Club in Central City.

In 1900, the present kitchen and the upstairs balcony were added. The balcony, which had no access from any room upstairs except through a bedroom window, faced Eureka Street and offered a good view of the town and valley. A bridge led from a bedroom across the hillside to an outhouse.

Cornish Roses

It is said that the yellow Cornish roses that proliferate in the front yard and by the gate were brought from Cronwall by the miners. The roses bloom once a year.

Moving On

The Thomases moved to Denver in 1917 after the closing of the Sauer-McShane Company, but kept the Central City house as a vacation house. Central City was declining in population, so houses were not selling.

After Marcia's death in 1944, the house passed to her sister Anna Thurber of Boston, who passed it to her daughter, Gertrude Tanner. Gertrude summered there with her husband for twenty-five years. She was on the entertainment committee of the Opera Association and hosted many cast parties at the house. The Tanners took pains to preserve the house as a Victorian home. After the outhouse was stolen by a neighbor who thought it was unattractive, the Tanners converted an upstairs bedroom into a bathroom. The bathtub was moved from the kitchen to the new bathroom.

The house eventually went to the Tanners' daughters, Anne Schultz and Jane Hummer. In all, the house remained in the family for ninety-five years.

Becoming a House Museum

The house was purchased by Mike and Darlene Leslie in 1987 after it had been on the market for three years. They ran it as a museum until 1989. When the Leslies wanted to sell it, the Gilpin Historical Society raised funds from the *Denver Post* readers and purchased the home in 1990.Major donations came from Doug Morton and Marilyn Brow of Morton Publishing and from Swingle Tree Company. Most of the original family belongings remain.

About the Thomas House Museum

Address: 209 Eureka Street, Central City, Colorado 80427

Phone: (303) 582-5283

Hours: Memorial Day–Labor Day, Saturday and Sunday, 11:00 a.m.–4:00 p.m. Other times by appointment.

Admission: Adults $5, Children under 12 free

Driving directions: I-70 to Exit 243, toward Central City/Hidden Valley. Go 0.3 mile. Turn right on Central City Parkway. Go 8.0 miles. Turn left on Lawrence Street. It becomes Eureka Street when it crosses Main Street in Central City. The house is one and a half blocks up the hill past the opera house and on the right.

Parking: Parking lots on Eureka Street or in the Century Casino parking lot (free)

Memberships: Membership in the Gilpin Historical Society is available at varying levels of support. Call (303) 582-5283

Web site: www.gilpinhistory.org/thomas_house.html

35 Tomeo House

Grace Rossi and her six children lived in the three-room house for seventeen years.

Courtesy of Louisville Historical Museum

Felix Tomeo was born in Italy about 1873. He married Michalena Burtimocio in 1902. He and his two brothers, Mike and Nick, worked as coal miners and saloonkeepers. The Tomeo brothers built this 600-square-foot house with three rooms and a cellar. Though it eventually did have an electric light fixture in each room, the Tomeo House never had running water.

Felix and Michalena lived in the one-story house when their daughter Dominica Emelia was born. They had seven more children between 1905 and 1916. Around 1906, Felix built a two-story house next to the smaller one. At the

The Tomeo House, built circa 1904.
One-story, three-room frame house with cellar.

same time, the Tomeo brothers constructed the building that was to become Jacoe's Store, which stood on the corner on the other side of the larger house.

About 1910, the Tomeo family moved into the two-story house and rented out the smaller house to May LaSalle, who lived there until 1924.

The Rossi Family

In 1924, when May left, the Tomeos rented out the one-story house to Grace Rossi and her six children—Guy, Angelina, Frank, Mary, Daniel, and John. Her husband, Mike Rossi, had died of asthma, caused by or complicated by coal mining. Grace was around forty-four when he died, and the family moved to Louisville from the Monarch Mine area.

The Rossi family members lived in the house for seventeen years, from 1924 to 1941, through the children's high-school graduations at Louisville High School. Guy married Rose Tomeo, Felix and Michalena's daughter.

Making a Living

Rent on the little house was seven dollars a month. To make ends meet, Grace took in washing and ironing. John and Frank worked on farms, butchered hogs, and cleaned ash pits. Initially, Frank and Guy used a cart and donkey to collect the ashes, but later, they used a bicycle and cart. They also worked at Jacoe's Store. Barter was the system of payment, so instead of receiving money for their services, they were paid in meat, eggs, and groceries.

The boys slept in two beds in what is now the bedroom of the house. The girls slept with their mother in what is now the sitting room. A coal stove was used for heating. A sewing machine sat near the front window, presumably for light, with a trunk next to it. They also had a crystal radio that John made. The front room was also used for weekly baths in large galvanized tubs.

Grace DiGiacomo Rossi, mother of six

John's Visit

Of the Rossi children, only John and Frank were still living on April 17, 2005, when John Ross visited the Tomeo House. (John now goes by the name of Ross.). The visit brought back many memories. He said that the front door is the same as when he lived there, but there wasn't a front porch or steps at the time; he recalled railroad ties used as steps. Nor were there sidewalks or lawns back then.

The Rossi family did have a large garden and a chicken coop in the backyard. The garden extended all the way to South Street behind the Jacoe Store. Canned goods were stored in the cellar. They also had an outhouse, complete with a Sears catalog.

Frank made kitchen cabinets out of apple crates from Jacoe's Store. He also made the family's large kitchen table in a high school shop class. John recalled eating a lot of spaghetti in that kitchen. A long bench stretched along the west wall of the kitchen, and there were two washtubs and a washboard. The kitchen stove was used to boil water for laundry that was washed in galvanized tubs.

Brothers Daniel, Guy, John, and Frank Rossi

John remembered helping with everything, especially with the wash and in the vegetable garden. The family grew tomatoes, peppers, cucumbers, corn, cabbage, lettuce, and more. They also made their own sausages. An apple tree behind the store provided fruit.

John worked at the Jacoe Store after school and was paid with a roast once a week. He said, "Everything was so cheap, you didn't hardly need anything." There was no money for buying toys, but the children made up their own games.

After high school, John worked for a time at McCorkle's Grocery Store, then joined the Navy in March 1942. He married Martha Coet, who had worked at the Blue Parrot Restaurant in Louisville before marrying John. After the war, John worked at a sheet-metal business in Denver, then at the Rocky Flats nuclear weapons facility. His mother, Grace, died in 1959.

The two-story house was eventually torn down, but the one-story house and Jacoe's Store remain and today are part of the Louisville Historical Museum.

About the Tomeo House
Part of the Louisville Historical Museum

Address: 1001 Main Street, Louisville, Colorado 80027

Phone: (303) 665-9048

Hours: Tuesdays, Wednesdays, Thursdays, and the first Saturday of every month, 10:00 a.m.–3:00 p.m. Call ahead for current hours.

Admission: Free

Driving directions: I-25 to Exit 217, U.S. 36 West toward Boulder. Go 11.4 miles. Take the Storage Tek Drive exit toward Louisville/Broomfield. Go 1 mile. Turn left on South 96th Street. Go 1.7 miles. South 96th Street becomes Colorado Highway 42. Go 0.1 mile. Turn left on Pine. Go 0.1 mile. Turn right on Main Street. Go 0.4 mile. Turn left on South Street at the museum.

Parking: Free on the street and in the parking lot behind the museum

Memberships: Membership in the Louisville Historical Society is available at varying levels of support. Call (303) 665-9048.

Web site: www.louisvilleco.gov/. Select Visiting/Historical Museum

36 Underhill Museum

Lucy Underhill's delphiniums reached a height of twelve feet.

Courtesy of James Werner

James Underhill was born in New York City in 1871. He attended prep schools and graduated with honors from Harvard with a bachelor's degree in chemistry and geology in 1894. He arrived in Idaho Springs in 1897, and began his career as a mining engineer. His first office was above the Merchants and

Underhill Museum
Decorative brickwork on the façade called Cornish work, after the masonry work created by early settlers from Cornwall, England.

Lucy Underhill among her delphiniums

James Underhill surveying

Miners Bank. James was later commissioned as U.S. deputy mineral surveyor. He wrote several books on surveying and geology.

Lucy Caroline Stoller was born in Denver in 1875. Shortly after her birth, the family returned to Missouri, where her father was engaged in the cattle business. She began her public education at the Humboldt School in Kansas City, Missouri.

James and Lucy were married in San Francisco in December 1899 by the clerk of court, with Lucy's oldest sister as one of the witnesses. At that time, James was probably working as a consultant at the Copper Mountain Mine in Redding, California.

James went on to obtain a master's degree from the University of Colorado in 1905. A year later, he became the first person to receive a doctorate in geology from the same university.

From 1919 to 1946, Dr. Underhill served as an associate professor of mining at the Colorado School of Mines in Golden. In 1924, he was elected as the outstanding professor of the year. He commuted from Idaho Springs to Golden by train and bus, as he did not own a car. He also served as director of the Experimental School at the Edgar Mine Tunnel in Idaho Springs, where the School of Mines trained students.

House and Office

The present house museum served as both the office and home for James and Lucy Underhill starting in 1912. The office faced the street, and the living quarters filled the rear of the first floor and the upper floor. The door on the left side of the building was the entrance to the living quarters located down a hallway. The door on the right was for business. James' original desk remains in the office, which is lit by skylights.

James served as an alderman on the Idaho Springs City Council for fourteen years and as the Clear Creek County U.S. food administrator during World War II. He was active in the Christian Science Church both in Idaho Springs and Denver. He was a member of several honorary societies including Theta Tau, Sigma Xi, Square and Compass, and Scabbard and Blade.

Courtesy of James Werner

James Underhill's office was on the ground floor of the house

Pastimes

Lucy assisted her husband in his office on Thursdays and Fridays. She served as the clerk of the Christian Science Church in Idaho Springs in the early 1900s. She was known for her French cooking, which was favored by her husband. The museum owns a cookbook of her recipes. Her delphiniums, grown in the enclosed courtyard to the rear of the home, were magnificent. Some reportedly reached a height of 12 feet. One such plant from her garden is still living.

The Underhills were devoted to the Saturday Metropolitan Opera live radio broadcasts. On Sundays, the couple rode motorcycles in the mountains.

James died in 1954 at the age of eighty-three. After his death, Lucy remained in the home until 1963. The last six years of her life were spent in the care of a friend in Denver. The Underhills had no children.

Famous relation

James's half-sister was popular author Frances Parkinson Keyes. Keyes's home in New Orleans, the Beauregard-Keyes House, is also a house museum. *Letters from a Senator's Wife*, a collection of Frances Keyes' correspondence, includes a lengthy letter Keyes wrote to Lucy about social occasions in Washington and about women's rights and the proposed amendment to the Constitution drafted by the National Woman's Party.

Becoming a House Museum

In 1963, Lucy deeded the building to the Idaho Springs Library for use as a museum. It opened in 1964. One of her requirements was that it would become a museum and never be turned into a tavern. Her staunch support of the Women's Christian Temperance Union explains her very specific request.

About the Underhill Museum

Address: 1416 Miner Street, Idaho Springs, Colorado 80452

Phone: (303) 567-4382

Hours: June–September, Daily 10:00 a.m.–4:00 p.m.

Admission: Donations accepted

Driving directions: I-70 West to Exit 240, Colorado 103, toward Mount Evans. Go 0.1 mile. Turn right on 13th Avenue. Go less than 0.1 mile. Turn right on Miner Street. Go 1 block. Museum is on the left.

Parking: Free on street or in public parking lot a few blocks east

Memberships: Membership in the Historical Society of Idaho Springs is available at varying levels of support. Call (303) 567-4382.

Web site: http://www.historicidahosprings.com/attractions/underhill_museum.php

37 Wheat Ridge Historic Park

The photographer had to place a wooden ring around Frank White's neck to hold him still long enough to take the exposure.

Courtesy of Mrs. Barbara White Bright

"Back in those days, everyone depended on you for the chore that you had to do," said the tour guide of the sod house in Wheat Ridge Historic Park.

The soddy was built sometime prior to 1864 when there were trappers in the area and there was still tall prairie grass (the grass was gone by 1864). No one knows who built it. But it was made with tall prairie grass sod, and the roof was made of hand-hewn shingles.

The L-shaped soddy was quite roomy. It is 36 feet long and was originally three rooms. It represents 5,000 square feet of sod. The sod was cut in strips 30 inches wide and 6 inches deep. Woodbine covered the sod and still grows inside the stucco walls, out the eaves and chimney. Still, the interior gives a good idea of how the family would have lived.

At some point in the 1800s, the sod walls were covered with chicken wire and plaster. This prevented the house from eroding. Eventually, some of the

Etta, Leonard, Frank, and Bert White in front of the sod house. L-shaped sod and stucco with hand-hewn shingled roof.

plaster peeled off, exposing the dirt walls to the weather. The Chinook winds would blow so hard in the valley that after each storm, a little more plaster came off. Author Claudia Worth writes, "The kids picked at it too. Grandpa White was always yelling at them 'to quit picking the plaster'."[1]

In 1975, the plaster that covered both interior and exterior of the soddy was removed to expose the sod walls. The walls were rebuilt using new sod where necessary.

Farmer Baugh

James H. Baugh, a Missouri native, came west in the spring of 1859. He squatted on the land that had been granted to Private Polomia Garcia y Padilla, a veteran of the New Mexican Volunteers who fought in the Navajo Wars.

On August 15, 1859, Baugh located just north of Prospect Trail, the main road between Denver and Golden. There was no land office in which to file his claim of 160 acres, no survey, and no legally constituted recorder to record legal documents. Finally, in 1867, the land was legally assigned to Baugh.

Baugh was an honest man. He sought out Padilla and paid him $500 for the land. Few of the men who staked farming claims between Golden and the confluence of Clear Creek and the South Platte River stayed very long. But Baugh stayed. Starting in 1859, there was a demand for Colorado-grown produce to feed gold seekers and those who came in their wake. He built two ditches to convey water from Clear Creek to the fields. One of them still waters the historic park today. Baugh grew wheat, oats, vegetables, and strawberries, which he sold in Denver and in the mining camps.

By 1879, ten or fifteen families had moved into the valley. Farmer Baugh found things getting too crowded, and he moved on.

The White Family

Blizzards had ruined the crops in Plainville, Kansas, where Samuel Albert "Bert" White farmed in 1888. He started walking west, taking jobs along the way. Eventually, he came to Denver, where he worked for farmers in the area. But in his free time, he looked for land. Family history has it that when he saw the land around the soddy, he said, "It grows a fine crop of weeds, so why not grow truck farm vegetables?"[2] He bought the place, and his family came out in a covered wagon.

At that time, the agricultural college was in Fort Collins, and Bert experimented with fruit and vegetable varieties for them. He and his six-foot-tall wife, Etta, produced raspberries, dewberries, gooseberries, white grape, rhubarb, beets, carrots, parsnips, turnips, green beans, head lettuce, and

asparagus. His claim to fame was Pascal celery, which he is believed to have introduced into the region, having acquired the seeds from France.

The Bungalow

In 1910, Bert built a brick bungalow a little south of the sod house and moved his family into it. The big cottonwood tree that stood just south shaded the house with its wide branches. Then in 1913, the tree experienced a very heavy snowfall.

Worth's book tells us what happened next from the perspective of the tree:

> That following summer, a terrible lightning storm came out of the mountains. Lighting was hitting the ground all around the fields. Then, I heard a loud bang and the sound of splintering wood. I felt a horrible pain in my side.[3]

The northern branch had broken off, and it crashed into the house. Bert and the boys sawed the broken limb up for firewood. They mended the roof, and the tree "vowed to never let my branches fall and hurt anyone again."[4]

In 1924, Bert's son Frank brought his wife and six children to live in the soddy and assist on the farm. Altogether, Frank and his wife had twelve children. He, his wife, and four girls slept in the sod house. The boys slept in another frame building that was used to process celery and apple vinegar. The children liked to cool their feet in the ditch that ran beside the brick bungalow, until Grandpa White "would holler at them to stop playing in the ditch exclaiming that water was valuable and every drop was needed to water the crops."[5]

Frank's son Jim remembers trudging home from school one bitter cold winter day. Grandma Etta made him come inside and spread his hands on a piece of brown wrapping paper. The next day, he had a homemade pair of gloves and a pair of mittens that fit perfectly.

Courtesy of Wheat Ridge Historical Society

When Frank White (left) and his brother, Leonard, posed for this picture, the photographer had to place a wooden ring around Frank's neck to hold him still. Pictures took so long to expose that many children could not keep from wiggling—thus the yoke in the photographer's studio.

While Frank and his family used the soddy, Bert and Etta made their home in the brick bungalow until they died in 1933.

In 1939, the Whites sold the property and moved away. But they came back to visit often, and in later years felt it was an honor that their sod home had been made into a museum. "You can tell it was well loved and lived in," said the tour guide. "It's a comfortable house. You can tell that the people who lived in it were not angry."

Three families owned the property after 1939, and the sod house was occupied until 1970. There was no plumbing. A pump in the kitchen brought water inside, and the outhouse was behind the house. A Save-Our-Soddy campaign in 1972 saved the sod house and the brick house. In 1973, the property was entered in the National Register of Historic Places.

About Wheat Ridge Historic Park

Address: 4610 Robb Street, Wheat Ridge, Colorado 80033

Phone: (303) 421-9111

Hours: Friday 10 a.m.–3 p.m.

Admission: Free.

Driving directions: I-25 to Exit 209B for 6th Avenue West toward Lakewood. Go 4.9 miles on West 6th Avenue Freeway. Exit Kipling Street North. Go 3.7 miles. Turn left on 44th Avenue. Go 0.9 mile. Turn right on Robb Street (north). Go 0.2 mile. Turn right into park.

Or, I-70 to Exit 206 for Ward Road (CO 72). Turn south on Ward Road and then left onto West 44th Avenue. Go 0.5 mile. Turn left on Robb Street. Go 0.2 miles. Turn right into park.

Parking: Free parking in the drive and on the streets around the park.

Memberships: Membership is available in Wheat Ridge Historical Society at varying levels of support. Call (303) 431-1261.

Web site: http://www.wheatridgehistoricalsociety.org/Joomla/

Appendix A. The Smoky Hill Trail

The Smoky Hill River begins as two separate branches about fifty miles apart on the eastern plains of what is now Colorado. The north and south branches unite at a point about fifty miles east of the present Kansas-Colorado state line. The region of the Smoky Hill River that passes through present-day Kansas and Colorado was home to large herds of buffalo and the many Native Americans who hunted there. During the early 19th century, trappers and traders penetrated up the valley from the east. When waves of gold seekers and settlers began to flood the region, they were not welcomed by the Native American tribes who had fought among themselves over the region as well.

When gold was discovered in the so-called Pikes Peak region of the South Platte River in the late 1850s, two routes to the Rocky Mountain goldfields became popular. One route was the Santa Fe Trail, which travelers followed as far as the Arkansas River, where they turned north and went up the Arkansas River valley. (*see* sidebar and map of the Santa Fe Trail in Chapter 4 Baca House.) The second route was the Platte River Route, which traveled over a branch of the more northern Oregon Trail. Both these trails were heavily traveled and well known.

Despite being less well known, the Smoky Hill route was thought to be 200 miles shorter than the other two. At fifteen miles a day of wagon travel, this could save two weeks. At first there was no actual trail to follow, and there was progressively less wood and water as one approached the headwaters of the river in the plateau of the plains. Water disappeared for long stretches near the western end of the river.

The first official expedition along the Smoky Hill route was made by Captain John C. Fremont in May 1843. On his second expedition to the West, he documented the eastern portion of this route. In his report, he said, "The entire valley of the Smoky Hill is almost perpetually covered with a light blue haze that is most noticeable on hot autumn days and it is from this fact that the river got its name, we are sure. Some historians claim the Indians named it. Some think that [Francisco Vásquez de] Coronado named it when he reached the valley near present day Lindsborg when searching for the mythical Seven Cities of Gold. Others think that Lieutenant [Zebulon] Pike named it on his exploration trip to the west in 1806, when he discovered Pike's Peak. Whatever the source of the name, it is a fitting and descriptive choice."[1]

By 1845, it was a general route westward though not a well-defined trail.

After leaving Junction City, Kansas Territory, there were no forts and only a few scattered trading posts. Travelers followed the Kansas River as far as the Smoky Hill fork and then followed either the Smoky Hill River to the southwest or the Republican River fork in a northerly direction to Cherry Creek.

Gold

Several discoveries of gold at the foot of the Rocky Mountains in the early 1850s failed to awaken the storm of gold seekers—until William Green Russell's famous find at Dry Creek, which flowed into the Platte River about 7 miles south of the mouth of Cherry Creek. (*See* sidebar in Chapter 8 Byers-Evans House.)

Then the news spread rapidly. Entrepreneurs began to write guides to what was known as the Pikes Peak gold region, even though the first gold discoveries were not really sitting at the foot of Pikes Peak. Again, the routes west were mentioned: the Platte River route; the Santa Fe Trail and Arkansas Valley; and the Smoky Hill Trail.

But publications about the Smoky Hill Trail were written by those who knew nothing about it. There was no real trail after Fort Riley. Each party might take a different course, so no road was established. Those promoting travel usually suggested that the distance from the Missouri River in Kansas, where the railroad ended, to Denver was around 500 miles. It was more likely between 625 and 875 miles. Travelers ran out of provisions long before they reached the mountains, if they were lucky enough to survive. Many didn't. Stories of starvation and death abounded. Both the Platte and the Arkansas routes were partly guarded by soldiers. But on the Smoky Hill Trail, Native Americans plundered as they wished. By the summer of 1859, the Smoky Hill Trail had gained a very bad name.

In spite of this, not everyone gave up on the trail. In April 1859, the freighting firms of Russell and Majors began to use the route to freight goods into Denver. In addition, the people of Leavenworth rallied towns along the route to build a road up the Smoky Hill Valley. Lawyer Henry Green headed up a road-building crew to survey and build a real road. They surveyed and built as they went, finally reaching Denver in fifty-seven days.

Once the Civil War began, fewer people traveled the route, but the work had not been done in vain.

Butterfield Overland Despatch

David A. Butterfield lived with his family in Kansas in 1856. When the war began, he felt the safest place for his family was Denver, and he moved them

there in 1862. He operated a grocery and dreamed of a freight line from the Missouri River to Denver.

In 1864, he moved to Atchison, Kansas. He studied the survey maps of the Smoky Hill Road made in 1860 and decided he could use much of that same route. He made his route shorter, faster, and safer than the earlier road so that merchants in Denver could get fast service on the goods they ordered. He attracted interest in his freight line by establishing headquarters in New York City and putting up gigantic signs showing huge covered wagons pulled by mules or oxen. He succeeded in organizing the Butterfield Overland Despatch, with offices in New York, Boston, Philadelphia, Cincinnati, St. Louis, Chicago, Denver, and Salt Lake City.

He hired Lieutenant Julian R. Fitch as a surveyor. Fitch was able to avoid some of the hazards of the earlier trail. He planned way stations and marked which ones would provide stage passengers with meals. These stations would be run by a family.

On June 24, 1865, a small wagon train carried 75 tons of freight bound for Denver and other points in Colorado. There were no stations yet, so the animals that started the trip had to finish it. On July 15, another wagon train left for the mountains. Steamboats began to unload quantities of freight on the Missouri River landing in Atchison for shipment down the Overland Despatch.

The Native Americans along this route still waged attacks against those who were invading their Smoky Hill River hunting grounds. Stations were burned, and much blood was shed. But the businessmen were determined. They built new stations with new spacing between them.

Butterfield himself rode in the first stagecoach to travel over the new road on September 11, 1865. It arrived in Denver without any serious mishaps. Denver residents turned out in force to greet the arriving stagecoach. That same year, Theodore H. Davis, the artist for *Harper's Magazine*, wrote of his experiences when he came west to make sketches of life on the prairies. It is a colorful account of what it was like to travel on the Butterfield Overland Despatch in November 1865.

Indian raids continued as forts were built and the railroad crept west. Stagecoaches picked up passengers and freight at the railroad terminus and carried them west on the Smoky Hill Trail. The Indians attacked railroad crews and freight wagons in their effort to drive the white man out of traditional hunting grounds. General George A. Custer and "Buffalo Bill" Cody fought in these battles.

The Kansas Pacific Railroad reached Denver in 1870. The writer of one contemporary article noted, "Staging between Denver and the east ended when

the Kansas Pacific was completed last Monday. The coach has given way to the palace car and staging for the overland traveler is a thing of the past."[2]

Today

Interstate 70 follows the Smoky Hill Trail for many miles, and much of the land where the trail passes is under cultivation. Stone markers lie along 220 miles of the route in Kansas. In Colorado, markers stand near Aroya and Cheyenne Wells, and the end of the trail is marked by the Pioneer Monument in downtown Denver at Colfax and Broadway.

Four educational plaques tell the story of the Smoky Hill Trail where it passed through present-day Mayfair Park in east Denver. A gravel path and natural grasses and plants help re-create the feeling of what it must have been like to travel then. One of the plaques points out that a wagon pulled by oxen traveled between 10 and 15 miles per day—if you didn't break a wheel or stop to ford a stream. At that rate, the sign says, from that spot it would take three hours to reach the capitol in downtown Denver and almost two days to get to Denver International Airport.

About the Smoky Hill Trail Markers in Mayfair Park

Hours: 5 a.m. until 11 p.m.

Address: Jersey Street and East 10th Ave., Denver, Colorado 80220

Driving directions: Monaco Parkway to East 10th Avenue. Turn West on East 10th Avenue. Go 0.4 miles. The educational markers are located along the gravel path on the north side of the park between Ivanhoe and Jersey.

Parking: Free on street

Appendix B
Milestones in Colorado History

1803 — Louisiana Purchase is signed on April 30.

1821 — The Santa Fe Trail is established. Mexico declares independence from Spain on August 24.

1832 — Bent's Fort is built on the Arkansas River

1842 — Fremont Expedition explores parts of Colorado. The first of five expeditions.

1848 — Mexican War ends with Treaty of Guadalupe Hidalgo.

1851 — First permanent non-Native settlement established in San Luis Valley.

1854 — Kansas Nebraska Act established Nebraska Territory and Kansas Territory on May 30.

1858 — William Green Russell party discovers gold near Cherry Creek in July. Auraria Town Company is founded on the west side of Cherry Creek in October. In November, the William H. Larimer party from Kansas Territory founds the Denver City Town Company on the east side of Cherry Creek, jumping the earlier claim.

1859 — First issue of the *Rocky Mountain News* comes off the press on April 23.

Gold discovered near Idaho Springs

1860 — Auraria and Denver are consolidated, taking the name of Denver.

Leadville booms with stampede of miners

1861 — Kansas becomes 34th state on January 29. Colorado Territory is created on February 28. Charleston batteries fire on Fort Sumter to begin the Civil War on April 12.

1862 — Congress nullifies the Dred Scott decision of the Supreme Court by passing an act prohibiting slavery in the Territories in July.

First tax supported school opens in Colorado.

1864 — Cherry Creek floods, May 19.

Sand Creek Massacre, November 29.

1865 — The American Civil War ends with Lee's surrender to Grant at Appomattox Courthouse in Virginia on April 9. The 13th Amendment to the Constitution barring slavery is ratified on December 6.

1869 — Final battle between Native Americans and Colorado whites at Summit Springs

1870 — Denver, Pacific, Kansas Pacific, and Colorado Central railroads reach Denver in August.

Union Colony established in Greeley

1871 — General William Palmer begins building Denver-Rio Grande RR

Palmer establishes Little London, the town that would become Colorado Springs

1876 — Colorado becomes the 38th state on August 1.

1877 — Railroad connection between Cheyenne and Denver is completed.

1880 — A decade begins of Colorado growth and prosperity propelled by mining and railroads.

1890 — Denver's population reaches 106,000.

1891 — Robert Womack finds gold in Cripple Creek

1893 — Sherman Silver Purchase Act is repealed. Colorado fortunes based on silver mining are lost, and Denver plunges into a depression.

Consitiutional amendment granting women the right to vote passes by general election.

1902 — City and County of Denver are established.

1912 — The *Titanic* sinks on April 5.

1914 — The Ludlow Massacre takes place on April 20. World War I begins with the assassination of Archduke Francis Ferdinand of Austria-Hungary.

1915 — Rocky Mountain National Park opens.

1919 — Prohibition begins with passage of 18th Amendment to the Constitution on January, 16, 1919. World War I ends with the Treaty of Versailles on May 7.

1928 — Moffet Tunnel opens.

1931 — Colorado's population passes 1 million.

1933 — Prohibition ends on February 20, 1933, with passage of the 21st Amendment, which calls for repeal of the 18th Amendment.

1941 — United States enters World War II after the Japanese bomb Pearl Harbor.

1945 — World War II ends with Japanese surrender on August, 14.

1958 — Air Force Academy opens north of Colorado Springs.

1973 — Eisenhower Tunnel is built under the Continental Divide.

1976 — The Big Thompson River floods on July 3.

Glossary of Architectural Terms

acanthus — A plant whose leaves and flowers decorate Corinthian columns.

baluster — Upright, often vase-shaped support for a railing.

barrel vault — A ceiling or roof constructed of a single, continuous, unbroken arch in the form of a tunnel.

batten — A narrow strip of wood used as flooring or to fasten other pieces of wood together.

battlement — Low wall on a roof or tower with upright stone sections alternating with open spaces, originally used to shoot through.

board and batten — A type of exterior siding or interior paneling made of alternating wide boards and narrow wooden strips (battens).

Byzantine — Massive domes with square bases, rounded arches and spires, and much use of mosaics.

capital — The uppermost part of a column. It crowns the shaft.

capstone — A stone used at the top of a wall or other structure.

casement — A window frame that opens on hinges at the side.

chateauesque — Patterned after 16th-century French chateaux. Features include:
vertical proportions
thick masonry walls
mix of Gothic and Renaissance ornaments
high-peaked hipped roofs
elaborate dormers
tall chimneys

clapboard siding — Long, narrow, wooden boards having one edge thicker than the other. Used on the exterior of buildings.

Corinthian column — Fluted (grooved) column with an acanthus leaf capital.

cupola — A small structure on a roof, sometimes made of glass and providing natural light inside.

Denver Square — A style popular in Denver after the silver crash of 1893. The houses were usually brick rectangles that were less ornamented and more restrained than the mansions built before the crash. The composition reflects a desire for permanence and stability.

Doric columns — The simplest of the classical columns. The base of the Doric column is the floor, whereas other types of columns had an extra piece. It is topped by a plain capital—a convex disk underneath a square block formed from a single piece of marble instead of the intricate scrollwork of the Ionic column or elaborate acanthus leaves of the Corinthian column.

dormer — An opening in a sloping roof, the framing of which projects out to form a vertical wall suitable for windows or other openings.

dormer window — Window that protrudes from a sloping roof and has a roof of its own.

eave — Overhang of the roof.

English Tudor — Half-timbering with white stucco or brick infill; steep roof; tall, narrow, multi-paned windows; and large, decorated chimneys.

entablature — Horizontal moldings and bands located immediately above columns and other similar supports.

eyebrow dormer — A low dormer window set in the slope of a roof. It has no sides, only wavy roofing flowing outward from the roof itself.

fanlight — A semicircular or fan-shaped window above a door or window.

Flemish stepped gables — Gables that rise step by step like two flights of stairs meeting at the top in a small platform.

flying buttress — An exterior support that protrudes from the wall and is typically arch-shaped. Used on Gothic cathedrals to help withstand the outward thrust of the very high walls.

frieze — A band pattern that repeats in one direction.

gable — Triangular area of a wall formed by two sloping ends of a pitched roof. A gable may or may not have a window in it.

gambrel roof — A two-sided roof with a lower steeper slope and an upper less-steep slope on each side.

Georgian Revival — Symmetrical composition with classical detail.

Gothic — Characterized by pointed arches, flying buttresses, and high curved ceilings. Style used in Western Europe between the 12th and 15th centuries.

Greek Revival — Adapted from the classic Greek temple front with stately, pillared columns and decorative friezes.

groin vault — Formed by the intersection at right angles of two barrel vaults. The lines at which the two vaults meet are called groins.

half-timbered chateau — Unlike modern framed buildings where the walls are installed outside and inside the frame, half-timbered buildings have walls that are filled in between the structural timbers, sometimes set at angles. Most commonly, this infill was wattle-and-daub (upright branches interwoven by smaller branches and covered by a thick coat of clay mud), laths and plaster, or bricks.

hipped roof (or hip roof) — A four-sided roof that slopes down to the eaves on all four sides. It may have dormers or connecting wings with gables.

Ionic column — More slender than the Doric with opposing scrolls on the capital.

Italianate — Decorative brackets, low-pitched roof, tall narrow windows with elaborate crowns, wide overhanging eaves.

Italianate Vernacular — Two or three stories, a low-pitched roof and overhanging eaves. Windows may have arches or curves above them. Based on Italianate styling but uses local materials, techniques, or forms.

leaded glass — Refers to the technique of assembling pieces of cut glass into windows or lamps using strips of lead known as "cames". The material is soldered between each piece of glass. The space between lead and glass is filled with putty to seal out the weather.

mansard roof — A four-sided roof that has two slopes on each of its four sides. The lower slope is steeper than the upper slope. The upper slope is usually not visible from the ground. From

the French architect François Mansart (1598–1666) of the Beaux Arts School of Architecture in Paris. Mansart revived interest in this style, which had been characteristic of French Renaissance architecture roofing.

Moorish — Characterized by horseshoe arches, geometric calligraphy, and extensive use of decorative work, tiles, and mosaic, but no icons.

Neoclassical — Inspired by the classical architecture of ancient Greece and Rome. Features can include:
symmetrical shape
tall columns that rise the full height of the building
triangular pediment
domed roof

pediment — A low-pitched triangular gable on the front of some buildings in the Grecian or Greek Revival style. They are sometimes filled with relief sculpture.

piles — Long, slender timber, stone, steel, or reinforced concrete columns driven into the ground to carry a vertical load.

plat — *Noun:* An area surveyed into lots and blocks and filed for the record with the county clerk. *Verb:* To map or chart in detail.

Queen Anne — Asymmetrical with architectural accents such as fancy spindles, round turrets, towers, wraparound porches, bay windows, and gables.

Richardsonian Romanesque — Heavy, rough-faced stone masonry with squat towers and Roman arches. Inspired by Boston architect H. H. Richardson.

Romanesque — A round-arched style with massive walls and columns supporting stone vaulted buildings. The larger structure of a Romanesque building is composed of smaller square or rectangular spaces enclosed by groin vaults.

sash — A framework that holds the panes of a window in the window frame.

sash window — A window with usually two sashes that slide vertically open and shut.

section — Land one-square-mile in area.

shingle-style Queen Anne — Americanization of Queen Anne style. A quieter, more horizontal style. Continuous wood shingle surfaces, extensive porches, eyebrow dormers, round arches, and rusticated stone (masonry laid in large blocks with deeply sunk joints, usually on the basement or first story of a building).

shiplap siding — Siding with a groove or step cut along the length of the edge of a piece of wood to receive another board. The groove fits under an overlap.

spindle work — A long thin piece of wood, thicker in the middle and tapering at the ends.

spire — Tall, tapering conical, polygonal, or pyramidal constructions sitting atop a tower or roof and ending in a point.

vault — An arrangement of arches, usually forming a ceiling or roof. Usually made of brick, concrete, or stone.

Venetian Ogee — An Ogee arch formed by two reversed slightly S-shaped curves. Ogee moldings are made of both a convex and a concave curve.

Notes

Chapter 4, Baca House

[1] Marian Sloan Russell, quoted in Steve Grinstead, *Trinidad History Museum: A Capsule History and Guide* (Denver: Colorado Historical Society), 7.

[2] Colorado's Historical Newspaper Collection. The Collaborative Digitization Program in partnership with the Colorado Historical Society and the Colorado State Library have created a statewide historic newspaper database dating from 1859 to 1880.

Chapter 5, Barney Ford House

[1] Notes from Karen Musolf, Ph.D., docent at Barney Ford House, 2005–2006.

[2] Forbes Parkhill, "Colorado's Negro 'President Maker,' the *Denver Post*, September 15, 1963.

[3] Ibid.

Chapter 6, Bloom House

[1] Many of these stories come from Frank's daughter, Alberta, and others who knew him. However, Frank was known to have quite a flare as a storyteller. So, it is difficult to determine which stories are true, which were filtered through his imagination, and which he might have embellished, as is true with all spinners of yarns.

[2] Joanne West Dodds, *The Thatchers: Hard Work Won the West* (Pueblo, Colo.: My Friend, The Printer, Inc., 2001), 21.

[3] Judi Brandow, "Household Hints and Successful Tips," *Visits with a Victorian Lady*, taped presentation at Rocky Mountain Fiction Writers Conference, 1996.

Chapter 8, Byers-Evans House

[1] William Byers, "Ascent of Long's Peak," *Rocky Mountain News*, September 23, 1864.

[2] Don Etter, *Auraria: Where Denver Began* (Boulder: Colorado Associated University Press, 1972).

[3] Quoted in *Rocky Mountain News*, April 22, 1984.

[4] Camp Weld was established as a Civil War camp in 1861 and was abandoned in 1865. Its site was on the South Platte River at present-day West Eighth Avenue and Vallejo Street. Troops of the 1st Regiment of Colorado Volunteers were trained at this camp. They were mainly responsible for the defeat of the Confederates in New Mexico.

[5] "To Celebrate Anniversary of Notable Woman's First Trip to Colorado," Sunday, August 3, [year missing, publication missing from copy in file] clip files, biography, Western History Genealogy Department, Denver Public Library.

[6] Frank Hall, *History of the State of Colorado*, vol. 4 (Chicago: Blakely Printing Company, 1889).

Chapter 9, Cherokee Ranch and Castle

[1] Frances Melrose, "Tweet Kimball Gears for National Western Stock Show," *Rocky Mountain News*, January 6, 1980.

[2] Lee Pitts, *Livestock Magazine*, September 1981.

Chapter 10, Cozen's Ranch and Stage Stop Museum

[1] Grand County, 1885 Census, agricultural schedule.

Chapter 11, Four Mile House

[1] Bayard Taylor, *Colorado: A Summer Trip* (New York: G.P. Putnam and Son, 1867), 36. Note: the Booths were not drinkers, and whether or not they actually sold liquor when operating the stage stop is one of speculation.

[2] Gertrude Brown Working, *Levi Booth of Four Mile House* (Denver: G. B. Working, 1986), 13–14.

[3] Tom Gavin, "Denver Woman, 88, Recalls Early 4-Mile House," *Rocky Mountain News*, September 16, 1956.

Chapter 14 Hedlund House

[1] Cecil Clark, "Walter M. Clark Family at Kit Carson, Colorado—1900–1907," *Kit Carson, Colorado* (Kit Carson: Kit Carson Historical Society, 1974).

[2] Letter from Mertle Clark Hedlund to Jefferson Swanger, November 3, 1904

[3] E-mail from Fran Mitterer, April 27, 2006.

[4] E-mail from Fran Mitterer, May 19, 2006.

[5] Ibid.

[6] E-mail from Fran Mitterer, May 31, 2006.

[7] E-mail from Fran Mitterer, April 29, 2006.

Chapter 17 Jack Dempsey Cabin

[1] Smith, Toby, *Kid Blackie: Jack Dempsey's Colorado Days*, Wayfinder Press, Ridgway, Colorado, 2003, p. 18.

Chapter 18 John Gully Homestead

[1] O'Brien, Mary Gully, "First Let Me Tell My Grandchildren a Story," *Early Aurora* (oral histories), McFadden, Carl, McFadden, Leona M., editors, Aurora Technical Center, Aurora, Colorado, 1978.

[2] Ibid.

Chapter 19 Justina Ford House

[1] Mark Harris, "The Forty Years of Justina Ford," *Negro Digest* (March 1950): 42.

[2] Ibid.

[3] Ibid., 43.

[4] Ibid., 45.

[5] Ibid., 44.

[6] Petra Lopez-Torres, "The Last of a Kind," edited by Magdalena Gallegos, *Urban Spectrum*, Sept. 1988.

Chapter 20 Lula Myers Ranch

[1] Mary Ellen Gilliland, *LULA: A Portrait in Pictures and Prose of a Keystone, Colorado Family*, Summit Historical Society in cooperation with Keystone Resort, Keystone, Colorado, 1990, p. 53.

Chapter 21, MacGregor Ranch

[1] Muriel MacGregor, "Tales of Pioneer Days on MacGregor's Ranch," in *Early Estes Park Narratives*, Vol. 1, ed. James H. Pickering (Estes Park, Colo.: Alpenaire Publishing Inc., 2004), 118.

[2] *Boulder County News*, August 10, 1877, p. 1.

[3] Estes-Poudre Ranger District, *Homestead Meadows*, Estes-Poudre Ranger District, Fort Collins, Colorado.

[4] "Preemption Act," *The Columbia Electronic Encyclopedia*, 6th ed., Columbia University Press, 2007, www.infoplease.com/ce6/history/A0840041.html.

Chapter 22, Mayer House, South Park City

[1] Frank H. Mayer and Charles B. Roth, *The Buffalo Harvest* (Union City, Tenn.: Pioneer Press, 1958, 1995).

[2] E.J. "Gene" Amitrani, *A Town Is Born: The Story of South Park City, rev. ed.* (Fairplay, Colorado: South Oak Community Presbyterian Church, 1982), 90.

[3] Ibid., 90.

[4] Mayer and Roth, *The Buffalo Harvest*, (Denver, Colorado: Sage Books, 1957)

[5] Ibid.

[6] Robert W. Fenwick, "103 Years without Regret," *Denver Post Empire Magazine*, October 4, 1953, p. 7.

[7] Ibid., 7.

[8] Ibid., 38.

[9] Ibid., 38.

Chapter 23, McAllister House

[1] Henry McAllister, paper read on September 10, 1908, to El Paso County Pioneers Association. Quoted in Polly King Ruhtenberg and Dorothy E. Smith, *Henry McAllister: Colorado Pioneer* Freeman, S.D.: Pine Hill Press, 1972.

[2] Quoted in Ruhtenberg and Smith, *Henry McAllister: Colorado Pioneer*.

Chapter 25, Miramont Castle

[1] "Clad in Colonial Garments, Manitou the Scene of a Brilliant Social Event," *the Denver Republican*, February 23, 1897.

[2] *Manitou Springs Journal*, November 14, 1896.

[3] "Ancient Splendor, A Reproduction of Ye Olden Tyme In Manitou," the *Gazette Telegraph*, February 23, 1897.

Chapter 26, Molly Brown House

[1] Kristen Iversen, *Molly Brown: Unraveling the Myth* (Boulder, Colo.: Johnson Books, 1999), 38.

[2] Ibid., p. 38.

[3] *Denver Post*, August 9, 1923.

Chapter 28, Old Homestead House

[1] "Close of an Erratic Life," *Denver Republican*, June 6, 1897.

[2] "Pearl DeVere Dead, Too Much Morphine," June 10, 1897, article copied by Grace Sterrett from the files of the *Cripple Creek Gold Rush* in January 1965, WHC Bancroft Box 19, Folder 59, "Madams," Western History Collection, Denver Public Library.

[3] Mabel Barbee Lee, *Cripple Creek Days* (Garden City, N.Y.: Doubleday & Company, Inc., 1958), 81.

4 Ibid, 82–84.

5 Nell Kimball, *Her Life as an American Madam*, ed. Stephen Longstreet (New York: The Macmillan Company, New York, 1970), 276.

Chapter 29, Orum House

1 Present-day Sloan's Lake park features a basketball court, bicycle and pedestrian pathway, boating, fishing, flower gardens, football field, softball field, soccer field, lighted tennis court, picnic area, two playgrounds, and water skiing. For more information, click "Find a Park" at www.denvergov.org/parks

Chapter 31, Rosemount Museum

1 Joanne West Dodds, *The Thatchers: Hard Work Won the West* (Pueblo, Colo.: My Friend, The Printer, Inc., 2001), 3.

2 Letter from Sarah Thatcher to Frank Bloom, March 21, 1865, transcription from the Colorado Historical Society, Trinidad History Museum.

3 Frank Bloom, Original ledger remembrances of Frank G. Bloom, Trinidad, Colorado, of life in Colorado 1866–1880s, #M1589, Western History Collection, The Denver Public Library.

4 Letter from Sarah Thatcher to Frank Bloom, May 29, 1866, transcription from the Colorado Historical Society, Trinidad History Museum.

5 *Colorado Business Directory 1877*, 205.

6 Dodds, *The Thatchers*, 126–127.

7 Quoted in Dodds, p. 172-3.

Chapter 32, Streer-Peterson House

1 Chris Leppek, "Little House on the Front Range, the Streer-Peterson House," *Intermountain Jewish News*, September 26, 1997.

2 Elizabeth Nosek, Interview with Dorothy Street Goodstein and Ruth Streer Kobey, Denver, Colorado, 1997.

3 Ibid.

4 Leppek, "Little House on the Front Range," 114.

5 Ibid., 116.

6 Ibid., 115.

Chapter 33, Tabor Home and the Matchless Mine Cabin

1 Phillip Hauser, Letter to Mr. James French, Fire Marshall, Leadville, Colorado, May 19, 1934, no. M Hauser L., Western History Collection, Denver Public Library.

2 Mary Cassidy, "Divorce of H.A.W. Tabor," unpublished manuscript, undated, from the collection of Christian J. Buys. Cassidy wrote history columns for the *Leadville Herald Democrat*.

3 M.G. Riley "Sin, Gin, and Jasmine, The Controversial Career of Caroline Bancroft," *Colorado Heritage* (March 2002): 43.

4 David Karsner, *Silver Dollar: The Story of the Tabors* (New York: Crown Publishers, 1932): 268.

5 Ibid., 284.

6 Text on the back of Augusta's gravestone in Riverside Pioneer Cemetery transcribed from a photo by Lillie Baird.

Chapter 37, Wheat Ridge Historic Park

1 Claudia Worth, *The Cottonwood Tree, The 130 Year History of the Clear Creek Valley as Witnessed by the Tree* (Wheat Ridge, Colo.: Wheat Ridge Historical Society), 8.

2 Interview with Barbara White Bright, September 16, 2005.

3 Worth, *The Cottonwood Tree*, 6

4 Ibid.

5 Ibid.

Appendix A, The Smoky Hill Trail

1 John C. Frémont, *Exploring Expedition to the Rocky Mountains in the year 1842* (Washington, D.C.: Smithsonian Institution Press, 1988).

2 E. O. Davis, "Swan Song of the Stage Coaches," *The First Five Years of the Railroad Era in Colorado* (Golden, CO: Sage Books, 1948),111.

Sources

Books

Campbell, Helen. *The Easiest Way in Housekeeping and Cooking.* Boston: Little, Brown, and Company, 1903; the Project Gutenberg Ebook # 15360, re-released 2005.

Cornelius, Mary Hooker. *The Young Housekeeper's Friend, or A Guide to Domestic Economy and Comfort.* Boston: Charles Tappan, New York: Saxton & Huntington, 1846.

Danilov, Victor J. *Colorado Museums and Historic Sites.* Boulder: University Press of Colorado, 2000.

Hall, Frank. *History of the State of Colorado.* Rocky Mountain Historical Company, Blakely Printing Company, Chicago, 1889-95.

Homestead Meadows. Fort.Collins, Colo.: Estes-Poudre Ranger District.

McAlester, Virginia, and Lee McAlester. *A Field Guide to America's Historic Neighborhoods and Museum Houses, The Western States.* New York: Alfred A. Knopf, 1998.

Smoky Hill North Trail, Instructional Resource Materials for Elementary School Teachers. Denver: Denver Parks and Recreation and Colorado Historical Society, 1997.

Wilk, Diane. *A Guide to Denver's Architectural Styles and Terms.* Denver: Historic Denver, Inc. and Denver Museum of Natural History, 1995.

A.J. Eaton House

Eaton Centennial Celebration Committee. *Eaton Centennial Celebration Commemorating Eaton's 100th Anniversary.* Eaton, Colorado, 1992.

Avery House

Watrous, Ansel. *History of Larimer County Colorado.* Fort Collins, Colo.: The Courier Printing and Publishing Company, 1911.

Baca House

Grinstead, Steve. *Trinidad History Museum.,* Denver: Colorado Historical Society, Denver, 2002.

Stokes, Gerald H. *A Walk Through the History of Trinidad.* Trinidad, Colo.: Trinidad Historical Society, 1986, 2000.

Taylor, Morris F. *Trinidad, a Centennial Town,.* Trinidad, Colo.: Trinidad State Junior College, 1976.

Barney Ford House

Barney Ford House Museum. Breckenridge, Colo.: Saddle Rock Society.

Hall, Frank. *History of the State of Colorado,* Vol. 4, Chicago: Blakely Printing Company, 1895.

Bloom Mansion

Patterson, Paul E., and Joy Poole. *Great Plains Cattle Empire, Thatcher Brothers and Associates (1875--1945).* Lubbock: Texas Tech University Press, 2000.

Taylor, Morris F. *Trinidad, Colorado Territory,* Trinidad State Junior College, Trinidad, Colorado, 1966.

Byers-Evans House

Etter, Don. *Auraria: Where Denver Began.* Boulder: Colorado Associated University Press, 1972.

Hall, Frank. History of the State of Colorado, Vol. 4. Chicago: Blakely Printing Company, 1895.

Noel, Dr. Thomas. *Denver: Rocky Mountain Gold.* Tulsa, Okla.:Continental Heritage Press, Inc., 1980.

Walsh, Elaine Colvin, and Jean Walton Smith. *Victoria of Civic Center.* Denver: Colorado Historical Society, 1984.

Cozens Ranch Museum

Reich, Alice, and Thomas J. Steele, editors. *Fraser Haps and Mishaps: The Diary of Mary Elizabeth Cozens.* Denver: Regis College Press, 1990.

Justina Ford House

Lohse, Joyce B. *Justina Ford, Medical Pioneer.* Palmer Lake, Colo.: Filter Press, 2005.

Four- Mile Historic Park

Lee, Wayne C., and Howard C. Raynesford. *Trails of the Smoky Hill,* Caldwell, Idaho: The Caxton Printers, Ltd., 1980.

Peters, Bette D. *Denver's Four Mile House.* Denver: The Junior League of Denver, Inc., 1980.

Working, Gertrude Brown. *Levi Booth of Four Mile House.* Denver: G.B. Working, 1986.

Hamill House

Bradley, Christine. *William A. Hamill, the Gentleman from Clear Creek.* Colorado State University Extension Service, and the Georgetown Society, Inc.

Healy House.

State Historical Society of Colorado. *Healy House and Dexter Cabin.* Denver: State Historical Monument, 1956.

Hedlund House

Clark, Cecil. "Walter M. Clark Family at Kit Carson, Colorado—1900–1907," in *Kit Carson, Colorado.* Kit Carson, Colo.: Kit Carson Historical Society, 1974.

Jack Dempsey Cabin

Smith, Toby. *Kid Blackie: Jack Dempsey's Colorado Days.* Ridgway, Colo.: Wayfinder Press, 2003.

John Gully Homestead

O'Brien, Mary Gully. "First Let Me Tell My Grandchildren a Story." In *Early Aurora,* edited by Carl McFadden and Leona M. McFadden. Aurora, Colo.: Aurora Technical Center, 1978.

Stone, Wilbur Fiske. *History of Colorado.* Vol. 4. Chicago: S.J. Clarke Publishing Company, 1919.

Lula Myers Ranch House

Gilliland, Mary Ellen. *LULA: A Portrait in Pictures and Prose of a Keystone, Colorado Family.* Keystone, Colo.: Summit Historical Society in cooperation with Keystone Resort, 1990.

MacGregor Ranch

Mills, Enos A. *The Story of Early Estes Park.* Estes Park, Colo.: Temporal Mechanical Press, 1905.

Pickering, James H. *Early Estes Park Narratives,* Vol. iv. Estes Park, Colo.: Alpenaire Publishing, Inc., 2004.

Pickering, James H. *This Blue Hollow.*, Boulder: University Press of Colorado, 1999.

Mayer House and South Park City

Amitrani, E.J. "Gene." *A Town is Born: The Story of South Park City.* Fairplay, Colo.: E.J. Amitrani, rev. ed., 1982.

Mayer, Frank H., and Charles B. Roth. *The Buffalo Harvest.* Union City, Tenn.: Pioneer Press, 1958, 1995.

McAllister House

Ruhtenberg, Polly King, and Dorothy E. Smith. *Henry McAllister: Colorado Pioneer.* Freeman, S.D.: Pine Hill Press, 1972.

Miramont Castle

Copp, Shirley. *Miramont Castle.* Manitou Springs, Colo.: The Manitou Springs Historical Society, revised 1993.

Mensing, Marcia. *Miramont Castle: The First Hundred Years.* Manitou Springs, Colo.: The Manitou Springs Historical Society, 1995.

Molly Brown House

Iversen, Kristen. *Molly Brown: Unraveling the Myth.* Boulder, Colo.: Johnson Books, 1999.

Old Homestead Museum

Black, Celeste. *The Pearl of Cripple Creek.* Colorado Springs: Black Bear Publishing, 1997.

Lee, Mabel Barbee. *Cripple Creek Days.* Garden City, N.Y.: Doubleday & Company, Inc., 1958.

MacKell, Jan. *Brothels, Bordellos, & Bad Girls.* Albuquerque: University of New Mexico Press, 2004.

Orum House

Jones, Celora Jean; researched by Connie Jo Fox; edited by Irma Wyhs. *Edgewater, Colorado: A Centennial Celebration, 1901-–2001.* Edgewater, Colo.: City of Edgewater and the Edgewater Historical Commission, 2002.

Rosemount Museum

Dodds, Joanne West. *The Thatchers: Hard Work Won the West.* Pueblo, Colo.: My Friend, The Printer, Inc., 2001.

Matthews, Frances, and Kay Stillman. *Rosemount Museum.* Pueblo, Colo.: Rosemount Museum Association, 1995.

Tabor Home and Matchless Mine Cabin

Buys, Christian J. *Leadville.* Montrose, Colo.: Western Reflections Publishing Company, 2004.

Furman, Evelyn E. *My Search for Augusta Pierce Tabor, Leadville's First Lady.* Denver: Quality Press, 1993.

Furman, Evelyn E. *Silver Dollar Tabor: The Leaf in the Storm.* Aurora, Colo.: The National Writers Press, 1982.

Gandy, Lewis Cass. *The Tabors.* New York: The Press of the Pioneers, Inc., 1934.

Karsner, David. *Silver Dollar: The Story of the Tabors.* New York: Crown Publishers, 1932.

Moynihan, Betty. *Augusta Tabor: A Pioneering Woman.* Evergreen, Colo.: Cordillera Press, Inc., 1988.

Smith, Duane A. *Horace Tabor, His Life and the Legend.* Boulder, Colo.: University Press of Colorado, 1989.

Wheat Ridge Historic Park

The Wheat Ridge Historical Committee. *Biographical Sketches Early Settlers of Wheat Ridge.* Wheat Ridge, Colo.: Wheat Ridge Centennial-Bicentennial Commission, 1976.

Worth, Claudia. *The Cottonwood Tree.* Wheat Ridge, Colo: Wheat Ridge Historical Society.

Articles

Goldrick, Professor O.J. "Great Flood in Denver." *The Weekly Commonweath* (Denver, City, Colorado Territory), May 25, 1864.

A. J. Eaton House Museum

United States Department of the Interior National Park Service. "National Register of Historic Places Continuation Sheet." Section 8, page 9, Eaton, Aaron James, House, Weld County, Colorado.

Baca House

"Hispanic Pioneer, Don Felipe Baca Brings His Family North to Trinidad." *Colorado Heritage,* 1982 annual issue. (Interviews with Luis and Facundo Baca.)

Reyes, Richard. "Trinidad, Colorado Founded by Tome's Baca Family." *Herencia, The Quarterly Journal of the Hispanic Genealogical Research Center of New Mexico* 4, no. 4 (October 1996).

Barney Ford House

"Barney Ford Stained Glass Window and Plaque." *Memorials and Art In and Around the Colorado State Capitol,* Colorado Legislative Council (June 1992): 40.

Halass, David Fridtjof. "Barney Ford: From Plantation Slave to Denver Leader." *Colorado History Now,* Colorado Historical Society (October 2000).

Johnson, Harold. "From Bondage to Riches: The Saga of a Summit County Pioneer." Summit Historical Society archives, Dillon, Colorado.

Martin, Monica J. "Nuggets." *Summit Sentinel* (Breckenridge, Colo.), June 5, 1981.

Parkhill, Forbes. "Colorado's Negro 'President Maker.'" the *Denver Post,* Sunday Magazine, September 15, 1963.

Briggle House

"William Harrison Briggle Home Welcomed Many." *Voices,* A Summit Historical Society Publication (Spring/Summer 1986).

Byers-Evans House

Halass, David Fridtjof. "Elizabeth Byers: A Woman of Consequence." *Colorado History Now,* April 1998.

Melrose, Frances. "Byers Left a Brilliant Imprint." *Rocky Mountain News,* April 22, 1984.

Cherokee Ranch and Castle

Barker, William J. "The Castle West of Wildcat." the *Denver Post Empire Magazine,* Nov. 01,1953.

"Historic Charlford Castle Sells for $135,000." *Cervi's Journal* (May 20, 1954).

McPhee, Mike. "Grande Dame Tweet Kimball Dies." the *Denver Post,* January 16, 1999.

Melrose, Frances. "Tweet Kimball Gears for National Western Stock Show." *Rocky Mountain News,* January 6, 1980.

Pitts, Lee. "Cherokee Ranch: A Santa Gertrudis Story." *Lifestock* (September 1981).

Cozens Ranch Museum

Maddox, Teri. "Ranch Witnessed Century of Change." *The Good Life,* April 17, 1986.

Melrose, Frances. "Cozens Diary Reveals Frontier Life." *Rocky Mountain News*, October 7, 1997.

White, Sally. "Jesuits in Jefferson County: A Story of Regis College." *Historically Jeffco* 17, no. 25: 30–34.

Four Mile Historic Park

Gavin, Tom. "Denver Woman, 88, Recalls Early 4-Mile House." *Rocky Mountain News*, September 16, 1956.

Hamill House

De Pew, Kathryn. "W.A. Hamill and the Hamill House." reprinted from the October 1955 issue of *Colorado Magazine*, Denver.

Healy House

Kent, Lewis A. "Leadville: The city, mines, and bullion product, personal histories of prominent citizens, facts and figures never before given to the public." *Denver Daily Times*, Denver, 1880.

Hiwan Historical Museum

Grunska, Jerry. "Hiwan Homestead Museum." *Historically Jeffco* 13, no. 21 (2000): 36–37.

Humphrey Memorial Park and Museum

Grunska, Jerry. "Hazel Humphrey Museum." *Historically Jeffco* 13, no. 21 (2000): 34–35.

John Gully Homestead

"Aurora's Oldest House Gets New Home." *Rocky Mountain News*, July 29, 1983.

Justina Ford House

Harris, Mark. "The Forty Years of Justina Ford." *Negro Digest*, March 1950.

MacGregor Ranch

MacGregor, Muriel "Tales of Pioneer Days on MacGregor's Ranch." In *Early Estes Park Narratives*, vol. 1, edited by James H. Pickering. Estes Park, Colo.: Alpenaire Publishing, Inc., 2004.

Mayer House and South Park City

Fenwick, Robert W. "103 Years without Regret." the *Denver Post Empire Magazine*, October 4, 1953.

Melrose, Frances. "Col. Frank Mayer Tells of His Early Days History to Writer." *Park County Republican* (Fairplay, Colo.), August 26, 1948.

Meeker Home Museum

"Josie's Journey, Miss Meeker Gives an Account of Her Captivity." *Denver Daily News*, November 30, 1879.

Ford, Peggy A. "A Brief History of the 1870 Nathan Cook Meeker Home in Greeley, Colorado." *The Greeley Tribune*, August 18, 1999.

Miramont Castle

"Ancient Splendor, A Reproduction of Ye Olden Tyme In Manitou." the *Gazette Telegraph*, February 23, 1897.

"Clad in Colonial Garments, Manitou the Scene of a Brilliant Social Event." the *Denver Republican*, February, 23, 1897.

Kelly, Bernard. "Old French-Built Castle Now Apartment House." the *Denver Post*, December 28, 1950.

O'Connor, Ellen G. "Historic Montcalm in Manitou Springs Once Property of Mercy Nuns of Denver." Denver Catholic Register, April 25, 1946.

Museo de las Tres Colonias

Thomas, Adam. "Hang Your Wagon to a Star: Hispanics in Fort Collins, 1900–2000." State Historical Fund Project, Fort Collins, Colorado, August 2003.

Old Homestead House Museum

"Close of an Erratic Life." *Denver Republican*, June 6, 1897.

"One Million Laid in Ashes. 8 Blocks Devastated in 2 Hrs., No Lives Lost." *Cripple Creek Morning Times*, April 26, 1896. Typescript from Mabel Barbee Lee papers, WHC759, Box 1, Folder 5, Western History Collection, Denver Public Library.

"Pearl DeVere Dead, Too Much Morphine." June 10, 1897 article copied by Grace Sterrett from the files of the *Cripple Creek Gold Rush* in January 1965, WHC Bancroft Box 19, Folder 59, "Madams," Western History Collection, Denver Public Library.

"Too Much Morphine." *Rocky Mountain News*, June 6, 1897.

House, Myron. "House with a Past." the *Denver Post Empire Magazine*, May 27, 1959.

Orum House

Fox, Connie. "Orum House in Edgewater." *Historically Jeffco* 12, no. 20 (1999): 33.

Wyhs, Irma. "Edgewater—A Romance," *Historically Jeffco* 13, no. 21 (2000): 22–27.

Rosemount Museum

Parmenter, Cindy. "From Mansion to Museum." the *Denver Post, January 19, 1969.*

Streer-Peterson House

Kehmeier, Clevenger. "A Moo from the Past." the *Denver Post*, November 15, 1998.

Leppek, Chris. "Little House on the Front Range, the Streer-Peterson House." *Intermountain Jewish News*, September 26, 1997.

Tabor Home and Matchless Mine Cabin

"Barth Held in Spell of 'Bad Luck' Jewel: Isabella Diamond, Sold by Queen of Spain That Columbus Might Find New World, Brought Woe to Widow of Tabor and Now to Millionaire." *Denver Post*, May 29, 1914.

"Carpenters Restore Baby Doe's Cabin." *Denver Post*, June 18, 1953.

"Peter McCourt, Pioneer in Theater Business, Dies." *Denver Post*, April 5, 1929.

Pomeroy, Earl. "There's New Life at the Matchless." *Denver Post*, 1953.

Teetor, Henry. "The Silver Theatrical Circuit: Or, All the World's a Stage." *Magazine of Western History* 13, no. 6 Dudley (April 1891).

Thomas House

Ditmer, Joanne. "Gifts Save Central City Museum." the *Denver Post*, July 23, 1990.

Interviews and lectures

A.J. Eaton House

Nancy Donahoo (curator). Tour of A.J. Eaton House Museum, Eaton, Colorado, March 9, 2006.

Avery House

Jane Hail (docent). Tour and interview, Avery House, Fort Collins, Colorado, November 19, 2006. Priscilla Opper (docent at Trinidad History Museum)

Baca House and Bloom Mansion

Priscilla Opper (docent). Interview, September 21, 2005.

Barney Ford House

Edna Pelzman (manager of Visitor Services). Visit to Barney Ford stained glass window behind Speaker's Desk, House of Representatives, Colorado State Capitol, Denver, Colorado, November 8, 2006.

Karen Musolf (docent). Notes, 2005–2006.

Sheryl Cutter. Tour and interview, Barney Ford House Museum, Breckenridge, Colorado, June 17, 2007.

Cherokee Ranch and Castle

John Lake (Tweet Kimball's butler of 20 years). Tour of Cherokee Castle, Sedalia, Colorado, March, 25, 2006.

Healy House

Maureen Scanlon (director). Tour of Healy House, Leadville, Colorado, May 28, 2006.

Hedlund House

Karen Hedlund Scott and Thomas Hedlund. Interview, Hugo, Colorado, May 13, 2006.

Humphrey House

Lois Lange (historian). Interview and tour of Humphrey House, Evergreen, Colorado, June 22, 2007.

John Gully Homestead

Michelle Bahe (curator of Collections). Tour of John Gully Homestead, Aurora History Museum, May 12, 2006.

Miramont Castle

Tina and Scott Nowlin. Interview with Virgil Pineda, Miramont Castle, Manitou Springs, Colorado, October 28, 2005.

Molly Brown House

Kerri Atter (director and curator). Tour of Molly Brown House, Denver, March 23, 2006.

Mary Rose Shearer (owner). Talk and event at Molly Brown Summer House, February 10, 2007.

Museo de las Tres Colonias

Juliet Romero Chavez. Interview at Museo de las Tres Colonias, Fort Collins,

Colorado, November 19, 2006.

Streer-Peterson House

Elizabeth Nosek. Interview with Dorothy Street Goodstein and Ruth Streer Kobey, Denver, Colorado.

Tabor House and Matchless Mine Cabin

Dr. Judy Temple. "Baby Doe Tabor: Finding Lizzie's Voice," Colorado Historical Society lecture, Denver, Colorado, May 16, 2006.

Tomeo House

Bridget Bacon (museum coordinator). Tour of Tomeo House, Louisville, Colorado, January 15, 2006.

Underhill Museum

Marjorie Bell (curator). Tour of Underhill Museum, Idaho Springs, Colorado, June 10, 2006.

Wheat Ridge Historic Park

Claudia Worth, president, and Charlotte Whetsel, vice president. Interviews, September 16, 2005.

Barbara White Bright. Interview, Arvada, Colorado, September 16, 2005.

Manuscripts and Oral Histories

Avery House

"Avery House History." Docent script, July 1995.

Baca House

Archibald, Albert William. "Notes by A.W. Archibald on himself and other persons and matters." Papers ca. 1900–1921, M14, Western History Collection, Denver Public Library.

Baca House and Bloom Mansion

Smith, Honora DeBusk. "Early Life in Trinidad and the Purgatory Valley." Master's thesis, University of Colorado, Boulder, 1930.

Barney Ford House Museum

Barney Ford House Museum Volunteer Handbook. Saddle Rock Society, Breckenridge, Colorado, 2004.

Bloom Mansion

Iliff, Alberta Bloom. "Don Colorado and His Times." Paper prepared for the Denver Fortnightly Club, November 21, 1961,

Colorado Historical Society archives at the Trinidad History Museum.

Manini, Paula. Unpublished transcript of interview with Alberta Iliff Shattuck. Colorado Historical Society Archives at the Trinidad History Museum, July 21, 1993.

Bloom Mansion and Rosemount Museum

Bloom, Frank. Original ledger remembrances of Frank G. Bloom, Trinidad, Colorado, of life in Colorado 1866–1880s. M1589, Western History Collection, Denver Public Library.

Cozens Ranch Museum

Sturn, Mayme G. "The Story of Mary York" as told to Mrs. Mayme G. Sturn by Mary, Sarah, and William Z. Cozens Jr. M166, Western History Collection, Denver Public Library.

Four Mile Historic Park

Johnston, William Crane, Jr. "Smoky Hill Trail." Master's thesis, Denver University, 1927.

Hedlund House

Hedlund, Mertle Clark. Letter from Mertle Clark Hedlund to Jefferson Swanger. November 3, 1904.

John Gully Homestead

Swiatosz, Susan. "Interpretive Plan for Gully Homestead." Aurora History Museum, Aurora, Colorado, summer 1982.

Meeker Home Museum

Meeker, Mrs. N.C. Letter from Mrs. N.C. Meeker to her children, Greeley, Colorado, March 5, 1898. Papers [manuscript], 1839–1917, Western History Collection, Denver Public Library.

Rock Ledge Ranch Historic Park

Chambers, Dorothy. Oral history, "The Ben Chambers Family Still Lives in Colorado." Recollections of Ben Chambers as told by Dorothy Chambers, wife of Robert Chambers II.

Delong, Grace. "A Ranch Begins: The Chambers Period 1874–1900," an account based on the Chambers history and other memories.

DeLong, Mary Chambers. Oral history from "The Chambers Family History as told by Mary Chambers Delong."

Tabor Home and Matchless Mine Cabin

Adams, Allen John. "Peter McCourt, Jr. and the Silver Theatrical Circuit, 1889–1910: An Historical and Biographical Study." Doctoral dissertation, University of Utah, 1969.

Hauser, Phillip. Letter to Mr. James French, Fire Marshall, Leadville, Colorado, May 19, 1934. No. M Hauser L., Western History Collection, Denver Public Library.

Neill, Sandra Kay. "Matchless Mine and Baby Doe Tabor Museum." Docent script, summer 1963.

Thomas House

"The Thomas House." Thomas House docent script.

Tomeo House

Ross family visit, April 18, 2005.

Wheat Ridge Historic Park

White, James R. "Henrietta (Etta) Mathews White, Recollections of her by her Grandson." Unpublished remembrance, Wheat Ridge Historical Society.

Historic Newspapers

Baca House and Bloom Mansion

Colorado's Historical Newspaper Collection. The Collaborative Digitization Program in partnership with the Colorado Historical Society and the Colorado State Library statewide historic newspaper database 1859–1880.

Baca House, Bloom Mansion, Molly Brown House, Tabor Home and Matchless Mine Cabin

Colorado Prospector. Trinidad issue, vol. 7, no. 9 (September 1976). Baby Doe Tabor, vol. 19, no. 4. Molly Brown, vol. 21, no. 1 (January 1990). Molly Brown, vol. 26, no. 3 (Summer 1995) Western History Collection, Denver Public Library.

Tapes/Videos/Online Resources/Historic Markers

Byers-Evans House

Chariot Productions. *"The Byers and Evans: First Families of Denver. V,"* video script. Chariot Productions, September 1988.

Cherokee Ranch and Castle

Wruck, Dave, editor. *A Jewel in the Rockies, the Story of Cherokee Ranch.* Jess Stainbrook, producer; David Schler, writer/director. Douglas County Television, 1999.

Four Mile Historic Park

Berry, Dave, editor. *A Moment in Time, Living History at Four Mile Historic Park.* Produced by Four Mile House, Harvey Productions.

Museo de las Tres Colonias

Chacon, Esmeralda, interviewer. Romero Family Oral History, Warren Berman studio, Fort Collins, Colorado, February 2006.

Old Homestead House Museum

The 12th Census of Population, 1900, Colorado, Precinct 16, Cripple Creek, June 13, 1900.